Welcome to Washington

2nd Edition

by

Clem Buckley and Jim Bruner

© 1998 by Jim Bruner, Publisher
All rights reserved
Printed in the United States of America
Library of Congress Catalog Number: 98-073962

ISBN 0-9628251-1-5

For further information, send inquiries to
Jim Bruner, Publisher
1849 North West Beach Road
Oak Harbor, WA 98277
E-mail: jbruner@oakharbor.net
URL: www.pioneernet.net/jbruner

Book Production and Design: Jim Bruner, Publisher

Edited by Jim Bruner

Cover

    Sunset from West Beach, Whidbey Island: Linda Bruner

    State Capitol photo: Harry T Halverson, Olympia, WA

    Orchard in The Okanogan, Palouse panorama, ferry, and Space Needle: Clem Buckley

Color Section

    Flag photos: Melanie Ashe

                   J and M Photography

                   P.O. Box 1455

                   Coupeville, WA 98239

    Capitol and Vietnam Veterans Memorial: Harry T Halverson, Olympia, WA

    Courthouses and other photos: Authors

Black & white photos: The authors, Melanie Ashe (pp.112 and 116), and Mike Boggs, Whidbey Island Dive Center, Oak Harbor, WA (p. 114)

Contents

Welcome

Welcome to the Evergreen State and the second edition of *Welcome to Washington*. After I had spent considerable time in real estate activities—especially those involving people who relocated here from other parts of the country—I sensed a need for one publication, without advertising, that presented information on a broad spectrum of topics. As a result, I wrote and published the first edition. By then, I was in the groove of collecting information about the state, so I continued.

Although I had already traveled the state extensively and participated in many of its activities when I began preparing this edition, I set out again specifically to visit each county seat and courthouse. I ended up doing that twice because I decided to include pictures of the courthouses and I wanted to introduce my new associate, Jim Bruner, to all of these fine places.

Knowing that Washington's population and its activities are severely skewed geographically toward the Puget Sound area, I considered how I could present, somewhat evenhandedly, all areas of the state. My solution was to focus, in part, on the counties. Even though some counties have fewer than 10,000 people, they are all interesting places to visit, with many things to see and activities to enjoy.

Because of expanded information on each county as well as on many other areas of interest, this edition is more than twice the size of the first, contains many more graphics, and has a new section on the environment. Now, it is a publication for a wider audience—longtime residents, students, and those in other parts of the country who want to know more about this northwest corner of the "lower 48," or more appropriately, the 48 contiguous states.

What this book is *not* is a compilation of nitty-gritty statistics about each housing market and school district and a list of places to stay or to eat. That information frequently changes and is readily available in phone books, chambers of commerce, and real estate offices. Yes, we do present *some* statistics, courtesy of the recently released 1997 Data Book from the state Office of Financial Management, but only for general information and comparison.

A couple of conventions used in the writing are worth noting:

1. In discussions of activities, names of counties are inserted in parentheses (Asotin) to provide a sense of location within the state.

2. Figures are generally rounded for ease in reading. Most constantly change anyway (e.g., population and financial/tax matters).

There were a few glitches in the first edition, which were quickly brought to my attention by Cheri Brennan, Sylvia Maurer, Dick Pattison, Jean Sexton, Lorrie Dutcher, John Puckett, and Loren McIntyre. I promised to mention them if a second edition came into being, so thanks.

To fully appreciate this state, you need to get out and explore it. Welcome to this book—and welcome to Washington!

Clem Buckley

Overview

In many ways, Washington is unique among all the states. It's a land of tremendous variety and startling contrasts, a place of lush rain forests and desert-dry prairie, of great rivers and soaring mountains. Washington's cultural diversity takes in major cities and tiny farming communities, busy seaports, and quiet college towns. From the huge inland sea called Puget Sound to the rolling wheat fields of the Palouse, it's a Yin-Yang land with living at its best.

Bordered on the north by Canada, to the west by the Pacific Ocean, and on most of the south by the Columbia River, it has much in common with neighboring Idaho on the east and Oregon on the south.

The one distinctive feature that has done the most to shape the weather and population patterns of the entire region is the imposing Cascade Range. This rampart, which includes Mount Rainier and Mount St. Helens, runs north and south, border to border, essentially dividing the state into two very different parts. The west has a mild, rain-rich climate, the "wet side," whereas the east is "the dry side," with greater temperature extremes. More than half of the people live in the metropolitan areas around Puget Sound, while the wide-open spaces of the east are home to much of the agricultural industry. However, both sides of the mountains provide endless opportunities for an enjoyable lifestyle.

In Washington, you can

- Ski during the day on an 80- to 100-inch snow base and then cruise off to dinner on the never-frozen waters of Puget Sound.

- Take one- to three-day driving tours, ride the ferries, take a hydrofoil trip, or get an eagle's-eye view by seaplane.

- Go mountain climbing in the morning and windsurfing in the afternoon.

- Attend a rodeo or logging show during the day and then the theater, opera, or ballet in the evening.

- Tour the largest dam (by volume) in North America (Grand Coulee) during the day and, on summer nights, watch a huge laser show projected on white water cascading from the spillways.

- Travel from the misty shores of the Pacific over the mountains to the dry winds of the Inland Empire all in one day.

The forests and wildernesses are never far away. A large part of the state is devoted to national and state parks and forests and the reservations of various Indian tribes. Camping, fishing, hiking, hunting, and winter sports are favorite recreational activities, in addition to all the pleasure boating in the many waters. Clear air and water, astounding natural beauty, a thriving civic and cultural base, and a healthy economy—that is why people want to live in Washington.

In 1997 and 1998, several cities in Washington were listed among the top ten "most livable" in the nation, according to their size—Seattle being first among large cities and Mount Vernon first among small cities.

Perhaps the best way to view and analyze the state is by region and the counties that compose each one. The state has from two to nine regions, depending on who is partitioning it and why. The two are, of course, the east and west. Most of the departments of state government do their managing in several regions. We have arbitrarily broken it up into eight.

Southeast

The sunny southeast has the Snake River, rolling Palouse hills and wheat fields, and the Tri-Cities, where the Snake joins the Columbia. The region has eight counties: Adams, Asotin, Benton, Columbia, Franklin, Garfield, Walla Walla, and Whitman. Most of the economy is agriculture plus the Hanford Site. The Blue Mountains give some height to the region and snow for winter skiing. Where the Clearwater and Snake Rivers join at Clarkston was the entry point into the state of the Lewis & Clark expedition in 1805. The population is sparse, except for the cities, but there is a lot of sun and plenty of space for quiet living or retirement.

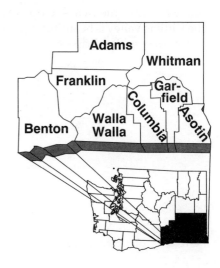

Northeast

The focal point of this region is Spokane, the headquarters of the Inland Empire. The five counties—Ferry, Lincoln, Pend Oreille, Spokane, and Stevens—offer a mixed economy. Agriculture, especially wheat, is a big part of it, but timber and mining in the northern reaches contribute, as do government and business activities in Spokane. Water has a big role, notably the Spokane River and the Columbia, with its Grand Coulee Dam and Lake Roosevelt. There are two large Indian reservations, Spokane and Colville. In the mountains and forests are big game, and many lakes and streams provide excellent fishing. Some of the coldest winter temperatures in the state are recorded in this region.

North Central

Four counties make up this region, two of which cling to the eastern slopes of the Cascades. Okanogan and Chelan Counties are the state's first and third largest and together have about 4 million acres of public lands. With Lake Chelan, the Okanogan and Columbia Rivers, and five dams, water is the main support of the economy. Orchards continue to expand up the slopes from the rivers and lakes, and where fruit is not growing, cattle are. In summer, Route 20 over the North Cascades is open and delivers visitors into the heart of what is known as "The Okanogan." Year round, Route 2 and Stevens Pass provide access to the Wenatchee Valley. The region has plenty of sun, but its northern region gets cold in the winter.

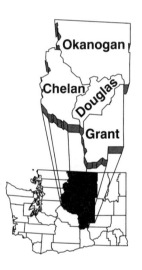

South Central

This three-county region contains Kittitas, Yakima (the state's second largest), and Klickitat. All three border the Cascades on the west and descend into some of the driest parts of the state. Thanks to sun and irrigation, agriculture is big, and the Yakima Valley is one of the richest crop areas in the nation. The Kittitas Valley is beautiful, and much of Klickitat County lies in the Columbia River Gorge National Scenic Area. Many wineries along the Yakima River offer tastings of some of the state's finest wines.

Southwest

Moving from the dry side to the wet side brings a big change: trees and more trees, a bit of open space for agriculture, and the ocean. This seven-county area consists of Clark, Cowlitz, Lewis, Pacific, Skamania, Thurston, and Wahkiakum. The state capital, Olympia, anchors the north end, and Vancouver nudges Oregon on the south. On the east is the Cascade Range and the state's newest natural

attraction, Mount St. Helens. On the south, the mighty Columbia ends its journey to the Pacific, and the west is home to much wildlife and a major stopping place for migrating birds on the Pacific Flyway. The low, coastal mountains soak up moisture, nurturing large tree farms that continue to renew a precious resource. The I-5 corridor continues to build and attract business, thanks to the excellent and still improving transportation network of ocean shipping, highways, rail, and air from Portland.

Olympic Peninsula

The Olympic National Park and Forest and several wilderness areas dominate four of the Peninsula's five counties: Grays Harbor, Mason, Jefferson, and Clallam. The remaining county, Kitsap, is adjacent to and more readily identified with Puget Sound. On the west side of the Olympic Mountains is a temperate rain forest that receives up to 180 inches of rain each year. A journey around the peninsula on U.S. Highway 101 should take a couple of days for full enjoyment of the sights, sounds, and solitude as it winds its way along Hood Canal, skirts the park, continues through or by several Indian reservations, and heads south along wild, scenic beaches. Midway across the Strait of Juan de Fuca is the international boundary. Across the Strait, Canada's Vancouver Island and popular city of Victoria are accessible via ferry from Port Angeles. Several ferries connect across the Sound to the east. Logging, shellfish, the Navy, and tourism are major components of the economy.

Northwest

Water on the west, mountains on the east, and the Canadian border define this region of many islands and an inland sea that is great for boating. Two of the counties, San Juan and Island, consist of tranquil islands that are popular with tourists and retirees. San Juan County's lifeline is the Washington State Ferry system. Island County's two main islands connect to the mainland via bridges, but a ferry is a popular option from Whidbey Island. A commuter airline offers another option to the few who are in a hurry. The Navy has a base in Island County. The remaining two counties—Whatcom and Skagit—extend to the crest of the Cascade Range. The major border crossing to Canada is at Blaine in Whatcom. The I-5 corridor through these two counties is growing rapidly and joins the region to the Seattle megalopolis and British Columbia's busy port and metropolitan center of Vancouver.

Central Sound

On the east shores of the Sound lie the Big Three counties in terms of people: #1 King, #2 Pierce, and #3 Snohomish, which contain Seattle, Tacoma, Everett, and dozens of other cities. Together, the three contain about 50% of the state's population. They extend from saltwater to the Cascade crest and include much of the Snoqualmie National Forest plus Mount Rainier National Park. Two of the nation's biggest businesses, Boeing and Microsoft, dominate the region, but there are thousands of other booming enterprises plus many governmental regional offices. Seattle and Tacoma are two of the West Coast's busiest ports, and Everett is a homeport for a Navy aircraft carrier and its supporting vessels. Air traffic continues to grow at Sea-Tac Airport, which is in the process of adding a third runway. What some consider the signature of the state is the Space Needle at the Seattle Center, built in 1962 for the World's Fair. People keep coming, and the prices of homes continue to rise.

Some Washington Statistics

Sixth fastest growing state (1990–1996)

Population (1997):	5,700,000
Land area, mi² (ranked 20th in U.S.):	66,582
Water area, mi²:	4,055
Total area, mi² (ranked 19th in U.S.):	70,637
County density, people/mi²: Highest:	774
Lowest:	3
Mean:	84
County per capita income: Highest:	$31,300
Lowest:	$14,300
Mean:	$23,700

Location

Of the 48 contiguous states, Washington is the farthest northwest, but if all U.S. states are considered, Washington is pretty centrally located. This is important because it is easier to get to a lot of places from Seattle than from any other major port in the country.

For instance, Seattle is 3,000 miles closer to any Asian city than New York City is, 800 miles closer to Anchorage and London than San Francisco is, and 200 miles closer to Tokyo than Los Angeles is. This is a big help in international commerce, and it makes the Seattle–Tacoma area a major U.S. transportation center.

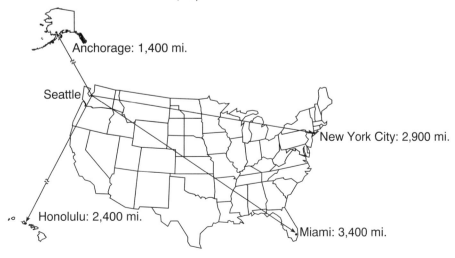

History

In 1989, the state of Washington celebrated its centennial year. However, the recorded history of the 42nd state to join the Union actually goes back more than four centuries, beginning with one of the great explorers of the Elizabethan age.

1579
Sir Francis Drake sails up the Pacific Coast and names the area New Albion.

1592
Juan de Fuca (a Greek navigator in the service of the Viceroy of Mexico) discovers the strait that will later be named in his honor. For the next two centuries, there is little recorded history of the region. Then, in the late 1700s, European and American seafarers began coming to trade for valuable furs.

1607
Jamestown settled.

1642
Cromwell becomes dictator of England.

1775
Bruno Heceta and Juan Francisco de Bodega lay claim to the coast in the name of Spain.

1776
Declaration of Independence signed.

1789
George Washington chosen first president.

1792
George Vancouver, British sea captain, explores the area in detail, naming many landmarks. Captain Robert Gray discovers the Columbia River.

1803
Captains Meriwether Lewis and William Clark begin their overland journey to the Pacific from St. Louis, after the Louisiana Purchase excites new interest in the Northwest.

1805
Lewis and Clark reach the Pacific, at the mouth of the Columbia River.

1807
Robert Fulton invents the steamboat.

1807
First trading posts are built on the Columbia River.

1810
The Spokane House post is built by the North West Fur Company.

1811
British explorer David Thompson is the first person to navigate the Columbia River from its origin in Canada to the Pacific Ocean.

1813
North West Fur is acquired by the Pacific Fur Company, owned by John Jacob Astor.

1818
The United States and England agree to a policy of joint occupancy in what is being called the Oregon Territory (an agreement that will last for nearly 30 years). The North West Fur Company establishes Fort Walla Walla, meaning "many waters."

1819

Spain relinquishes all claims to the area, as part of the Florida Treaty with the U.S.

1821

The faltering North West Fur Company is forced to merge with the powerful Hudson's Bay Company.

1823

Monroe Doctrine enunciated.

1825

Erie Canal opens.

1825

Fort Vancouver, a major trading post, is built on the Columbia River.

1836

Led by missionaries Marcus and Narcissa Whitman and Henry Spaulding, the first major migration of settlers over the Oregon Trail begins. The Whitmans found the Waiilatpu Mission near Walla Walla.

1842

First message sent over telegraph.

1843

Settlers of the Oregon Territory form a provisional government, precipitating a border dispute that nearly develops into a war between England and the U.S. The famous boundary slogan "fifty-four forty or fight!" becomes a rallying cry, but the dispute is finally settled in 1846 when the northern boundary of the Territory is fixed at latitude 49°N.

1845

Portland, Oregon, is born as a trading post across the Columbia from Vancouver, Washington.

1847

The Northwest Indian wars begin with the Whitman Massacre at Waiilatpu. Peaceful coexistence is not established for another 30 years.

1848

Gold discovered in California.

1848

Oregon Territory is established as a U.S. possession.

1853

Washington, with a non-native population of about 4,000, is granted separate territorial status. Isaac Stevens is appointed Territorial Governor and Supervisor of Indian Affairs. In this capacity, he negotiates treaties with Indian tribes throughout the area to assure valid claims to land taken by the settlers. Olympia is chosen as temporary capital.

1859

The Indian treaties are ratified by Congress. Oregon is granted statehood. Relations between England and the U.S. in the Northwest remain uneasy. When an American shoots an Englishman's pig during a dispute over San Juan Island, war nearly breaks out (an incident that will come to be known as "The Pig War").

1861

The South secedes from the Union; Civil War begins.

1861

Territorial University (later to become the University of Washington) opens in Seattle.

1863

Idaho Territory is formed, and the eastern boundary of Washington Territory (and later, state) is established. The first transcontinental telegraph is completed, linking California, Oregon, and Washington Territory with the rest of the country.

1866

First salmon cannery opens on the Columbia River.

1870

The Territory's population is approaching 24,000, and many of its principal cities—Seattle, Tacoma, Spokane, Walla Walla, Olympia—have been established. Railroads have arrived, and the Territory begins its campaign to be granted statehood.

1880

The fertile fields of the Palouse are yielding enough wheat for the Territory to begin exporting it. Statehood campaign intensifies.

1883

First transcontinental rail link with the eastern U.S. completed.

1885

George Fitch builds a small, water-driven generator at Spokane Falls—the first hydroelectric plant in the Northwest.

1889

Washington is granted statehood on November 11.

1897

The great Yukon Gold Rush commences, with most of the people and goods bound for the gold fields moving through Seattle. While the rest of the country is suffering a severe depression, the rush to Alaska and the Yukon keeps the Washington economy relatively healthy.

1899

Mount Rainier National Park is established.

1900

The forest-products industry gets a big boost in Washington when Frederick Weyerhaeuser buys 900,000 acres of forest and founds the company that bears his name. Mammoth sawmills are built around Puget Sound and in the lower Columbia region to harvest and process the readily accessible timber.

1909

The Alaska-Yukon-Pacific Exposition in Seattle is both a financial and social success.

1910

Women gain the right to vote in Washington.

1916

The Boeing Company (so named in 1917) flies its first aircraft (a seaplane) in Seattle.

1928

Olympia's permanent capitol building (modeled

1867
Russia sells Alaska to U.S.

1869
Transcontinental Railroad completed.

1903
Wright Brothers make first powered flight in a heavier than-air vehicle.

1917
The United States declares war on Germany.

1929
Stock market crashes: Great Depression begins.

after the one in "the other Washington") is completed.

1933

First dam on the Columbia, Rock Island, is built.

1935

First flight of the Boeing Model 299, prototype of the B-17 Flying Fortress bomber.

1938

Bonneville Dam is completed.

1941

1941 — WW II begins.

Grand Coulee Dam, then the largest concrete structure in the world, is finished.

1942

First flight of the Boeing B-29 Superfortress bomber.

1943

Construction begins on the Hanford nuclear facility.

1945 — WW II ends.

1951

First irrigation water from Grand Coulee moves to Columbia Basin.

1954

First flight of the Boeing Model 367-80, prototype of the Boeing 707 jetliner and the KC-135 military tanker. Building of five public utility district dams on the Columbia starts; completed in 1963.

1956

Construction started for four Lower Snake River dams; completed in 1975.

1962

The World's Fair brings the Space Needle to Seattle—along with millions of visitors seeing the Northwest for the first time. This is just one of the factors that will cause the state's population to jump from 2.8 million to 3.5 million by the end of the decade.

1963

1963 — President Kennedy assassinated.

First flight of the production Boeing 727-100.

1967

First flight of the Boeing 737.

1969

A major economic downturn takes place, prompting the famous billboard that reads, "Will the last person leaving Seattle please turn out the lights?" First flight of the Boeing 747.

1970

A decade begins in which Washington will experience both economic expansion and considerable population growth. The Trans-Alaska pipeline project is launched—and, as in the gold rush of 1897, most of the people, equipment, and supplies will pass through the Puget Sound area. Trade with the Pacific Rim countries increases dramatically.

1973 — Last U.S. combat troops leave Vietnam.

1979
American embassy in Iran seized.

1990
Berlin Wall falls; Cold War ends.

1997
Dow-Jones Average reaches 9000.
Hong Kong is turned over to China.

1974
Judge George Boldt issues a landmark decision entitling Washington Indians to half of the Northwest salmon and steelhead catches, based on treaties dating back to territorial days. Expo 74 held in Spokane.

1975
Seattle native Bill Gates and Paul Allen found Microsoft in Albuquerque, NM.

1980
On May 18, Mount St. Helens erupts, capturing the attention of the world. Congress passes Northwest Power Act, giving top priority to energy conservation and restoration of fish runs.

1981
First flight of the Boeing 767-200 jetliner. MS-DOS (*Micro*Soft *D*isk *O*perating *S*ystem) is introduced.

1982
First flight of the Boeing 757-200 jetliner.

1983
Microsoft Word and the "mouse" are introduced.

1986
Columbia River Gorge National Scenic Area created by Congress.

1990
The Goodwill Games are held in Seattle, bringing competitors and visitors from around the world to the Northwest. Microsoft becomes the first computer company to exceed $1 billion in annual sales.

1993
Final leg of Interstate 90 completed across Mercer Island and Lake Washington.

1994
The Boeing 777 twinjet rolls out.

1996
Boeing acquires Rockwell's aerospace and defense business.

1997
Boeing and McDonnell Douglas merge. The new Boeing Company employs more than 200,000.

In 400 years, Washington has progressed from a mysterious and largely unexplored land to a center of modern American life. In less than a century, its people have made the leap from the prairie schooner to the Boeing 777. And, the concentration of high-tech industry that has been developing in the state over the past two decades is an indication that the 21st century will continue to be an exciting and interesting time in which to live in Washington. Now, on to the future!

Geography & Climate

A great deal has been said and written about Washington's weather—and one very common theme seems to be rain! Contrary to popular conception, however, the amount of annual precipitation in the Evergreen State depends largely on the geographical location, and the intensity varies with the seasons.

When considering Washington meteorology, it's important to remember the difference between "climate" and "weather." The latter refers to the immediate state of the atmosphere with respect to heat or cold, wetness or dryness, wind or calm, and so forth. Climate is more general, referring to the average condition of the weather over a period of time.

Washington's location on the windward coast has resulted in a climate that is quite mild, considering the state's northerly latitude (46 to 49°N). The elements that most strongly influence Washington's climatic patterns include the onshore terrain, semipermanent high- and low-pressure regions located over the North Pacific, and the Pacific Ocean itself. These elements combine to produce a predominantly marine climate west of the Cascades, while the climate on the eastern side of the range possesses both continental and marine characteristics. Washington is, therefore, an area in which entirely different climatic conditions can coexist within a surprisingly small area.

The biggest (in terms of sheer size) contributor to Washington climate is, of course, the Pacific Ocean. The seasonal temperature changes in the Pacific are less than those that take place ashore. Thus, the ocean is warmer in winter and cooler in summer than the adjoining land mass, with average water temperatures ranging from 45°F in winter to 53°F in summer. (Some bays and coves may be warmer—but not warm enough to attract many swimmers!) Another important marine-related climatic element is found in the masses of moisture-laden air that move inland from the ocean.

This moving air is almost immediately lifted by mountains (orographic lifting), and much of its moisture is released along the western slope of the Coast Range, which includes the Olympics. A second dose of heavy precipitation from rising air occurs on the windward slopes of the Cascade Range, 90 to 120 miles inland. This great mountain barrier, which ranges from 4,000 to 14,000 feet in height, has only one break—the Columbia River Gorge. The Cascades also protect the western part of the state from cold air moving south from Canada, although some of it does occasionally spread across the border through the Fraser River Valley in southern British Columbia.

As air loses its moisture, moves over the mountains, and descends the eastern slopes, it warms and dries, causing near-desert conditions in the lowest section of the Columbia Basin. But another orographic lifting of the air takes place as it flows eastward from the lowest elevation of the inland basin toward the Rocky Mountains. The result is a gradual increase in precipitation in the higher country along the state's eastern border.

The location and intensity of the semipermanent high- and low-pressure areas over the north Pacific also have a definite influence on the climate. During the spring and summer, the low-pressure cell becomes weak and moves north of the Aleutian Islands, while the high-pressure area spreads out over most of the North Pacific. Because air circulates clockwise around high-pressure cells and counterclockwise around low-pressure areas, the prevailing flow in the spring and summer is westerly/northwesterly, bringing comparatively dry, cool, and stable air into the Pacific Northwest. As the air moves inland, it becomes warmer and drier, creating a dry season that begins in late spring and reaches its peak in midsummer.

In the fall and winter, the Aleutian low-pressure center intensifies and moves southward, reaching its maximum in midwinter. At the same time, the high-pressure cell weakens and moves farther south. The airflow at this season is mostly from the west and southwest, and the air is very moist and is close to the temperature of the ocean itself. As the air moves over the cooler land and rises along the western slopes of the mountains, it produces the wet season, which begins in October, peaks in midwinter, and gradually diminishes during the spring.

Regional Variation

Western Region

West of the Cascades, the summers are cool and fairly dry, whereas winters are mild, cloudy, and wet. Days with sunshine range from 4 to 8 per month in winter to about 20 per month in summer. Some precipitation can be expected 130 to 190 days each year, but seasonal variations are extreme —that is, it may rain for 20 to 25 days in one winter month, but summer can bring weeks of solid sunshine, with no rain and few, if any, clouds.

Coastal Area (West of Olympics)

This area runs south from the Strait of Juan de Fuca to the Columbia River, along the slopes of the Coast Range (including the Olympic Mountains) and the Willapa Hills. This is the region that gets the Northwest's heaviest rainfall—in fact, the western slopes of the Olympics receive upwards of 180 inches of precipitation annually and are cloaked by the world's largest temperate-zone rain forest. Snow falls at the highest altitudes during most of the year, whereas temperatures at the lower levels reach the 70s in summer and drop into the 30s and 40s during winter.

Northeast Olympics/San Juan Area

Because of its unique climate, the east slope of the Olympics—along the Strait of Juan de Fuca and into the San Juan Islands—is known as Washington's "banana belt." Both the Olympics and the Coast Range, extending to Vancouver Island (British Columbia) to the north, protect this area, causing most of the rain to fall to the west. As a result, annual rainfall in this area is only around 20 inches, and much of it comes in the form of a mild drizzle often called "soft rain" because the size of individual droplets is 1/4 to 1/5 that of normal raindrops. Temperatures here are slightly higher in summer and lower in winter than those along the coast.

Puget Sound Area

Farther east than the first two subregions, this area extends to about the 1,000-foot level of the Cascades, and from the Canadian border south to Chehalis (Cowlitz). Here, a difference of a few hundred feet in elevation can mean the difference between rain and snow in winter. Annual rainfall in the area ranges from 35 to 37 inches in Seattle (King) in the north to as much as 45 inches in Chehalis in the south. Although annual snowfall of 10 to 20 inches is about average,

Annual rainfall (inches) in the Olympics/San Juan/Puget Sound Area

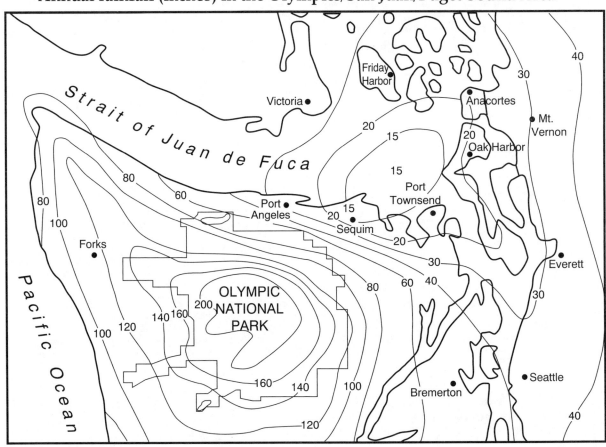

many winters pass with no snow hitting the ground near sea level. What snow does fall usually melts quickly.

Clean air is a notable feature of this region, as there is usually enough wind to disperse most air pollution. If there is not, no-burning restrictions are put into effect, which include wood stoves and fireplaces unless they are a sole source of home heat. Temperatures in the Puget Sound area sometimes move into the 90s in summer, and winter temperatures occasionally drop to the low 20s or upper teens.

Southwest Area

The two prominent features of this area, which is located south of Chehalis between the ocean and the Cascades foothills, are the Willapa Hills along the coast and the Columbia River Gorge. The low hills don't lift the air as much here as in the north, so more rain covers the whole area. The Columbia Gorge allows an exchange of air between the two sides of the state. In winter, colder air moves from east to west, causing ice storms as rain falls into the cold air around Vancouver (Clark).

Western Slopes of the Cascades

Along these slopes, the rising air releases most of its remaining moisture. Annual rainfall ranges from 60 to 100 inches or more, and snowfall, starting at 50 to 75 inches at the lower elevations, can rise to 500–600 inches at the 5,000-foot level. More than 1,000 inches has been recorded at Paradise, 5,500 feet up on Mount Rainier. Because snow remains on the mountains' higher peaks all year, several of the state's major ski areas are located in this region. When snow is still in the mountains and warm rains move in, many of the western region's rivers spill over their banks. But it's this abundance of rain and snow that provides much of the state's vital year-round water supply—and, in a too-dry year, the danger of summer forest fires increases dramatically.

Eastern Region

This portion of the state encompasses part of the large inland basin between the Cascades and the Rocky Mountains. The Rockies shield the region from most of the winter's cold-air masses that travel southward across Canada. The air that does get through combines with air moving across the Cascades from the ocean, producing a climate that possesses both marine and continental characteristics. In summer, the air moving across the continent results in low humidity and high temperatures. In winter, clear, cold weather prevails. Extremes of temperature are much greater than in the western part of the state.

East Slope Area

This is a strip 50 to 75 miles wide, running from Canada to the Columbia River. Rainfall decreases quickly going down slope, making it possible to record annual rainfall levels of 80 to 100 inches in one of the passes and only 20 inches just 30 miles away. Subzero temperatures are not uncommon in winter, and summer temperatures frequently soar into the 90s.

The Okanogan

This north-central area of the state includes the Waterville Plateau and the valleys along the Okanogan (spelled Okanagan in Canada), Methow, and Columbia Rivers. Toward the east, elevations begin to rise, up to 5,000 feet. Winter can bring annual snowfall of 30 to 70 inches and rainfall of 11 to 16 inches. Humidity levels are generally low. Temperatures in January will average between 28 and 32°F, with some subzero days to be expected. In July, the average maximum temperature is between 85 and 90°F, with a few days over 100°.

Northeast Area

Elevations continue to rise, with the Selkirk Mountains reaching 6,000 feet. Continental air moving in from Canada has a greater effect here than in other parts of the state, with minimum temperatures dropping as low as –10 to –20°F each winter. The state's lowest temperature, –42°F, was recorded in this area. Summer temperatures average in the high 80s. With snowfall of 40 to 80 inches per season, the high terrain offers magnificent cross-country skiing.

Central Basin

This, the lowest and driest part of the state, includes the areas around Ellensburg, Yakima, and the Tri-Cities. In some locations, annual rainfall is less than 10 inches, with winter snows of only 10 to 30 inches. The average high in January is near 30°F. In July, temperatures routinely reach the 90s but are somewhat alleviated by frequent summer thunderstorms.

Palouse/Blue Mountains

This area covers the southeast corner of the state, bordered by Spokane on the north and Idaho and Oregon to the east and south. Again, as elevations rise toward the east, from 3,500 feet in the Palouse Hills to 6,000 feet in the Blue Mountains, so does rainfall, reaching 20 inches per year in the hills and 40 inches in the mountains. Average winter temperatures are higher, and summer temperatures lower, than in the central basin.

Initially, the state's economy was based on natural resources of furs, fish, and trees, closely followed by land (agriculture) and mining. Except for fur, natural resources still play a significant role and now include water (hydroelectric power). Now, however, the diversity is greater and the base is much broader, with manufacturing, government, services, transportation (including international trade), construction, and wholesale and retail trade. Listed by number of people employed, the major industries are

Industry	# people	%
Services	612,000	25.4
Retail trade	437,400	18.2
Government	426,000	17.7
Manufacturing	339,300	14.1
Wholesale trade	140,100	5.8
Finance, insurance, real estate	121,000	5.0
Construction	119,200	5.0
Transportation, utilities	118,000	4.9
Agriculture, forestry, fishing	88,400	3.7
Mining (incl. sand and gravel)	3,300	0.1

The state follows closely the nation in per capita income, unemployment, average wages, and the changes in various economic indicators.

The principal goods-producing industries are aerospace, food products, lumber, wood and paper products, primary metals, computer software, and agriculture, which also is a national leader in crop diversity and production volume.

Increasing diversification in recent years has made the state less sensitive to cyclical changes, especially in manufacturing. The state's location, a day or so closer to the Far East and Alaska for shipping, has a positive impact. The service sector benefits from many regional offices of the federal government and private companies.

Some companies with a local base and recognition beyond the state's borders are Boeing, Microsoft, Weyerhaeuser, Paccar, Costco, Adobe, Immunex, Safeco, Egghead, Holland America, Eddie Bauer, Alaska Air Group, Washington Mutual, REI, Nordstrom, and Starbucks.

Products from Nature

Climate, geography, and other factors give the state a variety of agricultural activity (more than 140 different crops) and some of the country's most productive farmland. The result is that Washington farmers lead the nation in the production of many commodities and rank very high in others:

Rank	Commodity (% of national output)
1	Spearmint (98), hops (77), red raspberries (74), dry peas (62), lentils (56), apples (53), sweet cherries (45), asparagus (42), pears (38), carrots (32)
2	All grapes, seed peas, peppermint, fall potatoes, apricots
3	Processed sweet corn, processed green peas, prunes
Top 10	Wheat, milk, onions, cranberries, mint, barley, peaches, strawberries, beans

Yields are another way to determine productivity, and farmers here produce more potatoes and wheat on dryland fields per acre than in any other state. Milk production per cow is consistently high and is moo-ving upward.

Washington's 35,000 farms occupy about 16 million acres. More than half are small (i.e., under 50 acres), and many of these are part-time businesses. At the other end of the scale are the vast, dryland crop farms and ranches in the eastern region, often thousands of acres in size. Less than 2% of the state's workers are actually employed on farms, but each farm job creates jobs for 11 other people, such as those who manufacture farm equipment, process foods, stock produce in stores, process loans, staff restaurants, drive trucks, or load freighters.

The Palouse region in the state's southeast produces the dryland crops: wheat, barley, lentils, and dry peas. The central area, with the Columbia River irrigating 500,000 acres, produces potatoes, alfalfa hay, asparagus, vegetables, and tree fruits. The Yakima Valley, with many areas irrigated, ranks among the best in its bountiful output of hops, tree fruits, and grapes. It also has a large dairy industry. From Yakima to Wenatchee are apple orchards and other tree fruits. Livestock are raised throughout the eastern part of the state. West of the Cascades are many of the highly productive dairy herds that benefit from the milder climate and long grazing season. The Skagit Valley and its delta have excellent soils for veggies and flowers (tulips and daffodils), and it is the nation's leader in seed crops. Christmas tree farms stretch west from Olympia, and on the coast are cranberry bogs.

The value of Washington's agribusiness is now $29 billion (5% of its economy) and growing as more land is placed in use. In ranking, by millions of dollars, are apples (700) followed by milk (650), cattle (510), wheat (460), potatoes (350), and hay (260). It was originally estimated that the Columbia Irrigation Project would irrigate 1 million acres of virtual wasteland. Half of that land is now enormously productive. Improve-ments in yields and farming methods continue through the efforts of agricultural research at Washington State University.

The state's agricultural commodities are consumed about 25% locally, 50% in other states, and 25% in foreign lands. The transportation available

Number of Farms			Average Size of Farms			Total Land in Farms		
Rank	County	No.	Rank	County	Acres	Rank	County	Acres
1	Yakima	3,651	1	Ferry	3,876	1	Yakima	1,639,965
2	Spokane	1,708	2	Lincoln	2,070	2	Lincoln	1,465,788
3	Grant	1,696	3	Asotin	1,933	3	Whitman	1,404,289
4	Whatcom	1,367	4	Garfield	1,750	4	Okanogan	1,291,118
5	Okanogan	1,344	5	Adams	1,656	5	Grant	1,086,045
6	Clark	1,257	6	Columbia	1,596	6	Adams	996,742
7	Snohomish	1,255	7	Klickitat	1,358	7	Douglas	918,033
8	Chelan	1,240	8	Whitman	1,262	8	Ferry	748,088
9	King	1,221	9	Douglas	1,034	9	WallaWalla	710,546
10	Benton	1,128	10	Okanogan	961	10	Klickitat	689,639
11	Whitman	1,113	11	Walla Walla	954	11	Franklin	670,149
12	Lewis	1,067	12	Franklin	782	12	Benton	640,370
13	Pierce	1,059	13	Grant	640	13	Spokane	625,769
14	Stevens	1,054	14	Benton	568	14	Stevens	546,303
15	Douglas	888	15	Stevens	518	15	Kittitas	355,360
16	Franklin	857	16	Kittitas	469	16	Garfield	325,472
17	Thurston	811	17	Yakima	449	17	Columbia	304,928
18	Kittitas	758	18	Spokane	366	18	Asotin	274,546
19	Skagit	754	19	Pend Oreille	270	19	Whatcom	118,136
20	Walla Walla	745	20	Pacific	132	20	Lewis	112,263
21	Lincoln	708	20	San Juan	132	21	Chelan	112,085
22	Adams	602	22	Skagit	122	22	Skagit	92,074
23	Klickitat	508	23	Grays Harbor	116	23	Clark	82,967
24	Grays Harbor	385	24	Wahkiakum	115	24	Snohomish	74,153
25	Kitsap	366	25	Lewis	105	25	Thurston	59,890
26	Cowlitz	365	26	Cowlitz	98	26	Pierce	58,750
27	Clallam	328	27	Chelan	90	27	Pend Oreille	55,360
28	Island	278	28	Whatcom	86	28	Grays Harbor	44,742
29	Pacific	248	29	Jefferson	83	29	King	42,290
30	Pend Oreille	205	30	Mason	76	30	Cowlitz	35,678
31	Ferry	193	31	Clallam	74	31	Pacific	32,637
32	Columbia	191	31	Thurston	74	32	Clallam	24,253
33	Garfield	186	33	Island	70	33	San Juan	20,529
34	San Juan	155	34	Skamania	67	34	Island	19,526
35	Mason	145	35	Clark	66	35	Wahkiakum	12,611
36	Asotin	142	36	Snohomish	59	36	Mason	10,965
37	Jefferson	116	37	Pierce	55	37	Kitsap	10,302
38	Wahkiakum	110	38	King	35	38	Jefferson	9,603
39	Skamania	60	39	Kitsap	28	39	Skamania	4,043

for exporting is outstanding: barging down the rivers or trucking to relatively close deep-water ports, and then the shortest sea routes to Asia. Wheat, including 90% of the soft-wheat crop, accounts for half the value of exports. Apples are the number-two export. Thanks to new compression techniques, hay is also being shipped to overseas markets.

Apples

In value, apples are Washington's number-one crop, with annual production climbing toward $1 billion, and the state is known as "The Apple Bowl of the World."

Apples found their way to Washington in 1826, on a Hudson's Bay Company sailing vessel. Seeds of a "good luck" apple given to the vessel's Captain Simpson, on the eve of his departure from London, were planted at Fort Vancouver, Washington, in the spring of 1827.

From this humble beginning (not Johnny Appleseed!), Washington's apple production has grown to about 6 billion apples each year, some 30% of all of the apples grown commercially in all 39 apple-producing states. If the apples diverted to processing for apple juice and other ends are not considered, the remainder constitutes 45% of the nation's production of apples sold fresh. Apples are the state's second-largest agricultural export (by volume), after wheat.

The state's 180,000 acres of apple orchards are mostly in the vicinity of Yakima (80,000), Wenatchee (60,000), and the Columbia Basin (31,000). The Red Delicious variety currently is the most popular, but other varieties are coming on strong.

Wheat

Wheat is the state's number-one field crop. Over 2 million acres are planted, mostly in the central and eastern counties, producing around 150 million bushels. About 90% of the wheat grown is winter wheat, planted in the fall and harvested the following summer. The winter variety normally gives a higher yield than that planted in the spring and harvested in the fall.

Washington wheat comes in three classes: soft white, hard red winter, and hard red spring. "Soft" and "hard" refer to the density of the kernel. Each class is different in protein content, bran coat, and milling and baking qualities. About 85% of the state's harvest is soft white, which has two distinct types: club and common. Club has shorter and more compact heads. Together, they are sold in a mixture called Western White, which is quite popular on the world market and is grown only in the Northwest.

Approximately 90% of the state's crop is exported. Wheat accounts for nearly half of the total volume of all of Washington's farm exports, more than five times as much as the second largest export—apples.

Washington ranks fourth (after Kansas, North Dakota, and Oklahoma) in wheat production, and four Washington counties are in the top ten counties.

Most Washington wheat is grown on dryland farms without irrigation (see figure). With low rainfall, farmers seed about half their acreage, leaving the remaining ground fallow to collect moisture for the next year.

Mint

Mint oil is a natural flavoring for which there is no adequate substitute. Native spearmint is different from the other crops in which Washington leads the world. Anyone can grow it, but only about 250 farmers can sell it. In 1979, farmers in seven western states created the Farwest Spearmint Marketing Order, approved by the USDA, to match production

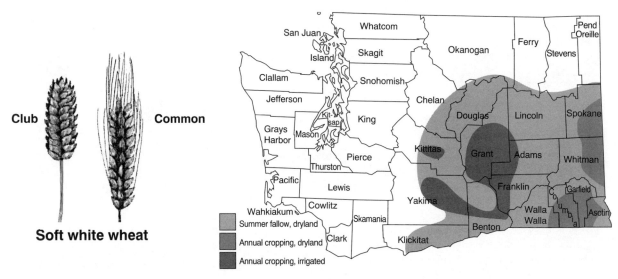

Soft white wheat — Club, Common

Summer fallow, dryland
Annual cropping, dryland
Annual cropping, irrigated

to world demand. This was done to stabilize prices, which previously fluctuated from $3 to $20 a pound. Now, only farmers with FSMO permits can sell it.

The Yakima Valley—with its 300 days of sun and deep, loamy soil—is well suited to mint growing, and the authorized grower/sellers are lucky folks indeed. Not only do they not have to worry about selling their crops, but it is a relatively clean, sweet-smelling crop that doesn't require messy, dusty threshing. Mint is processed by steaming the finely chopped plants and extracting the oil, after which the residue is returned to the fields as compost.

According to the Mint Industry Research Council in Stevenson (Skamania), mint has been found in ancient Egyptian tombs and has been used in Chinese medicine even longer. Early Romans ate it to increase intelligence, and sniffing it is still believed to improve concentration. Manufacturers blend various mint oils to flavor chewing gum, mouthwash, candy, and toothpaste.

Wine

Washington's wine industry, or viniculture, has grown in recent years to be a major component of the state's economy and is recognized almost everywhere for the quality of the product. The state has four appellations, federally recognized vineyard districts where there is a commonality of taste, basically a result of a combination of climate and geographic features. The three in the east are the Columbia, Yakima, and Walla Walla Valleys. The newest, on the "wet side," is Puget Sound.

It is where the grapes are grown, not where the winery is located, that gives a wine its distinctive varietal character. The state is fortunate to possess all three of the elements critical to successful wine growing: geography, climate, and soil.

Geography. The state lies on one of the "wine bands" located around the globe between latitudes 30° and 50°N. During the critical ripening period, the vines enjoy long, warm summer days, with an average of more than 17 hours of daylight in June. The vines then "rest" during the cool nights to maintain high acidity in the fruit. This combination produces grapes with excellent sugar/acid balance and distinctive varietal character.

Climate. Washington's vineyard temperatures fall within "Wine Region II," as do those in the great wine regions of the Napa Valley, Bordeaux, and Burgundy. The appellations on the dry side of the Cascades receive an average of only 8 inches of rain each year. This sparse rainfall, combined with controlled irrigation, allows each vine to receive just the right amount of water. Although the west side has lower temperatures and more rainfall, many varieties still provide an ample harvest.

Soil. The eastern soils are light-textured, mineral-rich, silt loams, which allow rapid warming and good water penetration. Western soils have a higher clay content and more organic material.

Within the four appellations is a wide array of microclimates, resulting in a broad range of classic European grapes grown by more than 60 wineries, with outputs ranging from a few to many thousands of cases each season. The eastern wineries are rather clustered, with more than 30 in the Yakima Valley along I-82 from Yakima to the Tri-Cities. Most offer tasting, and many host cultural events. Touring wineries is a popular activity.

Wine lovers are invited to join the Oenological Society of the Pacific Northwest. *The Grapevine* is the visitors' guide to the Yakima, Columbia, and Walla Walla Valleys.

Fish/Shellfish

Although most of the fish/shellfish that contribute to the state's economy are actually caught in Alaskan waters, much of the labor and capital involved comes from within the state. In the state itself, in 1995, about 170 million pounds were harvested, with a value of about the same magnitude.

Aquaculture

A decline in annual salmon runs has adversely affected both commercial and sport fishing. The number of licensed fishing boats has decreased by more than 50% in the last 15 years, mostly those smaller than 50 tons. The number of boats larger than 50 tons has actually increased slightly.

Fish farming, in which floating netpens are anchored close to shore, has undergone a large increase worldwide, but has grown slowly here. Opponents claim these farms cause visual pollution and carry the threat of disease.

The state is a major source of oysters and mussels. With reduced pollution in some areas of the lower Puget Sound, shellfish beds are being brought back into production.

Forest Products

The Northwest was built on timber. Although this resource industry is not as dominant as in the past, it still is ever present. Total timber harvest in 1996 was 4.2 billion board feet, down from a recent high of 7.0 billion in 1988. A large percentage of this was from the national forests, in spite of designated wilderness areas and old growth issues (e.g., spotted owl). About 75% of the harvest is from west of the

Cascades. Most of the 25% from the east is from the northern counties.

Employment levels have dropped as a result of a decrease in the amount of timber harvested and the introduction of automated plants and equipment. While this has been occurring, the industry has been working hard to improve its operations with regard to environmental matters. Harvesting is closely controlled, as is replanting. Research has revealed ways to use almost every last twig and piece of bark of each tree, and highly automated, laser-controlled machinery can create lumber from smaller trees.

Christmas trees contribute to some economies such as Mason County, as do special forest products of evergreen boughs, greenery for the floral industry, cones, moss, and burls. Hybrid cottonwood trees are now being planted for harvest in 10 to 15 years.

Overall, controversies involving this industry appear to be subsiding. Because trees are renewable and only about 2% per year are harvested, stability at about the present level of production is likely.

Government

In at least one way, our state is no different from the others: There's a lot of government, and it employs a lot of people (almost 18% of the total labor force). Included in this sector are all levels of government, education, and the military. The federal government is greatly in evidence. Seattle has a veritable alphabet soup of government agencies: HUD, GSA, FAA, VA, EPA, NOAA, SBA, and INS. There is no sign of any significant decrease in this category.

The impact of the U.S. Department of Defense and military bases is considerable. The state ranks in the top 10 in DoD personnel, both military and civilian, number of military installations and number of military retirees. The impact on the state from base closures during the 1990s was minimal, and some local installations actually gained from transfer-in of units and personnel. A notable closure was that of the Sand Point Naval Station in Seattle. National Oceanic and

Atmospheric Administration regional facilities are located on a part of that facility. A significant addition was the building of a new Naval Base at Everett. Major installations are

- Coast Guard, 13th District Seattle (with several small stations)
- Fairchild Air Force Base, Spokane
- Fort Lewis, Tacoma
- Indian Island Naval Weapons Station (Jefferson)
- Naval Undersea Warfare Engineering Station, Keyport (Kitsap)
- Madigan General Hospital, Tacoma
- McChord Air Force Base, Tacoma
- Naval Air Station, Whidbey Island (Island)
- Naval Base, Everett
- Puget Sound Naval Shipyard, Bremerton (Kitsap)
- Trident Submarine Base, Bangor (Kitsap)
- U.S. Army Yakima Firing Center, Yakima
- Reserve training centers at several locations

There are no scheduled closures as of this writing.

High Technology

Since its infancy in the mid-70s, the "high-tech" industry has virtually exploded in the state. Thousands are employed in hundreds of companies, ranging from giant Microsoft (more than 12,000) to one- and two-person firms with bright ideas.

High tech is a diverse industry encompassing electronics, manufacturing, telecommunications, biotechnology, computer software, etc. (High tech doesn't include applications in other industries. For instance, Boeing did almost all design of the 777 on computers, without paper drawings. This is a high-tech application, but the industry is aerospace manufacturing.) Companies are attracted to the state by such factors as previous successes, a highly productive labor force, proximity of major universities, location relative to the Far East, and quality of life.

Most of the state's high-tech firms are in the greater Seattle area, especially along the corridor from Redmond north along I-405 to Everett, and around Vancouver (across the Columbia from Portland, in Clark County). As the density of people continues to increase in these locations, smaller companies are relocating to or starting up in other places.

Aviation/Aerospace/Boeing

Washington has been into aviation since the century's second decade, when William Boeing, a

Seattle timberman, became interested in flying machines. In 1916, he formed the Pacific Aero Products Company and then changed its name a year later to Boeing Aircraft. Today, there are more than 30,000 licensed pilots and 7000 registered planes in the state.

In March 1919, Boeing pilot Eddie Hubbard flew the first international airmail from Seattle to Vancouver, B.C. During the 1920s, Boeing continued to build planes and, by August 1928, was carrying a quarter of the airmail in the United States. Then, the company was taken public to finance future expansion. Various mergers and acquisitions created the United Aircraft and Transportation Corporation, with Boeing and United Airlines as two of the components. In 1934, as a result of antitrust activity, this group was divided into United Air Lines, United Aircraft (manufacturing), and Boeing. In the mid 30s, Boeing built the famed "Clipper" for Pan American World Airways. With a range of over 3,000 miles, it flew Pacific Ocean routes and was used well into World War II. Then came the Model 307 Stratoliner, the first passenger plane with a pressurized cabin.

With World War II came the B-17 Flying Fortress, and thousands of workers thronged to Boeing's Seattle plants. Almost 7,000 B-17s were built, but only a few survive in flying condition today. Another plane of the times was the B-29 Superfortress. The best known B-29 was the Enola Gay, which dropped the atomic bomb on Hiroshima. During the war, development started on jet aircraft, with first the B-47 Stratojet and then the B-52 Stratofortress, which first flew in April 1952. The newest B-52 has served in the Air Force longer than any of the pilots now flying it, and it is older than most of them.

The commercial jet age was ushered in with the Model 367-80, called the "Dash 80" and soon to be given the famous 707 designation, the first of the 7XX series. It was placed in service in 1957, and more than 800 planes were delivered. A military version of this aircraft, the KC-135 tanker, has been re-engined and is still active. Since then have come the 727, 737, 747, 757, 767, and 777.

Although Boeing invested considerable resources in a supersonic transport (SST), federal support was cancelled in March 1971, and the plane never flew. Since 1960, with the purchase of a helicopter company in Philadelphia, Boeing has manufactured rotary-wing aircraft for both the military and civilian markets.

Activity in the space program has been extensive. Lunar orbiters, built in the 1960s to circle the Moon, sent pictures back to Earth that helped in selecting Moon landing sites. The powerful Saturn V launch vehicle came from Boeing's facility in Huntsville, Alabama. Much of the systems integration and building of the Lunar Roving Vehicle for NASA's Apollo Program was done at Boeing's facility in Kent. The Air Force and Navy cruise missiles have been major contracts for the company.

The company has also been involved in building hydrofoils, urban rapid rail mass transportation, and large wind turbines.

To support all the company's efforts, Boeing Computer was formed in 1970. Now, planes are being designed almost solely by computer, with few paper drawings being created. The company has several plants in the state, most in the Seattle area. The largest one, in Everett, is the largest building in the world, by volume. Boeing allows visitors to go inside and watch actual production in process.

The size and extent of the company, except for some peaks and valleys, remained about the same until 1996, when it acquired Rockwell's aerospace and defense units, worth about $3 billion. In 1997, a merger with McDonnell–Douglas created a giant company with more than 200,000 employees around the world and annual revenues exceeding $50 billion.

One interesting result of this was that a former McDonnell–Douglas airliner received the Boeing designation of 717. Programs underway include working on new fighter planes for the 21st century, an airborne laser (ABL), a tilt-rotor plane, the space station, and upgrades and new models of various planes in production. New production orders are announced almost weekly. With this giant firm and all its resources, nobody is surprised about any announcement by Boeing of new products and programs.

International Trade

The state's strategic location, transportation systems, and excellent port facilities have all contributed to major increases in this sector in recent years. Pacific Rim countries, consumers of much of the state's exports, are one or two days closer to our ports than others on the West Coast. Because of rail lines connecting Washington to eastern states, inventory tied up in the pipeline is significantly reduced. European trade also is significant, because flight time over the North Pole to London is the same as to Tokyo.

And then there is Canada. The U.S. and Canada are the world's largest import/export partnership, and much takes place in the western region. International trade is as, or more, important to Washington than any other state. The per capita value of exports originating here is more than twice that for the rest of the United States. A large percentage of the employment market directly depends on foreign trade. The full impact of the free-trade agreements is yet to be reported.

Energy

Washington's electric power system differs in a number of ways from those in the rest of the country. It can be broken down into three basic, physically integrated components:

- *Generation*, the production of energy.
- *Transmission*, the high-voltage transportation of energy from the generators to load centers.
- *Distribution*, the low-voltage delivery of energy from load centers to homes and businesses.

Federally owned hydroelectric power plants on the Columbia and Snake Rivers produce over half of the electricity used in Washington. This electricity is sold to distributors by the Bonneville Power Administration (BPA), which, under law, must market first to utilities serving the Northwest.

In addition, substantial hydro facilities are owned by other public entities such as the cities of Seattle and Tacoma, Washington Water Power, PacificCorp, and Puget Sound Energy. In total, two-thirds of Washington's electric power comes from hydroelectric power plants. Most of the rest comes from plants fired by natural gas. Attempts to build nuclear power plants generally have been financial disasters..

Hydro power is substantially different from other sources of power:

- It is cheap: Washington's average cost is less than 2.5¢ per kilowatt-hour, compared to California's 4¢ and 3.5¢ in the rest of the West.

- It comes from a renewable resource that has alternate and concurrent uses.

- It is most efficient when the dams and generators are operated cooperatively, not competitively. Because one dam affects the next dam downriver and so on, competition would not only be impractical and uneconomical but also damaging to the rivers and other resources.

The Federal Energy Regulatory Commission (FERC) has adopted regulations to ensure that the transmission systems of investor-owned utilities are accessible to all competitors and that no utility can operate its transmission to benefit its own power generation. This is called "open access." However, 80% of Washington's power transmission system is owned by the BPA and is exempt from FERC rules.

About 60 utilities serve retail customers in Washington. Three of these are investor-owned, providing about a third of the electricity sold in Washington and serving about 40% of the customers. Investor-owned utilities are regulated by the Washington Utilities and Transportation Commission.

The remainder are locally controlled city, county, or cooperative utilities. This is the highest proportion of publicly owned utilities in any state except Nebraska, where *all* utilities are publicly owned.

No state franchises for exclusive, monopoly service territories are granted. Instead, Washington's utilities have evolved in competition with each other for service territory. Based on a vote of the people, new publicly owned and locally regulated utilities can be formed through municipalization of the existing service territory of investor-owned utilities. This absence of monopolies, and the possibility of municipalization, has served as a competitive force that has helped to keep both public and private utility rates lower than they might otherwise have been.

Retail

This sector is holding steady in its percentage of the total. This is not surprising, considering the large numbers employed in resource and manufacturing.

Services

The percentage of people employed in this group continues a slow rise. Puget Sound cities provide almost all services for the Pacific Northwest.

Tourism

Tourism has become a major element of the state's economy, but not without help from energetic people and nature. Expo '62, the Seattle World's Fair, was one of few such expositions to turn a profit. Its legacy can still be seen at the Seattle Center, home of the popular Space Needle. Spokane got its turn in 1976. Its World Expo produced Riverfront Park and civic buildings, all much used today. Vancouver, B.C., helped with its Expo '86, which drew millions to the region and sparked an interest in cruises to Alaska.

In 1980, Mother Nature provided the eruption of Mount St. Helens. This gave the state the nation's first National Volcanic Monument, which draws thousands of visitors each year. Now, Mount St. Helens, Mount Rainier, the Olympic Mountains and Rain Forest, and the San Juan Islands provide more then enough major, unique, natural attractions for a two-week vacation.

Sports play a role, with major league teams in basketball (Supersonics), baseball (Mariners), and football (Seahawks). Also, Pac-10 college teams are popular.

Seattle can handle all but the largest events and has sufficient hotel rooms for attendees.

Washington tourism has an unofficial motto: "Keep Washington green—with money."

Government

Washington definitely does not lack for government. Many federal regulations were already in place when statehood was granted in 1889. Also, the writers of the state constitution were reluctant to place strong powers in the hands of a privileged few. The result is a long, very detailed constitution that has been amended more than 70 times.

Several levels and many special features of government within the state cause a lot of fragmentation and considerable overlap. However, this "open structure" has a major advantage, in that almost any one who really wants to participate in the state's governing process may do so as actively as desired.

The basic documents that the state uses to govern are the Constitution, the Revised Code of Washington (RCW), and the Washington Administrative Code (WAC). The RCW contains the basic law, and the WAC contains the rules and regulations used by the many departments and agencies to implement the RCW.

Three special features (few other states have all three) assist citizens in active participation:

Initiatives, basically citizen-written legislation, allow voters to place proposed laws on the ballot. They require petitions with signatures equal to 8% of the votes cast for Governor in the last general election.

The *direct initiative*, submitted directly to the public, requires only a majority vote to pass.

The *indirect initiative* is submitted to the Legislature, which can pass it into law, put it to a public vote as it stands, or submit it to the voters along with a legislative alternative.

In choosing between alternative initiatives, things get really complicated! Upon receiving a ballot with both an initiative and its legislative alternative, the voter casts either one or two votes. The voter can vote "for either" or "against both." If the voter is "against both," that is the end of it. If the vote is "for either," then a second vote is cast for either the initiative or the legislative alternative. Okay, now—are you sure you've got all this firmly fixed in your mind? You will find out if you come across one of these either/neither issues on an actual ballot!

A *referendum* permits voters to reject a law passed by the Legislature. It requires signatures equaling 4% of the last gubernatorial vote and must be submitted within 90 days of passage. If the referendum receives a majority of the vote, the legislation will stand as passed.

Recall allows voters to recall elected officials, but a reason must be stated. Directed mostly at local officials, it is seldom used. Judges are exempt.

Governmental Entities

There are six distinct and separate categories or entities of government that affect almost all citizens. Four, which are layered, are town/city, county, state, and federal. To these, add special districts and Native American or tribal.

Cities/Towns

About half the people reside within town or city boundaries. For the others, the county is their first level of governance. Towns and cities are classified on the basis of population, and the powers and obligations of each are determined by its classification:

Classification	Population needed (when formed)
First	>20,000
Second	10,000 to 20,000
Third	1,500 to 10,000
Fourth (Town)	300 to 1,500

Cities must furnish police and fire protection; may enact building codes and zoning ordinances; purchase, lease, condemn, or otherwise acquire real and personal property for city purposes; and provide construction and maintenance of streets, alleys, parks, and sidewalks. Cities are authorized to levy sales and business taxes. They may require and issue licenses for regulation or revenue-generating purposes; grant various franchises; acquire and operate certain types of public utilities; and borrow money or issue bonds for special projects.

There are three principal forms of government in the cities: mayor/council, council/manager, and commission. The basic difference between them lies in the placement of responsibility for city administration and the relationship of the administrative office to the legislative or policy-making body—and, of course, to the citizen.

In the mayor/council system, the voters elect a mayor and council members. The mayor is the chief administrative officer as well as the political head of the city. Therefore, that person is responsible for both determining policy and seeing it carried out.

In the council/manager system, the council determines policy and hires a city manager to serve as the chief administrative officer. The manager is accountable to the council, which chooses a mayor from among its members.

Commission cities elect three commissioners for four-year terms. Each fills a specific office: public safety and mayoralty; finance and accounting; and public works. The mayor's powers are the same as those of the other two commissioners.

Counties

Each of the state's 39 counties operates as a political subdivision, exercising the powers and responsibilities granted by statute. These are similar to those of the cities, plus providing for the superior court system and conducting elections. Washington counties classified according to population:

Class	Population
AA	500,000
A	210,000 to 500,000
1	125,000 to 210,000
2	70,000 to 125,000
3	40,000 to 70,000
4	18,000 to 40,000
5	12,000 to 18,000
6	8,000 to 12,000
7	5,000 to 8,000
8	3,000 to 5,000

A typical county is organized as follows:

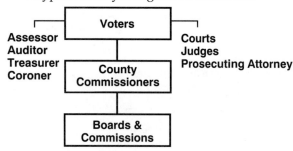

State Government

The makeup of the state government is similar to other states, with three separate but equal branches: Executive, Legislative, and Judicial.

Executive Branch

Nine officers serve four-year terms, and they are elected in presidential election years. Compensation is set by the Legislature. Each is relatively independent and can be from any political party.

Governor—Enforces the law and manages state government organizations that do not come under the other eight elected officials or agencies not under his jurisdiction. May fill vacancies that may occur in other elected offices between elections. Has line-item veto power.

Lieutenant Governor—Acting Governor when the Governor is out of state, with all the powers of the office. Acts as President of the Senate and chairs the Senate Rules Committee. First in line to succeed a Governor who vacates the office for any reason.

Secretary of State—Chief election officer of the state. Licenses all foreign and domestic corporations. Registers and attests to official acts of the Governor. Maintains various records and affixes state seal where required.

Treasurer—Establishes and carries out policy to manage state financial resources, chairs state finance committee, and manages state bond issues.

Auditor—Audits public accounts, prepares state financial statements, and conducts postaudits of state agencies and local governments.

Attorney General—Chief legal officer of the state and provides legal advice to the executive and legislative branches and county prosecuting attorneys. Represents administrative agencies at hearing and in court.

Superintendent of Pubic Instruction—Certifies teaching personnel, approves and accredits programs, apportions state and federal funds for K-12 schools and enforces laws relating to public schools.

Commissioner of Public Lands—Heads the Department of Natural Resources (DNR), which manages land, forest, and aquatic resources of the state, and is secretary of the State Capital Committee.

Insurance Commissioner—Regulates the insurance industry in the state and is the state fire marshal.

There are many departments, commissions, boards, and other smaller entities of the state. Major departments are Social and Health Services, Labor and Industries, Employment Security, Health, Corrections, Veterans Affairs, Licensing, General Administration, Revenue, Personnel, Retirement Systems, Ecology, Agriculture, and Fish and Wildlife.

Legislative Branch

The state has 49 legislative districts. The bicameral Legislature has a house with two representatives and one senator for each district. Senators are elected for four-year terms, with half up for election every other year. The 98 members of the House all stand for election every two years. The Legislature convenes every January with a starting schedule of 105 days in odd-numbered years, when the main focus is the biannual budget. In even years, it is a planned 60-day session. If the business does not get accomplished in the scheduled period, special sessions (30 days each) can be, and are frequently, called. Between sessions, many committees hold meetings and other activities. The legislative staffs are mostly full time, so the term "citizen legislature" is frequently debated.

Judiciary

The state's judicial system has four levels: Courts of Limited Jurisdiction, Superior Court, Appeals Court, and Supreme Court.

Courts of Limited Jurisdiction

These District and Municipal Courts hear misdemeanor criminal cases, traffic, nontraffic and parking infractions, domestic violence protection orders, and civil actions of $35,000 or less. Judges are elected for four-year terms and usually hear the cases, but a six-person jury may be requested. Small claims, in which people may represent themselves, also fall into this category. Any appeals from this level are made to a superior court.

Superior Court

In these courts, the major civil and criminal cases are tried, including civil matters, domestic relations, felony criminal, juvenile matters, and appeals from courts of limited jurisdiction. Judges are elected for four-year terms for the 30 judicial districts; each county does not have its own superior court. Juries normally consist of 12 members.

Court of Appeals

This court hears appeals from the lower courts, except those under the direct jurisdiction of the Supreme Court. There are three divisions: Spokane, Tacoma, and Seattle. Judges are elected for six year terms. A panel of three from the 16 elected appellate judges is selected to hear each appeal. Oral or written arguments are considered. The court may overrule, uphold, or modify decisions of lower courts. Actions of this court may be appealed to the Supreme Court.

Supreme Court

The highest court in the state has nine justices, each elected for a six-year term, with three chosen on a nonpartisan judicial ballot at the general election in even-numbered years. The Court may elect to reject or hear appeals, and its decisions have the force of nonstatutory law. In a few areas (such as constitutional questions), it is the court of original jurisdiction. The Court establishes rules for the state court system and governs admission to practice, conduct, and discipline for attorneys and judges. The Chief Justice is elected for a four-year term by a vote of the Court, and the senior remaining justice is the "Associate Chief Justice."

Laws, Rules, and Regulations

Two principal volumes set forth these matters. The Revised Code of Washington (RCW) contains the law as passed by the Legislature. Many of these laws are in general terms, enabling departments and agencies to conduct their business. To do their missions, these bodies adopt rules and regulations, which are codified in the Washington Administrative Code (WAC).

Federal Government

The state is represented in "the Other Washington" by two senators and nine representatives. The impact of the federal government in the state is much greater than might be supposed by the modest size of the congressional delegation. This is due to several factors:

- The Native American population in over 20 tribes and their reservations.

- The many navigable waters.

- Several large military bases.

- Canada on the north with adjacent waters, movement of fish, and border crossings.

- National Parks, forests, etc.

- Major ports of entry (customs).

- Regional headquarters of federal agencies.

Tribal Governments

Native Americans and their reservations occupy a unique position in both the state and federal systems and therefore have a large impact on various activities in the state.

Article 1, Section 8, of the U.S. Constitution states: "Congress shall have Power . . . to regulate Commerce with Foreign Nations, and among the several states, and with the Indian Tribes . . . ." Thus, the many treaties that were signed with the Indians in the past fall under the jurisdiction of the courts. The Washington Constitution, Article XXVI, is very specific on the subject of Indian lands: "That the people inhabiting this state do agree and declare that they forever disclaim all right and title to the unappropriated public lands lying within said limits owned or held by any Indian Tribes . . . and said Indian lands shall remain under the absolute jurisdiction and control of the Congress of the United States."

A common provision of the Indian treaties of the mid-1800s stated that "the right of taking fish at all usual and accustomed grounds and stations is further secured to said Indians in common with all citizens of the Territory." While there have been many changes over the years in the way the federal government has managed Indian affairs and lands, it was the tribe's ever decreasing share of the yearly salmon harvest that brought matters to a head in 1974. The federal government had brought suit against Washington State in federal court, on behalf of the state's Indian population. Judge Boldt ruled in favor of the Indians. The Boldt decision affirmed that treaty Indians are entitled to the opportunity to catch up to 50% of the salmon harvest in treaty areas under Washington State jurisdiction. The ruling also states that when Indian tribal governments are organized to regulate tribal fisheries and fishermen, they (rather than the state) will be responsible for that regulation within all "usual and accustomed places and grounds."

The Boldt decision has withstood many challenges. A later court ruling extended the original decision to include responsibility for environmental protection to preserve the salmon runs. As a result, tribal governments have become involved in decisions on logging practices, highway construction, and real estate development in several areas around the state. Now there is the matter of shellfish (clams, oysters) on all the beaches and tidelands and what the Indians are entitled to. And we have gaming casinos on reservations and smoke stores selling tobacco without certain taxes on reservations. Stay tuned, for there will be more to come.

Special Districts

These are established in various ways for a variety of purposes. Most are related to public services, are governed by a small group of individuals, and obtain operation funds from taxes, fees, or grants. Special districts include

School	*Irrigation*	*Port*
Parks and recreation	*Conservation*	*Fire*
Sewage	*Public utility*	*Water*
Hospital	*Library*	*Dikes*
Drainage	*Flood control*	*Cemetery*

Washington has more than 1,100 special districts—the eighth highest number of the 50 states. Consequently, populous counties may have scores of governmental bodies. King County has more than 200, whereas counties with small populations may have only 12 to 15. Special district boundaries may not coincide with those of cities and towns, a situation that causes some confusion during elections and when resources are allocated.

Port districts play a prominent role in many communities and the economy. Their history goes back to when the state joined the Union. Prior to that, waterfront development was privately done and sometimes monopolized. In the state constitution, title to the beds, tidelands, and shorelands of navigable waters was given to the state. Finally, in 1911, legislation was passed to enable the creation of locally controlled public port districts. These local special districts were authorized to acquire, develop, and operate facilities for all forms of transporting goods and people within the harbor lines. Along with that was the right to levy taxes and sell bonds to finance activities. In 1911, the Port of Seattle became the first of its kind in the country. In 1959, the Legislature authorized port districts to be established even where there was no appropriate body of water. Depending on size, port districts are governed by three or more commissioners who serve six-year, staggered terms. Daily operations are usually delegated to a port manager. The state now has more than 70 port districts in all but a few counties.

Making a Law in Olympia

A law starts as an idea or a need, either by a legislator or a citizen who communicates it to a legislator in either the House or the Senate. It is then drafted into a bill, usually by paid staffs who have expertise in writing in the proper form. The sponsor encourages as many cosponsors as possible to "sign on" before the bill is assigned a number, when it becomes a matter of public record. Then, it is referred to a policy committee by the majority party leadership. There is no guarantee the bill will receive a public hearing, because that is the decision of the committee chair. Many bills are introduced each session, and some are never heard.

After a public hearing, it moves to executive session of the committee. Again, there is the possibility that it may not be taken up. Here is the first opportunity to amend the bill. If the bill passes out of committee, it goes to the Rules Committee or, if money is involved, to the Fiscal Committee. If it passes Fiscal, then it goes back to Rules, where it again goes through a priority selection process. Passing out of Rules, it goes to a "second reading calendar" on the floor, where it can again be amended. Then, on to a third reading, when a vote is taken for final passage from the initiating chamber.

Next, the bill moves to the other chamber for essentially the same process. For final passage, the second chamber must approve it in exactly the same form, right down to each comma. If approved in spirit but not form, it goes back to the first chamber for a second approval. If it is not approved in its new form, it goes to a conference committee, which is closed to the public. The conference committee may do anything it wants, including a full rewrite. The conference committee report then goes to both chambers for a vote, no amendments allowed.

A bill that passes the Legislature goes on to the Governor, who may sign it, veto it, veto certain sections, or do nothing, in which case the bill automatically becomes law after ten days.

This is not an easy process and is why many ideas never become law.

Voting

Finally, those who don't care to be actively involved in government can at least vote. All state residents who are U.S. citizens over 18 years old and who have not been convicted of a felony may register. Each county auditor is also the registrar of voters. Every locale has several convenient places to register—the most widely used being driver's licensing locations. Registration is permanent unless it lapses because the registrant does not vote for a period of 24 months or does not vote in a presidential election.

In addition to a general election held each November, a primary election is held in September, and other special elections may be held as necessary.

Beware! Many special levies and other spending requests are put on the ballot at special elections, and low voter turnouts often allow minority groups to vote in their special interests.

Washington has a "blanket primary." That is, all candidates are placed on the same ballot, with party affiliation noted, and every voter can vote for any of them. Because of this, crossover voting frequently takes place and must be considered when analyzing primary results.

Growth Management

One of the more far-reaching pieces of legislation is called the Growth Management Act, passed in 1990. Its stated reason was, "The legislature finds that uncoordinated and unplanned growth, together with a lack of common goals expressing the public's interest

in the conservation of the wise use of our lands, pose a threat to the environment, sustainable development, and the health, safety and high quality of life enjoyed by the residents of this state." It calls for large and fast-growing cities and counties to plan in keeping with state goals on

Affordable housing	*Sprawl reduction*
Open space and recreation	*Economic development*
Environmental protection	*Regional transportation*
Natural resource industries	*Property rights*
Permit processing	*Historic lands and buildings*
Public facilities and services	*Public participation*

To date, extensive effort has been put into developing plans and, in some places and on some topics, controversy has and is taking place. One point that arises frequently is that the boards that review the plans are made up of nonelected members while the plans of the cities and counties are submitted by elected officials. This item will be with us—stay tuned.

Finance

The finances of the state involve everyone and center on the budget process, which encompasses revenues and expenditures. The state budget is based on a two-year cycle that officially starts on July 1 of each even-numbered year. Actually, budgetary action starts earlier, when state agencies develop budget estimates and submit them to the Office of Financial Management, which uses them to prepare the budget and submit it to the Governor on July 1. In turn, the Governor submits a recommended budget in December to the Legislature.

In January of odd-numbered years, the Legislature convenes for 105 days to receive and review the budget and prepare the appropriation bills. The Legislature then sends the bills to the Governor, who signs the biennial budget into law. All the time this is taking place, money is being spent, and reviews and forecasts of revenues are being made by such groups as the Economic and Revenue Forecasting Council, the Caseload Forecast Council, and committees of the Legislature. In even-numbered years, the budget in being is reviewed, and a supplemental budget is generally passed by the Legislature to reflect changes.

Revenue

The operative word here is "taxes," which affect all. A dictionary definition of *tax* is "a pecuniary burden laid upon individuals or property to support government, with the payment exacted by legislative authority."

Washington Tax History

The present tax structure took form during the Great Depression of the 1930s, when the government had to come up with new ways of gathering income. Up until then, more than 90% of state revenue came from property taxes. The 1935 Revenue Act added several new taxes: retail sales and use, business and occupation, public utility, tobacco and liquor, and admissions and conveyance. Since that time, several attempts have been made to institute a personal and/or corporate income tax. All of these attempts have failed either through State Supreme Court decisions or by the vote of the people.

In 1929, the State Supreme Court ruled that an income tax on financial institutions was unconstitutional because income, a form of property, must be taxed at the same rate as any other property. Then, in 1930, the voters approved the 14th Amendment to the State Constitution, which states that "all taxes shall be uniform upon the same class of property." Many believed that income would be considered different from tangible property and that an income tax would stand the test of the courts.

On this basis, the voters in 1932 approved both personal and corporate taxes, only to have the Court rule that all income falls into the same class of property and must therefore be taxed uniformly. There have been other efforts over the years, the latest being in 1982, but all have failed. There are still some who continue to advocate a personal income tax, but it is doubtful that it will ever make it past the voters. Since the 1930s, there have been changes involving rates, exemptions, modification of various tax bases, and other limitations.

Accounting Cycles

As already mentioned, the state has a fiscal biennium that commences July 1 in each odd-numbered year and ends on June 30 of the next odd-numbered year. School districts have a fiscal year that extends from September 1 to August 31. All other taxing districts operate on a calendar year basis.

Personal Income Tax

Washington is one of only seven states without a personal income tax. It does not impose a tax on in-tangible assets such as stocks, bonds, and bank accounts. In 1996, the U.S. Supreme Court ruled that no state could tax retirement income beyond its borders, which makes Washington a sort of tax haven for retirees from states such as California.

Consumer (Sales) Tax

A principal source of state revenue is the sales tax and other taxes on consumer items. The combined state and local sales tax ranges from 7.0 to 8.2 percent, depending on variable local sales tax rates. An excise tax applies to select products: gasoline (>20 cents per gallon), cigarettes (> 80 cents per pack), and alcoholic beverages. There is no tax on most food items or prescription drugs, nor is there a tax on most personal services (legal, medical, dental, etc).

Real Estate Tax

An excise tax (about 2%) is imposed on the sale of real property (paid by the seller). In building a new home, the purchase of the land is subject to the excise tax, while the material for construction is subject to the retail sales tax.

Property Tax

Personal property taxes are levied on business assets only. Taxes on real property are a primary revenue source and, while not as high as some states, still average about $13 per $1,000 of valuation. The exact amount varies over the state because of voter-approved special levies and some other factors (see Living).

Vehicle Taxes

The basic licensing fee is currently $54 and change for an original license for each private auto and $28+ for annual renewal. However, there is also a vehicle excise tax at 2.2% of the depreciated value, according to make, model, and age. Other vehicles—such as motor homes, trailers, and trucks—have other fees in addition. Some state residents consider this accumulation of fees to be exorbitant and try to evade them by licensing their vehicles in states such as Oregon, where fees are much lower. The state is cracking down on such shenanigans, however, and the penalties for getting caught are substantial.

Watercraft Excise Tax

Boats over 16 feet are subject to an excise tax if not used in business. If they are, they are subject to the personal property tax.

Business and Occupation (B&O) and Public Utility Tax

Businesses pay a B&O and/or public utility tax based on gross receipts of the business. The rates vary from 0.011 to 5.029 percent. Small businesses are par-

Sources of State Revenues (All governmental funds)
FY 1997 (annual amount)

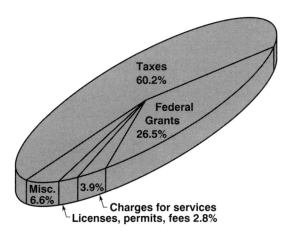

Sources of General Fund-State Revenues
1997–1999 Biennium Estimate

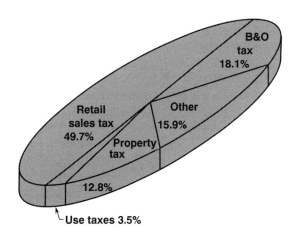

tially to totally exempt from this tax, according to a sliding scale.

Estate Tax

Estate tax is charged to the estate of a deceased person, but only if it exceeds the federal filing limit, now at $600,000. A person's estate is half of any community property plus any separate property.

Other Revenue Sources

The largest other source is federal grants. To this add licenses, permits, fees, etc.

Expenditures

The operation budget for the 1997–99 biennium from all fund sources is about $36 billion. Additionally, there is a capital budget (i.e., for major buildings, etc.) of $1.9 billion, funded mostly from general obligation bonds.

Operation expenses are grouped into seven broad categories:

Human Services   *Public Education*

Higher Education   *Natural Resources*

Transportation   *General Government*

Other

In 1993, passage of Initiative 601 placed very specific controls on spending and transferring funds between programs. It prohibits the state from imposing responsibility for new programs on local government without funding for reimbursement. There is now an emergency reserve fund, and a 2/3 vote of the Legislature is required to raise state revenues beyond that allowed by a "fiscal growth factor" to allow for inflation and population changes.

Distribution of 1997–1999 State Operating
Expenditures (all funds)

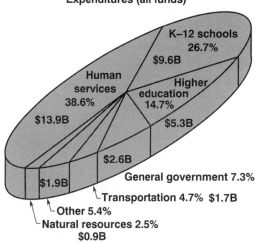

Environment

Land

The amount of land with which the state started has essentially remained unchanged except for some few acres reclaimed from tidelands or lost to erosion. However, tens of thousands of acres have changed in appearance and use, and much of it has been and is still being analyzed, almost as if under a microscope. In spite of the existence of huge tracts of wilderness, forest, and crops, land is actually a surprisingly scarce resource.

Much of the state's diversity lies with the land. It is a geologist's paradise as much as any state, with its mountains, volcanoes, lakes, rivers, falls, coulees, ocean shores, deltas, channeled scablands, glaciers, forests, minerals, and the Sound. Three different views of the land are life zones, ownership, and use.

Life Zones

Several major zones occur because of the wide range of altitudes (sea level to 14,410 feet) and various climates.

Arctic–alpine, a.k.a. *alpine* (5,500+ ft). Found only in the high peaks of the Cascades and Olympic Mountains. Heavy precipitation results in formation of glaciers above timberline. Covered by heavy snow more than eight months of the year. Plant season of a few flowers and lichens is short, and wildlife use is only for short periods in summer. Very sensitive to disturbance. These areas have no use except as snow pack reservoirs and limited recreation.

Canadian, a.k.a. *subalpine* (3,000–6,500 ft). Tall, dense conifer trees and a moderately long growing season for plants. Deep snow in the winter. Rich humus layer in the soil supports saprophytic plants. Many species of birds visit in the summer. Steep slopes and heavy precipitation may cause erosion.

Hudsonian, a.k.a. *subalpine* (2,000–5,000 ft). Open forest right below Arctic–Alpine zone. Trees are conifers with understory of shrubs. The short growing season of 3 to 5 months finds intense biological activity, resulting in rich and beautiful flower meadows. Sensitive to disturbance.

Humid transition zone (wet side), a.k.a. *montane and lowland forest* (sea level to 3,000 ft). Tall forests of Douglas fir, western red cedar, and western hemlock. Ocean beaches and lodgepole pine. Sitka spruce on west side of Olympic mountains. Shrub layers high. Considerable variety of vertebrates. Many birds are permanent residents that go into higher zones in summer. Winters are mild and wet. Growing season is long.

Arid timbered transition (dry side), a.k.a. *forests of dry climates* (1,800–3,000 ft). This region starts at the top with Douglas fir, descending to Ponderosa pine and finally grasslands. Winters are cold, and summers are long and hot. Can sustain heavy recreation use. Logging pressure high. Wintering area for big game, which spends summers at higher elevations.

Arid grassland transition, a.k.a. *steppe* (1,500–2,400 ft). A belt of grassland known as the Palouse. Prairie bunchgrass important. Some wetness from the snow, but arid summers limit growth. Used for wheat and grazing.

Upper Sonoran, a.k.a. *steppe lowlands of the Columbia Basin* (200–1,900 ft). Extremely arid, with grasses, herbs, and shrubs. Area too dry for dryland farming but excellent for irrigation.

Ownership

The total land area of the state is 66,582 sq. miles (176,617 sq. km) or 42,604,800 acres. This places the state 19th (with water) or 20th (without) in size of all 50. Here's who owns what and in what amounts:

Owner	No. of acres	%
Private	23,603,000	55
National Forests	8,888,000	21
National Parks	1,815,000	4
Indian	2,505,000	6
Other Federal	1,964,000	5
DNR and other State	3,541,000	8
County	345,000	1

National forests contain the land that has been established as wilderness.

Use

When Washington became a state, there were four principal uses for the land: forest, farming, rangeland, and settlement. While we can still look at those four broad general uses, many subcategories of use are now applicable. Zoning laws, ownership, and other rules and regulations require that each individual parcel of ground be given a detailed analysis before use or ownership change. What may be a permissible use today may not be so in the future. An example is a parcel of land that is being farmed, but which the owner wants to subdivide later into one-acre residential lots. A zoning change may be made to limit the lot size to five acres or more. Consideration must also be given to availability of water, sewer, roads, and many other items. Several of the changes that have taken place over the past 100 years:

- Vast areas have been logged. Initially, much of this land was turned into farmland or rezoned for settlement. Then, the practice of replanting of trees commenced. About 20 million acres of forest remain, with many square miles in parks, recreation areas, and wilderness.

- In the east, dryland farming techniques have enabled much of the land to produce wheat and other crops. One reason dryland farming works is that evapotranspiration, or the loss of water from plants by evaporation and transpiration, does not happen there as much as in most areas. The moisture from winter snow and any rain is able to sink deep enough to remain for winter wheat to sustain a vigorous spurt of growth in the spring. The big change there was the damming of the rivers to provide irrigation. More than 500,000 acres in the Columbia Basin receive water, with the potential of up to 1 million acres being able to receive the essential resource for growing.

- Ditching and diking of low-lying land and marshes in valleys such as the Skagit and Snohomish have created some of the most productive farmland in the state. Flooding still occurs in these places, but the good soaking the ground receives appears to do little long-range harm.

- Increasing urban areas and easements for transportation have consumed many acres of land. The pattern of land use continues to change, especially with the State Legislature's passage of the Growth Management Act in 1990. For the counties affected, this requires a complete review of land use with a major objective of stopping urban sprawl. This will result in a higher density of people residing within the borders of existing cities and towns.

Mountains

Mountains, especially the Cascade and Coast Ranges, contribute greatly to the character and the climate of the state. The Cascade Range bisects the state into really two states that differ in weather, climate, and vegetation, which further translates into different lifestyles and attitudes of the people. The Coast Range (which includes the Olympics), along the Pacific on the west, also has a direct effect on the weather and, in turn, the economy.

The *Olympic Mountains* on the Olympic Peninsula rise to 7,965 feet on Mt. Olympus. The proximity of the ocean and the quick rise in elevation combine to cause the annual rainfall to be upwards of 180 inches,

creating one of the few temperate rain forests in the world. No roads cross these mountains in any direction, but some roads go a short way into the interior. After that, there is hiking. Almost the whole area is in either a national park or forest, including wilderness. Hurricane Ridge provides a good view of the mountains, and a road from the west along the Hoh River leads to the Rain Forest Trail. Going south along the coastal range toward the Columbia, elevations decrease. The Willapa Hills rise about 1,500 feet and contain large amounts of timber acreage.

The *Cascade Range* contains mountains of all sizes and shapes. In the south, the hills are more rolling than in the north, where the peaks are steep and rugged. From south to north, there are five major volcanoes: Adams, St. Helens, Rainier, Shuksan, and Baker. The Transportation topic details the five roads that cross the range, providing access between east and west. Mount Rainier is "The Mountain," rising to 14,410 feet. It can be seen from much of the state on clear days. Many glaciers and streams are created from all the snow that permanently covers the higher elevations. The record snowfall in 1972 at the Paradise ranger station was 93.5 feet (1,122 inches). The lower areas are easily accessible, with a good road to Paradise and other camping and climbing areas. During the summer, many people take the guided climb to the top over a three-day period. One needs to be in good condition, and there is still danger. Remember: the Mountain is King!

Mount St. Helens has drawn the most attention since its eruption on May 18, 1980, at 8:32 a.m. For two months prior, there had been considerable earthquake and minor volcanic activity. The mountain was monitored by scientists, who warned that something major could happen. The blast was equal to an earthquake of magnitude 5 and reduced the height by 1,300 feet. The massive landslide destroyed 150,000 acres of forest and sent waters and mudflows to choke the Toutle and Cowlitz rivers and surrounding areas.

Mount Rainier

Hurdles at a high school appear to be the right height for elves after being inundated by mud flows from the eruption of Mount St. Helens.

About 4 billion board feet of timber was flattened or destroyed, of which 25% was recovered during the two years after the eruption. Much of the ash from the eruption landed in the eastern part of the state, hurting existing crops and vegetation but also adding nutrients to the soil. Sixty people either perished or were unaccounted for. In August 1982, President Reagan signed the law that set aside 110,000 acres centered on the volcano as the Mount St. Helens National Volcanic Monument, the nation's first such monument. The Corps of Engineers built massive earthworks along the rivers to prevent or reduce future flooding. Growth is taking place, and wildlife has returned to much of the area. Access roads, viewing sites, and visitor centers are available, with the main attractions being on route 504 off I-5 along the Toutle River.

In the southeast (Columbia, Garfield, and Asotin Counties) are the *Blue Mountains*, which rise to about 6,000 feet. The Umatilla National Forest and Wenaha-Tucannon Wilderness cover much of the area. These mountains extend well into Oregon.

The Northeast corner is anchored by the Selkirk Mountains, which are foothills of the Rockies. Again, we are looking at heights of only 5 to 6 thousand feet. There is considerable wildlife here in the Colville and Kaniksu National Forests, with a small area designated wilderness.

The mountains are a great natural resource and provide many benefits. They create subclimate zones, support all manner of wildlife, and provide many recreational opportunities and scenic views.

Forests

A forest is not just a dense growth of trees, but also undergrowth, insects, wildlife, air, soil, and water, with great diversity based location, climate, altitude, amount of water received, soil, etc. In the east, the drought-resistant Ponderosa Pine is dominant, while Douglas fir, hemlock, and cedar are common in the west.

Prominent in discussions about forests is the question: Is it an old-growth forest? There seems to be some consensus that old growth is defined by an age of at least 200 years and no significant disruption due to fire, disease, or other problems. However, trees do not live forever and are subjected to disease, fire, wind, and old age. The state has about 3 million acres of old growth, of which about 1.5 million is scheduled to be preserved forever.

Of the total land base in the state, about 40% is timberland, owned as follows:

Ownership	No. of acres	%
Federal		
National Forest	5,116,000	30
Other Federal	182,000	1
DNR	2,068,000	12
Indian	1,369,000	8
Timber industry	4,671,000	28
Small tree farmers	3,222,000	19
Miscellaneous	214,000	2
Total	16,842,000	100

A significant amount (5,815,000 acres) of the timberland in National Forests and Parks and some other areas is in preserves. This is 14% of the total state land area and is more than the area of some smaller states.

National forests are administered by the U.S. Department of Agriculture for wood production, recreation, wildlife, and wilderness. The wilderness areas are to be left in as natural a state as possible, with very limited human access.

Created in 1957 by the State Legislature, the Department of Natural Resources (DNR) manages all the state-owned lands, and regulates the forestry industry and wildlife on state and private lands. Much of the land it manages was granted to the state at the time of statehood as an endowment to provide funds for public school construction. Other land was acquired as a result of nonpayment of taxes, gifts, etc. These lands have been put into various trusts, with proceeds used for public purposes.

Most of the trees in the forests are conifers or softwoods that do not lose their leaves in the winter. The other main type is deciduous or hardwoods, which do lose their leaves in winter. The difference does not relate to the hardness or softness of the wood itself.

It is estimated there are about 10,000 different forest products, and the average American uses more than 600 pounds of paper in a year.

Trees are a renewable resource, and about three trees are planted for each one harvested. Through normal growth, more board feet are being added to the forests than are used.

For forest management, detailed planning considers the size of the area for cutting, terrain, watersheds, access to the area, and replanting. Different methods are used to harvest trees:

- Clear-cutting removes all trees from a specific area. It is the most economical and is the best for replanting shade-intolerant Douglas Fir.
- Partial cuts leave many mature trees behind to provide shelter for sun-intolerant seedlings and seeds for new trees. This is a common way to harvest Ponderosa Pine on the east side of the Cascades.
- Second-growth thinning is done every 10 to 15 years in a replanted forest. It removes weaker trees, providing more light and room for those remaining.

New seedlings are grown in nurseries from seeds selected from trees that have desirable characteristics. Millions of seedlings are planted each year. Nurseries can be visited, as can forests in all stages of growth and places where different harvesting methods have been used.

Laws governing the harvesting of timber include the following features:

- Permits are required before harvesting.
- All streams and wetlands to be protected with buffer strips.

- Permits are required before any burning is done.
- All lands harvested must be replanted with at least 190 trees per acre within three years.
- Excise taxes are levied on all timber harvests.

Aquatic Lands

A significant portion of the state, about 2 million acres (5% of the total), falls under the definition of aquatic land, which is owned by the state and managed by the Department of Natural Resources (DNR). These public lands are defined in Article XVII of the state constitution to be the "beds and shores of all navigable waters in the state, up to and including the line of ordinary high tide in waters where the tide ebbs and flows, and up to and including the line of ordinary high water within the banks of all navigable rivers and lakes . . . ." Under that article, they are called tide lands, but changing times and use have coined a new name.

Many states give upland owners the riparian right to build out over navigable waters. Washington, at the time of statehood, chose to become a nonriparian state and owns all the aquatic land, which requires abutting owners and others wanting to use such land to obtain authorization from the state. From 1889 to 1971, the state sold more than 60% of the tidelands and 30% of the shorelands to foster economic growth. Now, all aquatic lands are managed by the DNR in the public interest.

About 8,000 linear miles of aquatic lands are on navigable rivers, lakes, and tidally influenced areas. The term *navigable* means capable of and susceptible to use for commerce. Areas with state aquatic lands are

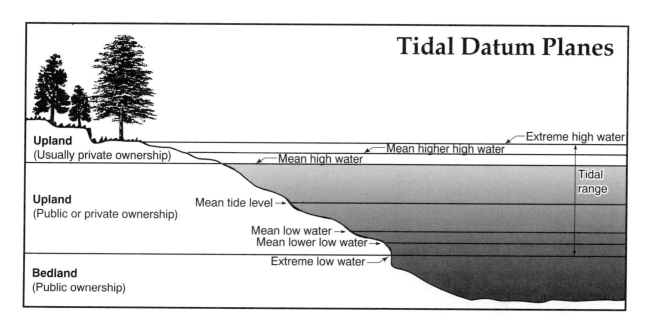

Tidal Datum Planes

Extreme high water

Mean higher high water

Mean high water

Upland
(Usually private ownership)

Tidal range

Upland
(Public or private ownership)

Mean tide level →

Mean low water →
Mean lower low water →

Extreme low water →

Bedland
(Public ownership)

- Hood Canal, Puget Sound, and the Strait of Juan de Fuca.
- Coastal areas, measured seaward three miles from mean high tide.
- Submerged lands of navigable rivers and lakes.
- Harbor areas.

Contained within these lands are resources of significant environmental and economic importance.

Aquatic Plants

Eelgrass, kelp, and seaweed grow in these areas, converting sunlight and carbon dioxide into plant material, which is consumed by animals. Salt marsh plants such as sedges and rushes contribute to the food chain and provide habitat and erosion control.

Aquatic Animals

Aquatic lands are the habitat of clams, oysters, mussels, scallops, geoduck, and shrimp. Crab and various fish use these waters as a nursery for their young.

Minerals

Within or on aquatic lands are minerals such as sand, gravel, petroleum, gas, gold, silver, and titanium, which may be available for extraction. Just leaving something like gravel in place can aid fish spawning.

The Division of Aquatic Lands of the DNR manages these lands to protect their environment, preserve the resource, and maintain access for commerce, travel, and recreation. Some of the land is leased, and the income is used for resource protection and to provide public access to aquatic lands.

To fully understand our surroundings requires information on those areas that have both land and water components.

Watersheds

A watershed is the entire area drained by a particular creek or river—a geographic unit of land that is defined by the flows of rainwater and melting snow within it. Thus, small, individual actions can affect the whole watershed. That is, we all live upstream from someone and downstream from someone else.

A given watershed comprises smaller ones and may be a component of a larger one. The Columbia River watershed encompasses not only eastern Washington but also parts of Idaho, Oregon, and Montana. Within that shed are hundreds of others such as the Snake, Spokane, Wenatchee, and Yakima River watersheds, each of which in turn has smaller components. Puget Sound is a watershed that drains an area from the crests of the Cascades to the Olympic Mountains, but it is part of one even larger called the Salish Watershed, which includes Vancouver Island and British Columbia. So, international boundaries are of no significance as far as nature is concerned.

Watershed analysis has become a major part of land and environment decisions. It is an inventory and analytical process to identify issues and processes, describe the condition of the watershed, and look at trends and the future. Identifying point and nonpoint pollution is one of the tasks in an analysis. Pollution is the collective result of many small actions that create undesirable conditions. An example of point pollution is an identifiable drainpipe that discharges an undesirable liquid into a stream. Nonpoint pollution is the aggregate of chemical flows from lawns, failing septic tanks, animal waste, and so forth.

Wetlands

In wetlands, groundwater is at or near the surface, or the land is covered by shallow water for all or part

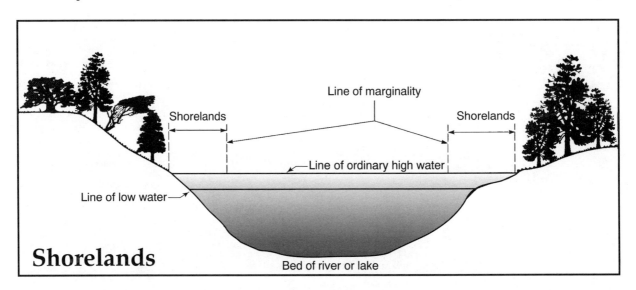

Shorelands

of the year, or saturation with water is the dominant factor of the nature of the soil and types of plants and animals living in or on the surface. Synonyms are marshes, swamps, and bogs.

The state has a large variety of wetlands. Along the Pacific Coast are the coastal salt marshes and tidelands in Grays Harbor and Willapa Bay. Nisqually Delta and Skagit Bay off Puget Sound are wetlands called tidal flats. Freshwater wetlands are widespread west of the Cascades. East of the mountains, the Potholes area around Moses Lake and the Turnbull National Wildlife Refuge near Cheney (Spokane) provide wetlands for many birds and mammals.

The benefits of wetlands are many: recreation, scenic areas, flood reduction and control, pollution control, fish and wildlife support (including a nursery for their young), storm and erosion control, and water for drinking and other household uses, agriculture, and aquaculture. Wetlands are well protected under a variety of laws and regulations.

Water

In our wondrous state of Washington,
Many waters do abound;
The ocean, lakes, and rivers,
And the beautiful Puget Sound.

With all these varied waters,
We certainly are blessed,
From the long and mighty Columbia
To the Pacific on our west.

Fishing, boating, barging, watching
Magnificent seals and whales—
The opportunities are endless
As every day unveils.

Barbara Buckley

When someone thinks or talks about the state, the subject of water in some context normally comes up. And with good reason, for it is a major component of our history, landscape, and economy. Most people live on or close by water of some sort, and their activities are oriented in some way, to salt or fresh water. The rich marine environment is shared with a vast number of animals and aquatic plants. Water is a major factor in the complex ecosystem in which we live and work here in the Northwest.

Coastal Waters

Pacific Ocean

The turbulent waters of the world's largest ocean, which occupies about one-third of the Earth's surface, dominate Washington's coast and helped form its rugged cliffs and long beaches. Although the direct coastline distance from the mouth of the Columbia north to the entrance to the Strait of Juan de Fuca is only 157 miles, the shoreline, including all the ins and outs, is 3,000 miles.

The impact of the Pacific goes far beyond the few miles of direct contact. It is the marine highway for shipping and contributes greatly to the moist, moderate climate of the western side of the Cascades. Its sheer size and vast expanse all the way to the shores of Asia, coupled with the westerly wind flow, creates the large and sometimes massive waves that batter the coast. The powerful seas have caused the north portion of the West Coast to be called the "graveyard of ships." Since the first known wreck in 1808, the coast has claimed at least 175 ships. Some passengers and crew survived, but many did not, especially in years before the coast was settled and the modern-day Coast Guard became available.

In July 1994, an area of 3,310 square miles along the Olympic coast from Cape Flattery south to the mouth of the Copalis River and extending out an average of 38 miles seaward was designated the Olympic Coast Marine Sanctuary. This was the 14th such designation since the inception of the program in 1975 and is now the only one in the Pacific Northwest. In this area live more than 25 species of whales, dolphins, and porpoises and some of the largest colonies of seabirds in the continental United States. It is a critical link in the Pacific Flyway. The Quinault, Hoh, Quillayute, and Makah tribes reside in this area. Within this same area are the Washington Islands National Wildlife Refuges, which include Flattery Rocks, Quillayute Needles, and the Copalis River. These seabird refuges—on 870 islands, rocks, and reefs—provide protection from human disturbance and are close to abundant ocean food sources. Prohibited in the sanctuary are seabed mining, oil and gas development, discharge of materials into the waters, and overflights of aircraft at less than 2,000 feet.

All along the coast, numerous rivers and creeks flow directly into the ocean. North of the Columbia are two significant estuaries, Grays Harbor and Willapa Bay. In the coastal waters from Grays Harbor south to the mouth of the Columbia are some of the best fishing and crabbing on the West Coast.

Strait of Juan de Fuca

Ocean-going vessels heading from the Pacific to the inland waters of Washington state or British Columbia first encounter the Strait of Juan de Fuca. This body of water separates the Olympic Peninsula and

Vancouver Island, with the International Boundary running down its middle. It was named for the Greek explorer Apostolos Varianos, who called himself Juan de Fuca when he was employed by Spain. From Cape Flattery east to the boundary of Puget Sound, the strait is about 60 miles wide. Most boaters consider themselves to be in the Strait between Point Hudson on the Olympic Peninsula (Jefferson) heading north for the sheltered waters of the San Juan Islands. The waters close to the south shore are heavily fished.

Puget Sound

Puget Sound is one of the world's great, unique, useful, and enjoyable bodies of water. The more you learn and experience about this estuary, you realize what a tremendous resource it is and how fortunate are the people who live, work, and play in its environs.

It has a defined boundary: all salt waters of the state of Washington inside the international boundary line between the state of Washington and the province of British Colurnbia lying east of 123°24' west longitude (just west of Port Angeles).

In May 1792, Lt. Peter Puget and several members of the crew of HMS Discovery, commanded by Captain George Vancouver, were sent to explore the inlet to the east and south of where they were anchored in Discovery Bay. They were the first Europeans to do such an investigation, and Captain Vancouver rewarded Lt. Puget by naming the waters Puget's Sound, now just Puget Sound.

But that only defines the water area. The Sound is really a region and a watershed made up of most of the land area of the 12 counties bordering the water portion. Nature knows few, if any, boundaries, so the waters to the north in Canada have an ever-imposing relationship. It is an ecosystem with a rich, marine environment. The focus here is on the water component. Some salient statistics of the Sound:

- There are over 1,330 miles of shoreline, around which more than 3 million people live.

- Most of the Sound is deep, with an average depth of 450 feet and a maximum depth of 930 feet just north of Seattle. The bottom consists of ridges and valleys called basins and sills. One notable sill, about 190 feet deep, is at Admiralty Inlet, the narrow passage between Port Townsend on the Peninsula and Fort Casey on Whidbey Island. This sill is a separator of the deep waters of the Strait and the southern part of the Sound. With tidal activity, the currents here are strong.

- Twice daily, some 1.46 cubic miles of water is moved in and out by the tides. This is about twice the average discharge from the Columbia River.

- More than 75 river systems make up the watershed.

- Nestled between the Cascade and Olympic Mountains, the basin covers more than 16,000 square miles of land and water, 80% of which is land and 20% water.

- The waters of the Sound are constantly at work, moving with the tidal changes. Although not the greatest tidal difference in North America, there is still a variation of about 12 feet between high and low tide during periods of maximum change. Fresh water flows into the estuary, remaining on top of the heavier salt water until movement gradually mixes the two.

- Several habitats in the Sound's ecosystem support a myriad of species: more than 200 fish, 100 birds and waterfowl, 25 marine mammals, and hundreds of plants and invertebrates. The habitats are open water, nearshore, benthic (bottom), intertidal, and freshwater. The vast food web throughout the Sound and the habitats provides for the survival of all plants and animals, from small to large.

The Sound is an integral part in the economy of the region and the state. The navigable waters support affordable and convenient transportation of all manner of goods and people. Thousands of commuters each workday use the largest ferry system in the country. Ocean shipping arrives and departs from major ports as Naval vessels steer for the Bremerton shipyard for repair or their homeport at Everett. Aquaculture and fishing, both commercial and recreational, are major industries stemming directly from the water. Washington residents own well over 600,000 boats and other watercraft, with the majority moored in the Puget Sound region. Finally, joining all the local people are the visitors and tourists who help keep Washington "green with money" and find much to do and see in this magnificent arena of flora, fauna, and marine activity.

Because the Sound is such a large, yet—in many aspects—fragile entity with so much human-generated activity, various elements of the ecosystem have been damaged by pollution, degradation, and misuse. Commencing back in the early 1980s, major programs were initiated at the state and federal levels relating to clean water and specifically to Puget Sound. There have been several evolutions in names and organizational structure, each building on the past. In 1998 was the Puget Sound Water Quality Protection Act, which established the Puget Sound Water Quality Action Team to develop a strategy to maintain and enhance the health of Puget Sound.

Hood Canal

The Hood Canal is a unique, beautiful body of water that seems to pierce the wooded hills as you enter its mouth near Port Ludlow and Port Gamble and travel south. At the mouth is Hood's Head, a spit except at high tide. Next is the Hood Canal floating bridge, built in 1961, which opens when a nuclear submarine is going to or coming from its home at Bangor. The canal extends south about 50 miles and, after a 90-degree turn to the east, then another 15 miles to its end in mud flats. It was originally named Hood's Channel by Captain Vancouver in 1792, but a transcription in the logbook said "Canal," and it has been that way ever since. The Olympic Forest comes right to the western edge in places, with mountain streams flowing into the Canal. It is one of the richest growing areas for shellfish. You can walk on layers of shells in Dabob Bay. Along the 242 miles of shoreline are small towns, parks, and many summer homes. A complete change of water takes about a year, whereas the Sound flushes twice in the same period. In the past was occasional talk about digging a trench from the end near Belfair to connect with the southern reaches of Puget Sound. It is doubtful that it will ever happen now.

Author's note: My first sighting of Washington State was early in the morning in June 1957 when my ship, the cruiser USS Bremerton, was on the way to Bremerton for drydock. We headed down Hood Canal, on water like glass, for Bangor to unload ammunition (the sub base was not yet built). A cruiser is a big vessel, and the wooded shores rose from the mist, coming closer and closer—so close I thought I could reach out the touch the branches.

Padilla Bay

Padilla Bay is a National Estuarine Research Reserve just east of Anacortes. An estuary is an area where fresh water from rivers meets and mixes with salt water. The habitat is diverse in plant and animal life and is a nursery for many species, including salmon and Dungeness crab. The seagrass meadow of 7,500 acres and salt marsh areas support large populations of wintering waterfowl. The Breazeale Interpretive Center on Bayview-Edison Road houses an array of interesting exhibits.

Rivers

"A river is more than an amenity. It is a treasure."
Oliver Wendell Holmes, 1920

The hundreds of rivers can be compared with the blood giving life to a person for it gives life to the state. They are a source of power, water for the fields and orchards, the medium for fish, a water highway for commerce and a reservoir for recreation. Most eventually flow into the Columbia or Puget Sound and thence to the Pacific. Space limits the discussion to only a few.

Columbia

Starting as a tiny rill in an ice field high in the Canadian Rocky mountains, the Columbia becomes a mighty river as it flows 1,200 miles to the Pacific Ocean. It was discovered in 1792 by Captain Robert Gray and named after his ship, the Columbia Rediva. While still in Canada, it is joined by the north-flowing Pend Oreille. In the "big bend" area of Lincoln County comes the waters of the Spokane River. Then, just before turning west near Pasco, it meets with the Snake and Yakima Rivers. From there, it forms the Washington–Oregon border. In all, the river drains a basin of about 260,000 square miles in all the Northwest states and receives waters from hundreds of rivers. It discharges about 2 million gallons of water per second into the sea—twice what the Nile in Egypt gives to the Mediterranean. The mouth of the river is more than four miles wide, and where its waters join those of the ocean is one of the most dangerous areas for boating in the world.

In the past 200 years, more than 2,000 boats have sunk where the river meets the ocean. Ocean swells that travel thousands of miles across the Pacific are hurled, by westerly winds that may reach 50 miles

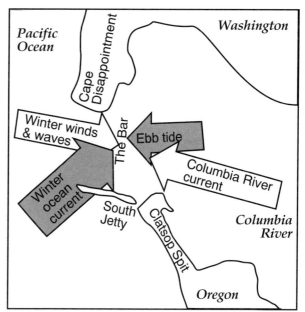

The Columbia is the most powerful river to empty into the Pacific between Alaska and Chile. Every day, its 150 billion gallons of water push tons of silt into a maze of sand bars. When the outgoing tide and river current collide with winter wind, ocean current, and waves, the result is chaotic.

per hour, against the river water flowing west, making 10- to 15-foot swells. The Coast Guard has its motor lifeboat school there at Cape Disappointment, training people for assignment at all their stations.

The last free-flowing part of the river, about 50 miles long, is the Hanford Reach in the nuclear reservation north of Richland (Benton) and by the Saddle Mountain Range. There is a good salmon run each year in this area, and extensive efforts are underway to preserve it and to designate this part of the river "Wild and Scenic."

Snake

The origin of the Snake River is in Yellowstone National Park, Wyoming. From there it flows south through Jackson Lake and into Idaho. After crossing Idaho, it forms the Idaho–Oregon border until it meets Washington's southeast corner and then forms the Washington–Idaho border for about 40 miles. At Clarkston, it turns west to join the Columbia near the Tri-Cities after a journey of 1,000 miles.

Along the way it drains a basin of over 109,000 square miles. Although the stretch of river known as Hell's Canyon, as deep as 7,900 feet, is just south of Washington, the river banks after it reaches Washington are still hundreds of feet high and provide excellent scenery.

With four dams on the Lower Snake River Project, numerous commercial port facilities are sited along the river. Much of the grain grown in the southeast counties is loaded on barges for the trip to the lower Columbia and transfer to ships to continue to the Pacific Rim. Young salmon also make the trip to the ocean in barges from their hatchery near Clarkston.

The Snake is a major tributary of the Columbia but is, itself, one of the largest rivers in the country—larger than the Colorado and the Sacramento combined. It delivers an average of 50,000 cubic feet of water into the Columbia every second, about one-fifth of the lower Columbia's total flow.

Skagit

The Skagit's headwaters are in Manning Provincial Park, just over the border in British Columbia. Its journey is much shorter than the Columbia's, for its waters arrive at Skagit Bay on the Sound in about 200 miles as the eagle flies. After three dams, the river continues southwest through the Cascades until reaching the broad Skagit Valley. Just west of Mount Vernon, the river splits into the North and South Forks, creating Fir Island.

All through the valley, dikes and drainage sloughs are in place to control high water—which they do most of the time. However, with a large rainfall and melting snow, the water can burst through the earthworks, causing flooding. The river is the water source for much of Skagit County and is the winter haven to the largest group of bald eagles in the contiguous 48 states. Whitewater rafting is popular near the towns of Marblemount and Rockport.

Yakima

Keechelus Lake, just east of Snoqualmie Pass in the Cascades along I-90, is the headwaters of the Yakima River, which flows southeast and east until it joins the Columbia at Richland. For 27 miles from Ellensburg to Yakima, it cuts through the Umtanum Ridge to depths of 1,700 feet, providing a slow, scenic stretch that is popular for rafting, with drops of only 14 feet per mile. Nearing Yakima, fruit orchards start to line its banks. Upon clearing Union Gap, it flows through the fertile Yakima Valley, where vineyards line the banks and some of the best agriculture production in the nation can be found. Some of the first irrigation in the state started with water from this river in ditches dug by hand.

Nisqually

This is a unique river and maybe the only one in the country that starts from a glacier in a national park (Mount Rainier) and ends at an estuary in a national wildlife refuge (Nisqually). Along its 78-mile path, it flows through forests, fields, towns, a military base (Fort Lewis), and an Indian reservation (Nisqually), and forms part of the border between Pierce and Lewis counties. It supports a wild salmon run.

Palouse

The two forks of the Palouse start in Idaho and join at Colfax. From there, the course is east through rolling hills of wheat and on to the Snake River. It helps form part of the boundaries of Whitman County with Adams and Franklin. Unfortunately the river is not clear, because eroding soil comes off the hillsides, resulting in a benign, brown river. Farmers are paid to forego farming along the waters, and almost a million acres have been taken out of production.

Elwha

Starting from glaciers on Mount Olympus, the Elwha descends to the Strait of Juan de Fuca at Port Angeles. Although not very long, it still has two dams. Unfortunately, they do not have fish ladders and have all but eliminated the salmon runs. Now, there are extensive efforts to take down one or both of the dams (see Dams).

Pend Oreille

One of only a few rivers in North America that

flow north, this river runs almost the length of Pend Oreille County in a beautiful valley. After entering Canada, it turns west and empties into the Columbia for the long journey to the Pacific. Two dams are in place to the north.

Toutle

This river is best known as the carrier of the waters of Spirit Lake and other material from the 1980 Mount St. Helens eruption down to its confluence with the Cowlitz River, just north of Castle Rock.

Lakes

There are many, many lakes in Washington, and this listing will not satisfy everyone because we don't have room to tell about everyone's favorite. However, we do discuss several more lakes in context with their surroundings. The ones discussed here are either especially large, unique, or important to the areas they serve.

Banks

A reservoir for the upper section of the Columbia Basin Irrigation Project. Named for Frank Banks, chief construction engineer of the Grand Coulee Dam, it lies in the Upper Grand Coulee, which is bounded by coulee walls on the east and west and earthfill dams on the north and south. It is 27 miles long, running from the city of Grand Coulee on the north to Coulee City on the south, and contains 1,275,000 acre-feet of water.

The water in the lake comes from Lake Roosevelt via pumps that lift the water 280 feet up to a feeder canal. It then flows 1.8 miles into the lake. Of the 12 pumps, 6 can be reversed to become generators during times of peak power needs.

Water released from the south end of Banks Lake goes into a canal and then through a maze of tunnels, siphons, and other channels. Some goes into Billy Clapp Lake for further distribution. Excess water ends up in the Potholes Reservoir south of Moses Lake. All water that is not used, for whatever reason, finds its way back into the Columbia River.

Chelan

Near the center of the state and nestled in one of the deepest gorges in North America, Lake Chelan is 55 miles long and covers about 50 square miles. Its width varies from 1 to 2 miles and is the third deepest, at 1,486 feet, after Crater Lake and Lake Tahoe. It is fed from the glaciers in the North Cascades. The water is cool, with a maximum of about 73°F at Wapato Point at the south end and only 60°F at Stehekin at the north end, but does not freeze in the winter. There are no roads to Stehekin. Visitors arrive by boat, plane, or foot. The round trip by boat takes a day, but the time is enjoyable because of the views of mountain scenery and orchards along the shore. The Chelan River dam controls the height of the water, which can vary by 20 feet. The water is pristine because there is little development.

Roosevelt

Lake Roosevelt is the largest of more than 140 lakes, ponds, and reservoirs related to the Grand Coulee Dam and the Columbia Basin Project. It extends north from the dam 150 miles to the Canadian Border and has 600 miles of shoreline. Part of it is in the Colville and Spokane Indian Reservations, and tribal authorities regulate activities in their areas. The lake is actually a reservoir, and the water level is carefully regulated. When water is drawn down, the shoreline changes dramatically. A vertical drop of 2 feet can expose hundreds of feet of lake bottom. A variety of recreational activities, including year-around fishing, are available. Almost all of the water in the lake has a planned use.

Ross

Ross Lake, created by Ross Dam, lies in the Ross Lake National Recreation Area in the Cascade Mountains in the eastern part of Whatcom County. The largest of three lakes on the upper Skagit River, it is 24 miles long and 2 miles wide. It covers 12,000 acres and extends a few miles into Canada. Various recreational activities are available.

Sacajawea

Lake Sacajawea, named for the Indian squaw who guided Lewis and Clark (1804–1806), is formed by the Ice Harbor Dam on the Snake River (Franklin and Walla Walla).

Soap

It's the water! This two-mile long lake is fed by groundwater and has no outlet. It has a high concentration of 16 minerals that leach from the surrounding rocks. People have been coming for years to bathe in and drink the water, hoping it will cure or alleviate their arthritis or psoriasis. It lies just north of the town of Soap Lake (Grant).

Washington

Lake Washington is Seattle's eastern boundary. Along its many miles of shoreline are thousands of homes, some valued in the millions of dollars. Lying in the lake itself is a self-contained, affluent city—Mercer Island—which is accessed via I-90. A fixed bridge connects it to the east side of the lake, and a floating bridge connects it to Seattle. The Evergreen

Point floating bridge crosses the lake several miles north, connecting the University of Washington and its fabulous Arboretum to Bellevue. At the south end is Renton and a Boeing plant. Thousands of pleasure boats are moored in the lake, with easy access to Puget Sound via Portage Bay, Lake Union, the Ship Canal, and the Hiram Chittenden Locks. Every August, hordes of people jam the shoreline and the lake itself to enjoy the Seafair air show and hydroplane races.

Dams

Washington has several hundred dams, ranging from small to the super-sized Grand Coulee. They are a major component of the economy, providing hydropower, irrigation, flood control, and recreation. Fewer than 100 of these produce over 24,000 megawatts of hydroelectricity. Yet, they are at the center of controversy because damming rivers affects wild salmon runs and otherwise changes the natural environment.

Upper Columbia

In the early 1900s, it was recognized that water was the only resource needed to turn the semi-arid Columbia Basin into productive cropland. Two plans were proposed: (1) a 134-mile, gravity-flow canal from Lake Pend Oreille and (2) a big dam at Grand Coulee. The fight raged for 13 years. Finally, President Roosevelt authorized $60 million to start the dam.

Building began in 1933, providing employment for thousands of people during the Great Depression. Towns were created overnight, and work was carried on around the clock until the dam was completed in 1942. In order of importance, the principal purposes of the dam originally were irrigation, production of electric power, and flood control. However, power production soon gained more importance because of the Manhattan Project at the Hanford nuclear site. Later, recreation became another benefit of the dam.

Four federal agencies are responsible for the operation of the dam and related matters. The U.S. Bureau of Reclamation built and operates the Columbia Basin Project, including the dam, and has final authority in all decisions. The Bonneville Power Adminstration (BPA) transmits the power generated to retail distributors. Since 1980, the BPA also has been charged with ensuring that the Northwest has an adequate supply of power from all sources. The National Park Service manages the Coulee Dam National Recreation Area, which includes Lake Roosevelt and adjacent land not within the Indian reservation. Finally, the U.S. Army Corps of Engineers is responsible for coordinating flood control in the Basin.

The Grand Coulee Dam, the key structure of the multipurpose Columbia Basin Project, is a study in superlatives. The dam is one of the largest concrete structures in the world, containing about 24 million tons of concrete. It rises 550 feet from bedrock to its crest and its width tapers from more than 500 feet at the base to 30 feet at the top. The dam forms the

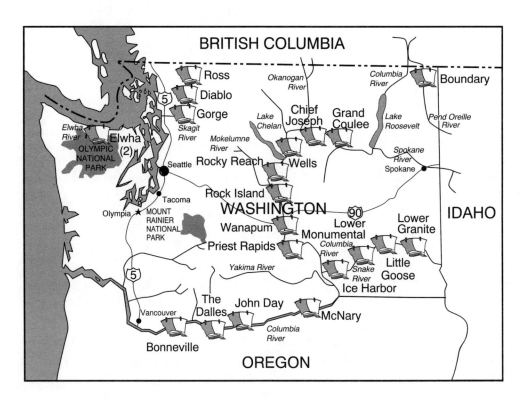

Chief Joseph Dam (Okanogan)

huge, 10-million-acre-foot, Franklin Roosevelt Lake, which extends 151 miles north to the Canadian border. The laser show at night during the summer is something to see when water comes over the spillway to provide a white background for laser graphics. In this mode, the dam is one of the largest projection screens in the world, rising more than 300 feet above the downstream water level.

Downstream from Grand Coulee, the Chief Joseph, Wells, Rocky Reach, Rock Island (the first major dam built on the Columbia, in 1933), Wanapum, and Priest Rapids Dams completed the Columbia Basin Project, bringing more than 500,000 acres of land into cultivation (see Grant County and Agriculture) in support of the state's largest industry.

Lower Columbia

Started in 1933, Bonneville was the first dam dedicated by President Roosevelt in September 1937. Built and operated by the Army Corps of Engineers at a cost of $88.4 million, it is the farthest downstream of the Columbia dams. The original powerhouse could not handle all the water when other dams were built upriver, so a second one with eight additional units was completed in 1981, doubling the power output.

Bonneville and the other three dams on the lower Columbia (The Dalles, John Day, and McNary) have turned the once wild river into a series of lakes that are vital to the area's commerce and recreation.

Lower Snake River Dams

Four dams on the Snake River were authorized by Congress in 1945. From the east, they are Lower Granite, Little Goose, Lower Monumental, and Ice Harbor, each about 100 feet high. Construction started on the series in 1956 and was completed in 1975. Power output commenced on the first, Ice Harbor, in 1961. All have navigation locks and fish ladders. These four plus the four on the lower Columbia form a water highway 470 miles long from Lewiston, Idaho, and Clarkston in Asotin County, Washington, to the Pacific Ocean.

Seattle City Light Dams

To provide power for the state's biggest metropolitan area, Seattle City Light operates four dams, the Boundary Dam on the Pend Oreille River and three on the upper Skagit River: Ross, Diablo, and Gorge. Seattle City Light's popular tour to Ross Lake not only provides information in an inspiring and entertaining setting but also an all-you-can-eat meal. Optional features include a ride on an incline railway and a cruise on Diablo Lake. The location is on Route 20 in the North Cascades (Skagit).

Elwha Dams

Two dams on the Elwha River are about to be removed in hopes of restoring salmon runs up the river, which springs from the heart of Olympic National Park. The dams provide energy to a pulp mill.

Summary

The following table summarizes the main hydroelectric projects in Washington, their responsible agencies or public utility districts, and their potential power output in megawatts:

Dam	Agency	Power
Grand Coulee	USBR*	10,309
Chief Joseph	USACE[†]	2,614
Wells	Douglas County	774
Rocky Reach	Chelan County	1,213
Rock Island	Chelan County	622
Wanapum	Grant County	1,330
Priest Rapids	Grant County	1,262
McNary	USACE	2,130
John Day	USACE	2,160
The Dalles	USACE	1,807
Bonneville	USACE	1,089
Lower Granite	USACE	810
Little Goose	USACE	810
Lower Monumental	USACE	810
Ice Harbor	USACE	603
Boundary	Seattle City Light	1,051
Ross	Seattle City Light	450
Diablo	Seattle City Light	510
Gorge	Seattle City Light	157
Elwha (2)	James River Corp.	19

* US Bureau of Reclamation [†] US Army Corps of Engineers

Salmon Types and Phases

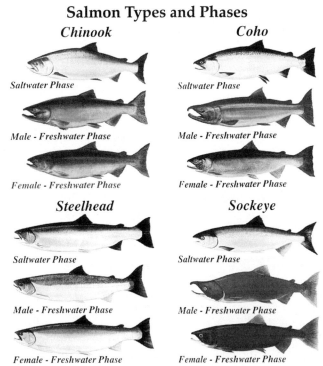

Chinook

Saltwater Phase

Male - Freshwater Phase

Female - Freshwater Phase

Coho

Saltwater Phase

Male - Freshwater Phase

Female - Freshwater Phase

Steelhead

Saltwater Phase

Male - Freshwater Phase

Female - Freshwater Phase

Sockeye

Saltwater Phase

Male - Freshwater Phase

Female - Freshwater Phase

Topics/Issues

Salmon

Decimation of salmon runs is a hot topic as this book goes to press. Although 95% of salmon may be successful in clearing each dam during a spawning season, a series of dams, each taking a 5% toll, do significant damage to an annual run. If a young salmon going downstream misses the fish ladder at a dam and exits one of the hydroelectric turbines, it may be stunned sufficiently to succumb to seagulls and other predators that have learned to wait just below the dam for easy pickings.

Investigation and work continue on all aspects of the juvenile and adult bypass systems of the dams on the Columbia and Snake Rivers to increase anadromous fish stocks. There are no "one size fits all" solutions because each dam and the river conditions surrounding it are different.

Turbine passage. Not all fish are able to bypass the turbines. The blades do not churn the water—rather, the moving water turns them at about 70 to 90 rpm. Pressure changes and turbine strikes kill some of the juveniles. A scale model of a turbine with plexiglas sides has been built to reveal what takes place inside.

Surface bypass. At some dams, sluiceways gather and channel surface trash and ice away from the turbines. Special screens and other modifications are being made to channel fish to these sluiceways.

Juvenile bypass. Large, underwater screens are placed in front of the turbine intakes to divert fish to a bypass channel and back into the river downstream. In some instances, the diversion can be to a pond and then into a barge or truck for transport downriver. Larger screens are being installed.

Spillways. Operational plans are underway to determine the best times and amounts of water to move over the spillways and thus pass the juveniles this way rather than via the bypass. Continual tests are conducted to determine optimums for fish survial.

Transportation. During movement by barges or trucks, the water is kept at the best temperature and properly aerated. With barges, fresh water is continually being run through the system. Information is being analyzed to determine if this program provides better results than bypassing the dams in the water.

The Chelan and Douglas County Public Utility Districts (PUDs) recently entered into a 50-year plan aiming for 100% survival of salmon runs. The plan mandates at least 91% survival at each of the dams under their control (Wells, Rocky Reach, and Rock Island), and any losses would be made up by production at hatcheries.

Because dams have varying designs that make uniform measures impractical, other PUDs operating on the Columbia feel the Chelan/Douglas plan is not feasible for them and have entered into agreements with federal fisheries managers and Indian tribes to develop different methods to reach similar goals.

Stormwater

Stormwater is any water that falls onto the ground and doesn't soak in but runs off and eventually enters streams and then the Sound and Ocean. It is caused by impervious surfaces (roofs, driveways, parking lots, etc.) or land that becomes saturated with water. It is a source of nonpoint pollution. Local governments in the state created some of the first stormwater utility districts, billing property owners and using funds to help diminish this runoff.

Snowpack

This refers to the accumulation of snow in the mountains during the winter that, in turn, supplies much of the water during the year as the snow melts. It takes 10 to 12 inches of snow to equal 1 inch of rain. Without a good snowpack, water shortages will occur during a warm summer in many places in the state.

Water Sources

The water we receive from precipitation (rain or snow) accumulates in snowpacks, rivers, lakes, reservoirs, or aquifers.

Wild and Scenic Rivers

The National Wild and Scenic Rivers System was created by Congress in 1968 to preserve certain rivers with outstanding natural, cultural, or recreational features in a free-flowing condition for the enjoyment of present and future generations. There are presently three such rivers in the state: Klickitat and White Salmon (both in Klickitat County) and the Skagit, including portions of the Sauk, Suiattle, and Cascade (Skagit). Being considered is the Hanford Reach Section of the Columbia, which lies in the Hanford Reservation (Benton and Grant Counties). Continued use and development is determined for each river.

Locks

Moving boats up or down to a different water level is done using one or more locks. They are part of many dams and sometimes are found between bodies of water such as Puget Sound and Lake Washington (via the Hiram Chittenden Locks and Ship Canal). They are really not that complicated. There are gates at both ends of the lock. If a boat is to be lowered, the gate on the high-water end opens, and the boat enters the lock. That gate then closes, and water drains out of the lock until the level inside the lock reaches the level of the body of water to be entered. Then, the other end of the lock opens, and the boat moves out into the lower level. The reverse happens in raising. The Chittenden locks at Ballard in Seattle are a good place to watch their operation, especially on a summer holiday weekend when all the pleasure boats are going through—a real circus sometimes! Beware of dive-bombing seagulls.

Boats going through the Hiram Chittenden Locks

Aliens Among Us

Water weeds Once started, water weeds become a serious problem by choking lakes and rivers. An example is milfoil, a non-native weed that came to the area in the mid-1970s. It has few natural controls and forms a mat so thick that it restricts swimming, boating, and fishing. Mechanical and hand harvesting, bottom screening, and special herbicides are the primary control methods.

Green crabs An alien from Europe, *Carcinus maenas*, a.k.a. the Atlantic green crab, eats baby shellfish like popcorn. So far, 50 of these omnivorous critters have been caught in Willapa (Pacific) and Grays Harbor, which produce 15% of America's oysters. Also, Puget Sound's $40 million annual shellfish harvest is in peril. An executive order is being prepared at this writing, requiring federal agencies to assess the problem and coordinate their alien-fighting. Meanwhile, for the green crab, it's chow time.

Fish & Wildlife

More than 600 fish and wildlife species in the state compete with the ever-increasing human population for space and natural resources. Management of these species and the interface with sportsmen and commercial activity is vested with the Department of Fish and Wildlife (WDFW), which was formed in 1994 by the merger of the Departments of Fisheries and Wildlife. The WDFW manages more than 80 fish hatcheries, 583 water access sites, and 850,000 acres of wildlife habitat and licenses 1.3 million sport fishers, 7,000 commercial fishers, and 270,000 hunters.

The Washington Fish and Wildlife Commission is the supervising authority, with the primary roles of establishing policy and monitoring the WDFW. Nine members from all over the state serve staggered six-year terms. Management of the species is both macro and micro. There are seven large geographic regions, but within those are scores of game management units, and each lake, river, and designated area of the Sound has specific rules and seasons.

Fish

Before the late 1800s, there were only a few freshwater fish in the state: trout, whitefish, suckers, and a few others. It was determined that more varieties were needed, so importing of other species began to go along with those in saltwater. Today, few other states offer the variety and quality of fishing found here. There is excellent fishing of one type or another year-round. The spring lake fishing traditionally starts on the last Saturday in April. Most rivers and streams open on June 1. The WDFW stocks the lakes and rivers so the fry will be grown by the time opening days arrive.

Trout Rainbow trout are the most popular. Others are Beardslee, cutthroat, brown, golden, Dolly Varden, eastern brook, and lake.

Kokanee Sometimes called silver trout, they are actually sockeye salmon that do not go out to sea.

Whitefish Native to the state and closely related to trout and salmon.

Bass Both largemouth and smallmouth were introduced to the state.

Walleye Often called "walleye pike," they are actually cousins to the yellow perch and were not introduced to the state until the 1960s.

Crappies, yellow perch, bluegill, sunfish, catfish, tiger muskies, and *burbot* are all available.

Sturgeon The largest of the freshwater species, this prehistoric fish is available in the Columbia and other large streams. They can measure up to 8 feet and weigh several hundred pounds.

Halibut This big saltwater fish can grow to 400 pounds. Found in various places along the Strait of Juan de Fuca.

Skate Similar to halibut.

Sharks Blue and dogfish are seldom fished for, but the dogfish is frequently caught when fishing for salmon.

Lingcod Very popular but closely controlled.

Rockfish Several varieties include yelloweye, canary, quillback, black, and copper. With depleted salmon runs, many go for this fish.

Greenling, Pacific cod, and *pollack* are other bottom fish.

Saltwater Perch Common varieties are pile, striped, and red-tailed.

Albacore A tuna popular with sport fishermen.

Steelhead (anadromous) Sea-going rainbow trout that return to fresh water at different times, frequently in the winter months. Can grow to 20 or 30 pounds. (Sometimes listed as a salmon; see the figure on the next page.)

Shad (anadromous) A member of the herring family found mostly in the Columbia River.

Forage fish This group includes herring, anchovy, sand lance and smelt. Growing to about 9 inches, they are the fish that other fish and wildlife feed on. Popular for bait. During a good smelt run, a rake is used at high slack tides.

Salmon (anadromous) The fish for which the state is famous. Several varieties are Chinook (King), Coho (Silver), Pink (Humpies), Chum (Dog), and Sockeye. Kings can grow to 100 pounds, but the large ones are now found farther north. The size of the runs, when fish return to spawn, varies each year (see Issues).

Shellfish

"When the tide is out, the table is set" speaks to the gathering of shellfish, which is almost as popular an activity as is the eating of them at the table. Again, the demand for them is greater than the natural population of the shellfish can satisfy, so many restrictions are in place. A separate shellfish license is required, which also allows harvesting of a limited amount of seaweed. Many of the beaches where shellfish are found are privately owned, and permission is necessary before gathering. Several of these shellfish are grown/harvested commercially in and around the Sound and in estuaries and ocean waters.

Hardshell Clams These include littleneck (manila), butter, house, and softshell. Harvested with a shovel or rake with good availability at low (minus) tides. Average 2 to 6 inches in size.

Razor Clams Elongated, thin shells up to 9 inches long; can dig rapidly. Dug with narrow shovels or a round cylinder called a "clam gun." Found on broad, sandy, coastal beaches.

Geoducks The largest burrowing clam, they can weight up to 10 pounds and live burrowed 2 to 3 feet deep. Need a minus tide of 2 feet or more.

Oysters are often found in groups attached to one another or to rocks. Recreational oyster gathering in the Hood Canal. Best not to collect in hot summer months.

Mussels are oblong, blue-black shells about 3 inches long. They attach themselves to solid objects. To eat, steam them or cook them like clams.

Abalone resembles a large, flattened snail and grows to about 6 inches. It is found subtidally attached to rocks in northern Puget Sound and the San Juan Islands.

Squid has ten arms and a cone-shaped body. Giant squid may be 20 feet from tip to tip of its tentacles. Squid move into the Sound in late summer and then on south by mid-winter. They are timid but are attracted to bright light at night and may be caught with unbaited squid jigs. The taste is similar to razor clams.

Octopus Some of the largest in the world are found in Puget Sound weighing up to 100 pounds. Have eight suction-cup studded arms used to catch fish and crab. Something for sport divers.

Shrimp Several species are all similar, with ten legs and long antennae, up to 8 or 10 inches long. Found throughout the Sound and off the coast and caught in shrimp pots in water to 300 feet deep.

Crab The most popular is the Dungeness, which reaches 10 inches across the back and has a purple-tinged shell. The red rock crab is slightly smaller, with heavy brick-red shells and black-tipped claws. Caught with crab pots or rings, or sometimes by wading in shallow water with a rake.

Whales

Orcas Members of three pods—J, K, and L—are resident in the Sound. They are the largest of the dolphins and are carnivorous. They are quite social and keep in defined groups. The males grow to 26 or 28 feet long and 15,000 pounds, and the females are slightly smaller. Their distinctive markings enable experienced watchers to keep track of individual whales and their pods. They are known to attack other whales in a cooperative hunt, surrounding and drowning them—hence the name "killer whale." Fish are one of their main menu items, and it has been estimated that one pod lunched on over 1,000 salmon in one day. They are protected by the Marine Mammal Protection Act, which makes it illegal to harass, harm, or kill them. Boat must stay 100 yards or more away. The orcas don't know that, however, so they will swim right under tour boats.

Gray Whales Much larger than the orca, they travel along the coast on their annual migration between Baja California and Arctic waters.

Seals and sea lions The waters are well populated with these clever pinnepeds ("feet resembling feathers"). Now protected by the Marine Mammal Protection Act, they just sit and wait for salmon in places such as the entrance to the Chittendon Locks in Ballard (a community in Seattle). One named Herschel was the object of many varied attempts to keep him from feasting on the fish. One time, he was captured and taken to Southern California waters, only to be back to his favorite buoy in a few days.

Orcas near San Juan Island

Miscellaneous Aquatic Information

Red tide A phenomenon caused by large groups of microorganisms, most of which are harmless, but a few are toxic and deadly. They multiply when nutrients and light are abundant, and in sufficient numbers, turn the water red. Shellfish through which this water pass can become contaminated and can, in turn, harm humans through paralytic shellfish poisoning (PSP). There are no set patterns as to when and where the toxic levels become too high. Marine waters are continually tested by the state, and warnings are issued. The hot line number is (800) 562-5632.

Hatcheries These are located throughout the state on public, private, and Indian lands. They raise millions of many species of both salt- and freshwater fish that are released into rivers and lakes. Hatcheries enhance fish survival only during their early life. Once released, they require clean, cool water and abundant cover to survive.

Licensing The state has many specific licensing requirements, but generally any resident over 15 years of age and all nonresidents need a ticket. (Seniors over 70 get a reduced rate.) There is a free fishing weekend early in June for everyone for all fish except steelhead. With a license comes a catch record card that is to be sent to WDFW at the end of the calendar year. All the details are in a pamphlet provided.

Indian fishing rights Since the Boldt decision regarding salmon and the right of Indians to have half of the harvest, the ruling has been extended to include shellfish on most beaches, public and private. This is quite involved and beyond the scope of this book. Of further note is that the Makah Nation (Clallam) is the only tribe in the country with a treaty right to hunt whales.

Wildlife

This topic covers a broad range of animals and birds from bear and moose to eagles and pheasants. Similar to fish, there is extensive management to preserve, protect, and enhance the stock we have while providing hunters and people who just want to look ample opportunities. Specific rules and seasons are in place for the three main types of equipment used in hunting; modern firearms, muzzleloaders, and bows and arrows. Trapping continues to be pursued by many. Wildlife refuges exist throughout the state.

Bear The state is home to both the grizzly and black bear. The grizzly population is small, with just a few dozen in the northern mountains and is endangered/threatened. Conversely, the black bear is abundant, with several thousand roaming most counties. This is a game species and is hunted annually. Being able to distinguish between the two is essential because killing a grizzly is illegal and could be costly. Color and size alone are not the determining factors, so consult local wildlife pamphlets and authorities before venturing into the wilderness.

Moose are the largest of the deer family, followed by elk, caribou, and then deer. They are seldom sighted and stay in the north and northeast mountain areas. Only a few moose permits are issued each year, and an individual is entitled to only one in a lifetime.

Elk, including the well-known Roosevelt subspecies, are thriving. One reason is the feeding at the Oak Creek Wildlife Refuge near Yakima, where fencing controls their movement. The herd of several hundred is fed daily during winter months, with public viewing adding to the spectacle.

Mountain goats Native to the Cascades, they were introduced by man into the Olympics. They prefer rugged, rocky, mountain terrain near the timberline so they have plenty of area to escape from predators.

Cougars, goats, and *big horned sheep* are other big game available for the hunt, all with various limitations. (The referenced cougar does not refer to the two-legged species that inhabits Pullman in the Palouse.)

Small game that all require a hunting license, are bobcat, coyote, fox, raccoon, rabbit and forest grouse. Hunting with hounds is allowed with a permit for coyote, fox and raccoon. Raccoons are so people orientated they will come up to a glass door at night and stand there watching TV and then go and tip over the garbage can looking for goodies.

Migratory waterfowl With all the water, wetland, grain crops, and forest areas, the state is a paradise for birds of many descriptions. The state being along the Pacific Flyway only enhances the number of species that bird watchers can view and count.

Eagles Since June 20, 1782 when the bald eagle became the symbol of the new country, it has always attracted considerable attention. Their population was so drastically reduced by hunting and toxic substances that the National Emblem Law was passed in 1940, which prohibited killing them. Alaska was excluded and continued paying a bounty until 1962, when DDT was banned and the eagle was placed on the endangered species list. Their population has now recovered, and they even appear in populated areas. It takes 3 to 5 years for the head to become white. They are territorial, mate for life, and frequently build

more than one nest high in trees that provide a good view. They come back to the same nest each year and continue to improve it. Nests may be 6 feet in diameter and 4 to 10 feet deep, weighing 200–300 pounds.

It's really an experience to watch an eagle glide down, grab a fish from the water, and then return to a tree branch to snack and wait for another morsel.

An eagle watching for prey in Skagit County

Spotted owl Since being placed on the threatened/endangered species list, this bird has been controversial. The controversy mostly relates to what some claim is their need for a large amount of "old growth" forest to sustain themselves. Others now say the birds will also reside in younger trees. Until the issue is resolved, many acres of timber are not being harvested where the spotted owl is found to be nesting.

Wild turkey Since 1960, three subspecies of wild turkey have been introduced to the state—Merriam's, Rio Grande, and eastern. They are further trapped and relocated to enhance populations throughout the state. Never wear red or blue clothes when hunting this bird, because they are the colors of its head!

Trumpeter swans This is another species that has made a big comeback since being hunted nearly to extinction. Besides grain, they like carrots, potatoes, and corn, all grown in the Skagit Delta, where the birds like to reside in winter months.

Ducks and *geese* The numbers of some, especially the Canadian Goose, are so great in some parks and people places that they are caught and relocated. Thousands of snow geese winter in Skagit County.

Upland game birds Ring-necked pheasant, chucker, partridge, and quail are abundant, especially on the dry side. There are special bird-dog training seasons and areas.

Falconry A falconry license and current hunting license are required for hunting with a raptor.

Air

In Washington, air quality is generally not given a whole lot of thought—mainly because it is great. Oh, some days are a bit smoggy in Seattle, and for those days there may be a restriction on incinerators and fireplaces.

In the western megalopolis and Spokane, emission tests are required to register motor vehicles. Such requirements are imposed regionally by ZIP Code. Ironically, traffic congestion in the big cities may be a help to the future of air quality. Some people in Seattle are getting rid of their cars because parking them is becoming a major expense.

Because of the widespread use of hydroelectric power and secondary power plants fired by natural gas, the most serious emission problems are from motor vehicles, lawn mowers, fireplaces, and pulp mills. Emissions from bakeries have been mentioned as contibuting to the depletion of the ozone layer.

Industries in various cities produce odors that assault the senses. Everett (Snohomish) used to be known for its bad-smelling air, but it has improved immensely in recent years. The well-known "Tacoma Aroma" is alive and well.

A major benefit to Washington's air quality comes in the form of winds from the Pacific Ocean. Pacific storms scrub the air well before the winds take it over the land mass. When forest fires or volcanic eruptions occur in Asia or the Pacific islands, Washington may experience uncharacteristically hazy skies and unusually colorful sunsets.

People prone to allergies, alas, have a problem because Washington's trademark greenery comes with an elevated pollen count and other airborne molecules that aggravate sinus conditions. Electrostatic air filters in home ventilation systems can help alleviate this problem.

Alternative Energy Sources

Some environmentally conscious individuals are now using alternative means of generating electricity that have great potential for future conservation of natural resources and reduction of air and water pollution.

Although the equipment needed for personal and home power generation was too expensive to be widely accepted only a short time ago, it is becoming more affordable and attractive to individual homeowners.

For instance, small, synchronous inverters designed to change the 12-volt dc power produced by solar electric panels into the 110-volt ac power used in typical homes are available and are compatible with power grids of electric utility companies. This means that, for less than $1,000, a homeowner can install one of these to produce much of the power needed in the home and feed any excess power generated on sunny days into the grid.

By law, utility companies must accommodate such devices, which reduce the overall cost of power purchased from the utilities and may even cause home electric meters to run backward at times. Utility companies are uneasy about home energy production, but only partly because of the prospect of lost revenue. There is also the potential for a line repairman to be electrocuted by a supposedly severed transmission line that is still live from power fed into it from a home generator.

In addition to solar generators, wind and water generators provide still more alternatives for days and times of the year when sunshine is not abundant. A combination of solar and wind generators holds the possibility of further reducing the cost of purchased power and even complete independence from electric utilities.

Various publications are available that contain in-depth articles on the subject and advertising from manufacturers of equipment that can make home power generation a viable alternative for the energy contrarian.

Air Pollution Sources and Their Contributions

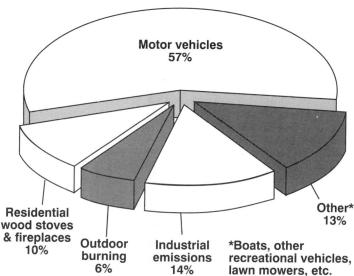

Motor vehicles
57%

Residential wood stoves & fireplaces
10%

Outdoor burning
6%

Industrial emissions
14%

*Boats, other recreational vehicles, lawn mowers, etc.

Other*
13%

Living

As suggested by Washington's growing population, everything necessary for enjoyable living is available in the state, and in great variety. It all comes down to what the individual or family desires. However, choices may be limited when the location of a workplace is factored in.

Lifestyles

The lifestyles of most state residents include some aspect of the outdoors and/or athletic activity. Even those who live and work in an urban setting typically head out of town as soon and as frequently as possible.

For those who are involved or interested in some aspect of the arts—music, theater, painting, or crafts—ample opportunities exist in or close to the cities and most towns. And if one just wants to relax, read, or garden, then that can be done in any location.

Water orientation is a must for many. Choices range from being on the water, to being able to see it, to being close enough so it takes just a short time to launch the boat, to being only concerned with drinking and washing.

Want to see sunshine most of the year? Just go to the eastern part of the state. How about a farm or ranch? Plenty of choices.

Then there are the islands—some connected to the mainland by bridge and others only by ferry. Each island has its own character and customs.

Solitude in the mountains among all the trees? No problem.

Need a small-town atmosphere? Many county seats in less-populated areas have fewer than 3,000 people, and many towns have fewer than 100 residents.

Living, for the most part, is relaxed and casual. A latte stand is generally close by. "Formal" attire frequently consists of jeans and hiking boots. Car horns are seldom used, even in heavy Puget Sound traffic. Want to get a business deal finished between three or more parties in the summer? Relax—it may be several weeks before everyone involved is back from boating.

Native Americans

The native peoples, like the state, are quite diverse. Before the white settlers arrived, they adapted their activities to the four seasons and to the state's geography, developing two distinct cultures east and west of the Cascades.

Those in the east, known as Plateau People, were seasonally nomadic and followed the food sources in the same fashion as other tribes throughout the North American heartland. They dug roots in the spring; fished and gathered nuts and berries in the summer; and hunted buffalo, deer, and elk in the fall; all in preparation for the winter.

The west side, with its wetter and milder climate and saltwater coastal region, provided a greater variety of plants, fish, and game year round. The natives of this region had permanent settlements, living in wooden structures in the winter and cattail mat dwellings during other seasons.

Frequently, the tribes from both sides of the mountains met to exchange food and various products and to hold social events.

The major change in their civilization took place in the 1850s, when Territorial Governor Isaac Stevens negotiated several treaties with the tribes. These treaties established most of the present tribes and confederations and laid out the reservation lands. Today, more than 20 Indian tribes live on reservations in the state. The largest tribe is the 6,400-member Yakima Indian Nation, with about 1.1 million acres of land on their reservation in Yakima County. The Confederated Tribes of the Colville have 1 million acres and 6,200 members in Okanogan and Ferry Counties.

Several museums feature Indian heritage and culture throughout the state. Tillicum Village on Blake Island in the Sound near Seattle is the highlight of a water excursion that ends with a traditional baked salmon dinner in a cedar longhouse.

Housing

Two words describe the housing market in the state—variety and change. A wide range is available in terms of style, amenities, views, price, and so on. The market is in a continual state of flux. Most homes are not very old—especially compared with the East Coast market. Don't expect to find "this old house" dating back to the early 1800s, when the territory was just being discovered.

Market

There is always a "housing market"—sometimes a buyers' market, sometimes a sellers' market, and sometimes a state of equilibrium. Many events cause the market to shift: level of economic activity , building moratoriums, zoning changes, and interest rates, to name a few. Within the state are hundreds of submarkets—small areas created by geography, topography, periods when the homes were built, zoning, price, etc. Moses Lake's (Grant) market is not the same as Omak's (Okanogan), and none are the same as Seattle's, where scores of submarkets exist.

Types

Housing types are widely varied; single-family detached, duplexes, triplexes, fourplexes, townhouses, ramblers, split-entries, multistory, highrise condominiums, homes on acreage, and others. One common structure—the daylight-basement rambler—is not found in many other parts of the country. This is a house cut into a hillside, with a complete rambler floorplan on the top (or entry) level, and a full basement with doors and windows on the downhill side. Normally the basement will contain bedrooms and recreation areas, but almost any combination can be found. The term "basement" is used here instead of "cellar." There is some manufactured housing, but zoning laws severely restrict where it can be placed.

Styles

There is a large array of architectural styles: traditional, Northwest, modern, contemporary, Tudor, New England and Cape Cod colonial, and California ranch. There are not many Southern Colonial or Spanish-style houses.

What is the Northwest style? Broadly speaking, it is a single-story or daylight-basement rambler with a shake roof and cedar siding. It usually has large windows, sliding glass doors and considerable roof overhang. The lines show a distinct Japanese influence, and the living room generally has a beamed ceiling.

Much new construction is modern contemporary, with wood exterior. Inside are one or more areas with cathedral ceilings to the roof and large areas partitioned by limited walls.

Ownership

Single-family, detached, is as popular here as anywhere. Condominiums are found mostly in areas of greatest population concentrations, and their demand is more constant now than in the past, when there was considerable fluctuation. The cooperative form of ownership is not common. There are a few

vacation timeshares—mostly water oriented. Leasing/renting is an option used by many coming into the market until they can acquire the capital or earning capacity to purchase.

Costs

Median Home Prices by County and Statewide

County	1st qtr, 1997	1st qtr, 1998	% chg.
Adams	$ 95,300	$ 95,200	–0.1
Asotin	$ 90,800	$ 88,000	–3.1
Benton	$102,800	$110,000	7.0
Chelan	$129,500	$123,900	–4.3
Clallam	$116,600	$113,300	–2.8
Clark	$129,000	$132,300	2.6
Columbia	N/A	$ 80,000e	N/A
Cowlitz	$ 83,800	$104,400	+24.6
Douglas	$129,500	$123,900	–4.3
Ferry	$ 85,100	$ 93,000e	N/A
Franklin	$102,800	$110,000	+7.0
Garfield	$ 90,800	$ 88,000	–3.1
Grany	$ 95,300	$ 95,200	–0.1
Grays Harbor	$ 69,000	$ 82,300	+19.3
Island	$139,800	$142,300	1.8
Jefferson	$147,100	$147,500	0.3
King	$177,300	$203,500	+14.8
Kitsap	$124,600	$135,000	8.3
Kittitas	$ 90,400	$121,600	+34.5
Klickitat	N/A	$ 90,000e	N/A
Lewis	$ 79,700	$ 78,000	–2.1
Lincoln	N/A	$110,000e	N/A
Mason	$ 90,000	$ 91,900	+2.1
Okanogan	N/A	$ 80,000e	N/A
Pacific	$ 80,000	$ 60,000	–25.0
Pend Oreille	$104,500	$ 88,500	–15.3
Pierce	$127,300	$138,000	+8.4
San Juan	$187,500	$190,000	+1.3
Skagit	$137,200	$138,900	+1.2
Skamania	N/A	$ 90,000e	N/A
Snohomish	$158,500	$165,000	+4.1
Spokane	$ 99,700	$ 96,300	–3.4
Stevens	$ 85,000	$ 85,800	+0.9
Thurston	$119,500	$125,000	+4.6
Wahkiakum	$ 73,500	$ 97,000	+32.0
Walla Walla	$ 91,000	$ 94,000	+3.3
Whatcom	$129,500	$137,900	+6.5
Whitman	$120,000	$126,700	+5.6
Yakima	$109,100	$ 99,800	–8.5
Statewide	$147,200	$155,800	+5.8

e: author's estimate

Source: Washington Center for Real Estate Research

Price range is considerable. We will only mention in passing the upper limit of about $60 million for Bill Gates' palace on Lake Washington. Others on the water are well over $1 million in price. Back to reality. The median price statewide for a home is about $156,000 (see table). Prices in urban areas, especially Seattle, are high and going higher. In small towns and rural settings, adequate housing is available for under $100,000. How much under depends on the highly personal opinion of "adequate." New construction continues to increase, mainly a result of land costs. These are rising, in part, as a result of the state's Growth Management Act, of which one stated purpose is to limit the population increase to urban area and keep rural areas rural.

Education

The focus on education throughout the state is extremely high. The first two sections of Article IX of the State Constitution provide the basis:

§1 Preamble. It is the paramount duty of the State to make ample provision for the education of all children residing within its borders, without distinction or preference on account of race, color, caste, or sex.

§2 Public School System. The legislature shall provide for a general and uniform system of public schools. The public school system shall include common schools, and such high schools, normal schools, and technical schools as may hereafter be established. But the entire revenue derived from the common school fund and the state tax for common schools shall be exclusively applied to the support of the common schools.

Superintendent of Public Instruction (SPI)

This position in the executive department of the state is one of nine officers elected by statewide vote for a four-year term. By section 22, Article III, this person "shall have supervision over all matters pertaining to public schools and shall perform such specific duties as may be prescribed by law." Some of the key functions of the office are (1) Secure needed laws and appropriations; (2) Apportion and distribute monies to local school districts; (3) Gather and disseminate information about the schools; (4) Administer the state school construction program; (5) Issue certificates for all teaching and support personnel of the K-12 program; (6) Be an ex officio member and chief executive officer of the State Board of Education.

State Board of Education (SBE)

This is one of the oldest parts of our state government, having been created by the Legislature of the Territory of Washington in 1877 and later reaffirmed by the State Legislature. The SBE has 11 members elected for four-year terms: one from each of the nine congressional districts, a private school representative, and the SPI. Members may not be employed in the field of education. There are also two ex officio student members, one each from the east side and west side. They are high school seniors and are the chair and cochair of the Washington Association of Student Councils.

The SBE duties, as prescribed by law, relate to establishment of rules, regulation, standards, and guidelines for certification of personnel, approval of professional education programs, allocation of state funds for school construction, approval of school district basic education programs, school accreditation, minimum graduation requirements, and approval of private schools.

Education Service Districts

These are nine regional bodies designed to assist local school districts in cooperative programs and act in an advisory capacity. They act as a conduit to assist the SPI and SBE in carrying out their duties. Programs include education of the handicapped, transportation, driver education, data processing, vocational education, and instructional materials.

Local School Districts

Local school districts are responsible for the delivery of instruction. Latest figures (1997) show 296 districts serving almost 1 million students. Each district is governed by a local school board of five to seven members who are popularly elected to staggered four-year terms in odd-numbered years. Functions of the Board are to make policy covering local needs, hire and fire the district superintendent, evaluate teaching materials, develop learning objectives for district courses, and much more. Since the state has full funding responsibility except for local special levies and certain mandated programs, school districts do not have full autonomy.

Public Education, K–12

Local districts are required to comply with basic education requirements as set forth in the statutes:

- A certain number of program hours at each grade level, with the percentages of these hours devoted to basic skills and work skills. The school year is to be at least 180 days.

- The basic skills are reading/language art, social studies, science, math, physical education, health art and music.
- Work skills include industrial arts, home and family life, business, health, agriculture, vocations, trade, and technical.
- Teacher contact with the pupil is to average 25 hours per week.
- District personnel to have current, valid certificates.

Various special programs are provided to support and enhance core basic education:

- *Highly Capable (Gifted)* for the student who has superior cognitive ability.
- *Drug and Alcohol Abuse Prevention* gives instruction on the effects of alcoholic stimulants and narcotics on the human system.
- *Early Childhood and Childcare Programs* provide young children with varied opportunities to solve problems, interact socially, develop large and small muscles, and explore their environment.
- *Learning Assistance* gives help to those who have been identified as deficient in basic skills.
- *Transitional Bilingual Education* provides funds for those who most need to develop English language proficiency.
- *Special Education* for children ages 3 through 21 who have disabilities.

Achievement Tests

Achievement tests are given to students in selected grades to determine how well the students are doing in comparison with others. District wide results are available by school in each district.

Graduation Requirement

There is no standard state requirement or mandatory testing for graduation from high school. Some LSDs require students to pass a minimum competency exam. Minimum requirements of the SBE are

English	3.0 years
Math	2.0 years
Social Studies	3.0 years
Science	2.0 years
Physical Ed	2.0 years
Occupational Ed	1.5 years

Transportation

To enable students to reach schools, the state reimburses LSDs to transport all students who must travel more than a mile to school or where walking hazards exist. Districts may further reduce minimum walking distances.

Home Schooling

This is a state-authorized method of providing instruction and is carefully regulated. Home based instruction may take place on a full time basis, as an extension program of an approved private school, or part time in conjunction with public school attendance. This program is under the general supervision of the SPI, with detailed supervision delegated to the LSD. Parents who home school must file with the local school district.

Kindergarten

Most kindergartens are half-day sessions, but some LSDs, mainly in the metropolitan areas, offer full days, with the parents paying half of the cost.

Extracurricular Activities

There are many activities before and after the normal school day at all levels. Several sports have play-offs at the state level according to the high-school classification (size).

Funding

More than 75% of funding comes from the state. Local sources provide about 15% through the special-levy process, with the remainder coming from federal sources. About 80% of the LSDs have one or more special levies to provide both operating and capital improvement funds. The formulas and allocations for how many dollars each LSD receives are somewhat complicated and beyond the scope of this text. About 80% of the budget goes for salaries and benefits.

Special levies, which can provide up to 30% of what the state pays, continue to be a subject of many debates. Some believe that each LSD should be able to spend as much as it wants and can afford, and the voters will allow. Others believe the state already controls so much of the educational funding process that it should provide all of the funds necessary for quality education.

Public Higher Education

The state has 6 universities, some with branch campuses, 27 two-year community colleges (CCs) and five technical colleges within the state system. The four-year schools use about 12% of the state budget, and the two-year colleges get 4%. The two major schools that bestow doctoral degrees are the University of Washington (UW) in Seattle and Washington State University (WSU) at Pullman (Whitman). Enrollment at UW is well over 30,000 and at WSU about 20,000. WSU is a Land Grant school, has an excellent agriculture program and extension service, and receives funds under the Morrill Act. The UW has sizable medical, dental, and law schools. Tuition for state residents is about 30% of costs.

The four other public universities are Central Washington University, Ellensburg (Kittitas); Eastern Washington University, Cheney (Spokane); Western Washington University, Bellingham (Whatcom); The Evergreen State College, Olympia (Thurston).

Almost anyone can attend a CC, but enrollment may be limited for a particular class or college. Entrance to the four-year schools is highly competitive, with a premium placed on good grades. It is common practice for a student to first go to a community college and then transfer to the four-year school. Some say that reduces the overall quality of a four-year institution.

Private Schools

A large array of private schools at all educational levels generally serves the metropolitan areas. While each has its specific offering, most have one thing in common—a significant tuition. The state has more than 400 private schools (K-12) providing instruction for about 80,000 students. More than 300 are elementary, and 60 are high schools. These schools are subject to the minimum requirements set by the Legislature and must be approved annually by the SBE. Most are church-affiliated and denominationally oriented, but some are secular.

For higher education, there are several well known privately funded colleges and universities: Seattle University, Seattle Pacific University, Gonzaga University (Spokane), Pacific Lutheran University (Tacoma), University of Puget Sound, Cornish College of the Arts (Seattle), and Whitman College (Walla Walla). City University has classrooms in various locations, with classes at night and on weekends for those who are employed.

Tomorrow

Continuing studies and planning are underway to improve the processes and quality of education. Major issues being addressed are

- Opportunities to learn
- High standards
- Assessment and accountability
- Career preparation
- Parent/community involvement
- Safe schools
- Advanced technology
- Local decisions
- Professional excellence.

Health Care

The central Puget Sound region is the health-care center of the Northwest and is one of the best and most complete centers in the nation. Among the many hospitals are Children's Hospital, Northwest Kidney Foundation, Fred Hutchinson Cancer Research Center, and the University of Washington School of Medicine. The Seattle Fire Department's Medic 1 Program, designed for quick response to medical emergencies, was the first, and still one of the fastest response systems in the country. Similar services are available throughout King and in other counties.

Licensing Drivers

A driver's license is required of all resident drivers 16 years of age or older. Anyone moving into the state, except an active-duty military resident of another state, has 30 days to apply. Instruction permits for those 15 years old are available with specific requirements.

Licensing Vehicles

Anyone moving a vehicle into and becoming a resident the state must obtain Washington plates within 30 days. Licensing requires the vehicle title (or copy if a lienholder holds the title), vehicle registration, and personal identification. No person may operate a vehicle registered in this state without vehicle liability insurance. Proof of insurance (or proof of financial reponsibility in cases where an individual is wealthy enough to weather any kind of financial catastrophe) must be available at all times in the vehicle. To be registered, a vehicle new to the state must pass an inspection by the State Patrol, and an emissions inspection is required if it is registered in a large population area (designated by ZIP code). Personalized plates and special plates for disabled veterans and other handicapped individuals are available for an extra fee. The licensing fee is mostly an excise tax based on the market value of the vehicle.

Fishing, a favorite recreation all over Washington.

Recreation

Recreation is available in nearly all areas of interest. Exceptions might be major league hockey (nearest is Vancouver, B.C.) and first-run shows and plays (but most get here rather soon). See the Facts & Fun section for details.

The Future

Looking forward two decades from the approaching millennium, we believe that some things are almost certain to happen and others are probable. Looking back at the first edition (1991), most of the predictions for the next decade were reasonably accurate. Now, let's try for the next 20 years.

- The state's population will increase by well over 1 million. This will come from people living longer, local births, and a net inmigration from other states and countries. Most of the increase will be in the western counties and along the I-5 corridor.

- Population densities in urban areas will increase as growth-management plans are implemented.

- Transportation, growth management, and the environment will be emphasized in the region known as Cascadia—the west side of the Cascade Range from Vancouver, B.C., on the north to Eugene, OR, on the south—i.e., all of the wet side of the state.

- The border between the United States and Canada (Whatcom County and British Columbia) will become more invisible as pressure grows from the people who live in the area and want freedom of movement.

- The two megalopolises, Vancouver–Portland and Tacoma–Seattle–Everett, will continue to expand, mostly in a north–south direction. The former will run from Kelso south to Eugene. The latter will extend from Mount Vernon on the north to Olympia on the south. It will also curl around to the west and pick up Bremerton and much of the Kitsap Peninsula. It is doubtful that the space between Bellingham and Vancouver, B.C., will fill in sufficiently to become a megalopolis.

- Two or more new counties may be formed. The principal reason for this is the skewed concentrations of people in some existing counties. The prime examples are King and Snohomish, which Seattle and Everett dominate. Petitions for such action have been submitted in four counties as of this writing. (Recently, the "Cedar County" faction removed its bid to split from King County.)

- If the state's population continues to become more skewed to the west, agitation may resume in the eastern part of the state to separate. There has been talk in the past about a state called Lincoln, which could include parts of Oregon and Idaho.

- Personal travel in the I-5 corridor will become increasingly time consuming and difficult, and more mass transit will be created.

- More businesses will move to the fringes of the urban areas and some to east of the Cascades.

- The timber industry will remain at about the present level of activity and could increase slightly as improved harvesting methods and faster growing trees are introduced.

- Agriculture, especially the dairy industry, will be an increasingly difficult business to conduct west of the Cascades, even with the purchase of development rights. Environmental controls will not allow residues from fertilizers or animal waste to enter the waters, and the cost will be too high to implement the necessary controls. As a result, dairy farms will continue to relocate to the east.

Counties

Washington's counties vary greatly in size, population, climate, and amount of private versus public land. In spite of the differences, we have tried to give "equal billing" as much as possible in presenting each county.

Throughout, you will find many words about the myriad bodies of water throughout the state. In this regard, we now offer an item of interest and note: all but one county has identifiable water as part of the boundary between it and at least one adjacent county. The only county that doesn't is Pend Oreille, and even there the Pend Oreille River runs almost the full length of the county. The Columbia River borders 17 counties, the Snake 6, and the Spokane 4. The Pacific is a boundary for 4, and Puget Sound 12.

The focal points of activity in many of the counties, especially the smaller ones, are the courthouses. Many are on the National Register of Historic Places and are in excellent condition. For this reason, we included pictures of the courthouses, both in this section and in the special color section.

Also, each county provided a flag to be placed in the state capital rotunda as part of the centennial celebration in 1989. Not all counties display their flags, so we have included all of them in the color pages.

Data are as of 1997 or as recent as research found.

Adams County

	Amount	Rank
County Population	15,800	31
Ritzville	1,775	
Othello	5,395	
Density/mi²	8	32
Per capita income	$17,789	13
Area in mi²	1,925	14
Area in acres	1,232,000	14
Acreage of Public Lands	86,400	
Public land as % of Total	7	37
Acreage of Federal Land	21,200	
Acreage of State Land	54,000	
Acreage of Indian Land	—	
Acreage of County Land	11,200	

On May 18, 1980, Ritzville was covered by ashfall measuring 3 to 6 inches from the eruption of Mount St. Helens. The ash is still evident along highways and in the fields.

Adams County is in the heartland of eastern Washington agriculture.

The first permanent white settler, George Lucas, arrived in 1869. In 1879, Jared M. Harris, a veteran of the battles of Gettysburg and Lookout Mountain, and James G. Bennett, later named one of Adams County's first commissioners, broke a small plot of land belonging to Philip Ritz (the founder of Ritzville) and sowed it to wheat. An army of squirrels devoured the grain. The next year, Bennett tried again on a plot of his own and harvested the first crop of wheat in the area.

In 1883, the county was carved out of Whitman County and named after President John Adams. Ritzville, the only town in the county at the time, was named the county seat.

With the arrival of German and Russian immigrants in the late 1800s, farming replaced cattle raising as the principal industry. However, livestock raising is still economically important to the county and the individual ranchers.

The terrain is rolling with a rich, light, loessal soil interspersed with basalt rock formations—characteristic of channeled scablands. Elevation ranges from 600 to 2,200 feet.

Most of the farming was in dryland wheat until the Columbia Basin Irrigation Project was started in the 1940s. This made water available to the western third of the county and greatly increased yields. It also permitted other crops that need more water than is provided by natural precipitation, which averages about 12 inches annually.

With the arrival of irrigation, the tiny railroad stopover town of Othello, in the western panhandle of the county, began growing and is now more than twice the size of Ritzville. However, the history of wheat and present-day oversight remains with the Washington Association of Wheat Growers in Ritzville.

A wide variety of crops is grown along with wheat, including apples, corn, dry beans, asparagus, and potatoes. Much of the processing after harvest, especially of potatoes, takes place in Othello.

Just northwest of Othello is the 23,100-acre Columbia National Wildlife Refuge, which contains a scenic mixture of canyons, buttes, grasslands, and wetlands. As a result of irrigation, wetlands comprise more than 3700 acres of lakes, ponds, and streams. The Refuge is the winter home of thousands of mallard ducks and some Canadian geese. Many other species of wildlife inhabit this area throughout the year. During the winter, major wildlife concentration areas are closed to the public to prevent disturbing the wildlife. Summer viewing in the Refuge is no problem.

There is exceptionally good fishing in the lakes and bird hunting throughout the county in the fall. Don't be surprised to see signs in the motels that say, "No bird cleaning in the rooms."

Asotin County

	Amount	Rank
County Population	19,700	29
Asotin	1,106	
Clarkston	6,870	
Density/mi²	31	20
Per capita income	$18,360	21
Area in mi²	636	34
Area in acres	405,100	34
Acreage of Public Lands	99,300	
Public land as % of Total	25	37
Acreage of Federal Land	65,700	
Acreage of State Land	31,300	
Acreage of Indian Land	0	
Acreage of County Land	2,300	

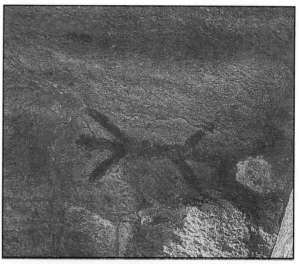

Ancient Indian art in Asotin County

Asotin County is where Washington's day begins—the anchor of the southeast corner of the state, with Idaho on the east and Oregon on the south.

The name is derived from a Nez Perce Indian word that means "place of many eels," which describes the confluence of Asotin Creek and the Snake River.

Early settlers were not attracted to the area. The first permanent resident (one Sam Smith) arrived in 1861. The population buildup was slow until the late 1870 because of problems with the Nez Perce. The county was chartered in 1883, when it was segregated from Garfield County to the east. Asotin and Asotin City were established within one mile of each other, about five miles south of where the Clearwater River joins the Snake. Asotin finally emerged as the county seat. Clarkston, which is directly across the Snake River from Lewiston, Idaho, has become the major population center.

It's easy to relate Hell's Canyon, America's deepest gorge, to Asotin and Clarkston because almost all boat trips into this national recreation area start from these locations (or Lewiston). The actual canyon starts more than 40 miles upstream in Oregon and Idaho. On land, the road along the Snake past Asotin, the last town, is very basic and does not go through to Oregon. The one road that does go through has two lanes and many curves and goes over the Blue Mountains.

Clarkston is the last inland port on the Snake, more than 400 miles from the Pacific Ocean, at an elevation of 736 feet. Agriculture plays a smaller role in this county than in others in the region. Most of the employment is in retail trade, services, and government. With plenty of sun, limited rain, and moderate temperatures, there is considerable and varied outdoor recreation activity.

Whitewater rafting in Hell's Canyon.

Benton County

	Amount	Rank
County Population	134,100	10
Prosser	4,840	
Kennewick	49,090	
Density/mi²	79	10
Per capita income	$22,072	6
Area in mi²	1,703	22
Area in acres	1,097,600	22
Acreage of Public Lands	372,300	
Public land as % of Total	34	
Acreage of Federal Land	31,800	
Acreage of State Land	46,000	
Acreage of Indian Land	10	
Acreage of County Land	8,400	

Benton County is famous, or maybe infamous, as the home of the U.S. Department of Energy's Hanford nuclear site, but hardly anyone outside the area knows it by name. On December 2, 1942, the first controlled nuclear chain reaction was conducted there. In January 1943, the Hanford site was chosen to produce plutonium for the Top Secret Manhattan Project's new atomic weapon. This major event shaped the economy and lifestyle of the whole area known as the Tri-Cities (Richland, Kennewick, and Pasco). Hanford was chosen because it was remote, yet near railroads, and had abundant water for reactor cooling and plentiful electricity from nearby hydroelectric dams. Thousands of workers streamed into the area, living in hastily built camps and housing.

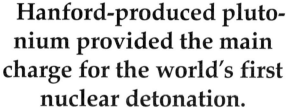

Hanford-produced plutonium provided the main charge for the world's first nuclear detonation.

Just 27 months after construction was started, Hanford-produced plutonium provided the main charge for the world's first nuclear detonation, near Alamogordo, New Mexico.

The atomic-energy-related buildup and activity at Hanford continued until 1965. Today, none of the original nine plutonium reactors are in operation, but occasional proposals arise to reactivate one or more to supply plutonium for fueling reactors to generate electricity or tritium for present or future weapons. Hanford's mission, as of now, is focused on three elements: site cleanup, science and technology, and economic diversification. The 560-square-mile site covers a third of the county. The Hanford Science Center in Richland has displays and hands-on exhibits related to atomic energy and other Hanford programs. There is also a visitor center at Plant 2.

There is considerable concern at this writing about the danger of radiation leaking into the Columbia River from old nuclear waste storage tanks at Hanford. Efforts to clean it up seem to go nowhere.

The Columbia River forms the north, east, and south borders of Benton County. The Yakima River flows through its middle (west to east) and joins the Columbia at Richland.

After Lewis and Clark visited the area in 1805, the fur trade became a prime livelihood for the first part of the 19th century. The first settler, J. B. Nelson, built his cabin near the mouth of the Yakima in 1863. In 1868, E. Bird moved 300 head of cattle into the Richland area. Then, in 1881, Colonel W. F. Prosser, special agent for the Interior Department, filed a homestead claim, platted the site, and obtained a post office for the town, which took his name and became the county seat.

After the Northern Pacific Railroad started construction of a main line up the Yakima River Valley, growth continued at a moderate pace. In 1895, the first European grapes were planted in irrigated fields near Kennewick. Carved out of Yakima County on March 8, 1905, Benton County was one of the last to be formed by the state legislature. It is named for Senator Thomas Hart Benton of Missouri, who was a champion of the West.

Besides Hanford, the county's principal employer, agriculture and related food processing continue to be the main economic engines. Just north of Prosser is the large Washington State University Irrigated Agricultural Research and Extension Center. The wine industry continues to grow, and many wineries welcome visitors. The state's largest winery is located at Paterson, overlooking the Columbia.

Chelan County

	Amount	Rank
County Population	62,200	18
Wenatchee	25,160	
Density/mi²	21	24
Per capita income	$21,590	7
Area in mi²	2,922	3
Area in acres	1,865,600	3
Acreage of Public Lands	1,510,900	
Public land as % of Total	81	
Acreage of Federal Land	1,434,150	
Acreage of State Land	71,100	
Acreage of Indian Land	1,440	
Acreage of County Land	4,170	

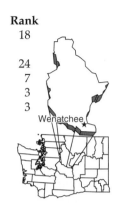

Wenatchee

At an elevation of 4,061 feet, U.S. Highway 2 crosses the crest of the Cascades and the western border of Chelan County at Stevens Pass amid mountain peaks rising to 9,000 feet. It then descends through Leavenworth and Cashmere to Wenatchee at 600 feet, where the Wenatchee River joins the Columbia. Chelan is the third largest county in the state, of which 77% is federal land (mostly national forest) and another 4% is under state and county control.

Fur traders and missionaries arrived in the area in the early 1800s, but significant settlement awaited the coming of the railroads and the discovery of gold in the hills later in the century.

The State Legislature created Chelan County in 1899 from portions of Okanogan and Kittitas Counties because early residents found it difficult to travel to the county seat of either one. The name Chelan is derived from an Indian word that means "deep water," an obvious reference to Lake Chelan. Wenatchee, now the county seat and the trade center of the north-central region, was born in 1892. Its name comes from a poetic description of the area, *wa-nat-chee*, meaning "robe of the rainbow."

This area is one of the best in the state for seeing the typical four seasons. In the spring, apple and other fruit trees provide a carpet of blossoms along the waters and up the slopes. In April, Wenatchee hosts the annual Apple Blossom Festival. Summer, with days in the 90s, is for enjoying water and other sports. In the fall, when the leaves turn gold and red, Leavenworth holds the Autumn Leaves Festival, and later in December the Christmas Lighting Celebration. Many winter sport activities emerge with the arrival of snow. Mission Ridge, a few miles from Wenatchee and Stevens Pass, has alpine skiing. Snowmobiles and dog sleds are two more ways to get around in the snow. A few zero-degree days can be expected in the winter.

The backbone of the economy is agriculture, with 70% involving fruit—the apple is king!—and the re-

mainder being grains and livestock. The area receives only about 9 inches of rain a year, but irrigation, sunshine, a 180-day growing season, and the right soils create an environment that produces about half of the state's apple crop.

Many attractions generate considerable tourist activity. In the 1960s without government help, the citizens of Leavenworth started transforming their town into a charming Bavarian Village in a distinct alpine setting. In Cashmere, named for the Vale of Kashmir, is an interesting pioneer museum and the factory where the jellied-fruit candies Aplets and Cotlets are made, mostly by hand. At the south end of Lake Chelan, which is a national recreation area, are many sites where people can swim, play golf, ski Nordic, or just plain relax. Many take the 55-mile boat trip to Stehekin, a small destination resort at the north end of the lake. Boat, plane, or hiking over the mountains are the only ways to get there. Another attraction is Rocky Reach Dam, one of eleven on the Columbia, with its fish viewing, dam tours, and park. Two other dams on the Columbia plus one at the end of Lake Chelan, all provide electrical power. There has been gold mining in recent years.

A relaxing, beautiful, scenic vista is the Ohme Gardens, which sit on a high bluff above the Columbia just north of Wenatchee.

In Manson, on the east shore of Lake Chelan, is a really basic weather station (if it is still in operation). A rock is suspended by a line from a sign that essentially says, "If the rock is moving, it's windy . . . if white, it's snowing . . . if wet, it's raining . . . if not visible, it's foggy . . ."

Clallam County

	Amount	Rank
County Population	66,400	17
Port Angeles	19,000	
Density/mi²	38	17
Per capita income	$20,597	12
Area in mi²	1,745	20
Area in acres	1,121,900	20
Acreage of Public Lands	718,400	
Public land as % of Total	64	
Acreage of Federal Land	521,800	
Acreage of State Land	161,000	
Acreage of Indian Land	30,000	
Acreage of County Land	5,400	

What interesting boundaries! The north boundary of the county runs from the most northwesterly point of the lower 48 states, Tatoosh Island and the Cape Flattery light, east about 90 miles along the international boundary with Canada in the middle of the Strait of Juan de Fuca, and into Puget Sound. On the west, the boundary is the Pacific Ocean and the Flattery Rocks National Wildlife Refuge. The south has Indian reservations and Olympic National Park. The border with Jefferson County on the south is mostly along a latitude of 27° 30' north, but it is fuzzy from a surveyor's standpoint as it goes through the Olympic Mountains. On the east, the line is just west of Protection Island but includes Diamond Point and a little of Discovery Bay.

The county was officially organized by the Washington Territorial Legislature on April 26, 1854, and named after the Indian tribe who called themselves the *Nu-sklaim*, meaning "strong people" or "big brave nation." The first county seat was New Dungeness, at times called "Whiskey Flat," until 1890. Then it was moved to Port Angeles (PA), where we find the headquarters of the Olympic National Park and the south terminal of a ferry trip (1.5 hours) to Victoria, B.C. As the deepest natural seaport north of San Francisco, it is the home of many fishing vessels, a major port for oceangoing vessels, and was for a time a home port of the U.S. Navy's Pacific Fleet. Due south from the city is the road to Hurricane Ridge, which provides an excellent site to view the Olympic Mountains and Park.

The second largest town, Sequim (pronounced Skwimm), recently has enjoyed a population boom as a result of publicity about Washington's "Banana Belt." Tucked into the "rain shadow" of the Olympic Mountains, it receives only about 20 inches of rain per year and is popular among retirees—especially military, who use the Navy facilities at nearby Bremerton and Bangor.

In the early years, land in this area was irrigated from the Dungeness River. From this activity rose the Irrigation Festival in 1895, which continues to this day, the state's oldest continuing celebration.

Adjacent to Sequim on the north is the Dungeness Spit, home to the tasty crab of the same name. A national wildlife refuge, it is the world's largest sand spit, extending 6 miles into the Strait. At the Olympic Game Farm near the Spit can be seen many animals featured in movies.

Heading west from PA along the Strait, State Route 112 is dotted with small towns catering to salmon and halibut sport fishermen. This road ends at Neah Bay and the Makah Indian Reservation. The Makah Cultural House contains some of the Northwest's finest Native American artifacts. From Neah Bay, a 3-mile trail to Cape Flattery offers views of rugged headlands, Tatoosh Island, and the entrance to the Strait.

West from PA, Highway 101 crosses the Elwha river, hugs the shore of Lake Crescent, and 40 miles farther, enters the city of Forks in the heart of logging country. On the way, a side trip to Sol Duc Hot Springs in Olympic National Park provides an opportunity for a relaxing hot bath and excellent viewing of salmon runs in season. From Forks, SR 110 leads to the coastal town of La Push and the Quillayute Indian Reservation. South from Forks, Highway 101 enters Jefferson County, where a side road leads to Olympic National Park's most-visited rain forest.

The economy of the county is in transition and is uncertain. Because of the mild climate in the eastern county, dairy was at one time a large business with over 250 herds. Recently, much farmland has been developed, mostly to make way for Sequim's retirees. Logging and timber processing have been greatly curtailed as a result of designated "wilderness areas" and environmental concerns. Fishing is severely limited because of depleted stocks.

Clark County

	Amount	Rank
County Population	316,800	5
Vancouver	127,900	
Density/mi^2	505	3
Per capita income	$23,013	3
Area in mi^2	628	35
Area in acres	401,000	35
Acreage of Public Lands	80,000	
Public land as % of Total	20	37
Acreage of Federal Land	10,400	
Acreage of State Land	59,200	
Acreage of Indian Land	0	
Acreage of County Land	10,600	

Fort Vancouver barracks

Named for Captain William Clark of the Lewis & Clark Expedition and created by the Oregon Provisional Government on June 27, 1844, this was the first county in the state. From its vantage point near the mouth of the Columbia, early inhabitants witnessed the initial exploration of the territory. In 1792, Lt. Broughton of the British navy sailed past, going up the Columbia. Then came Lewis and Clark. In 1825, the Hudson's Bay Company (HBC) relocated its regional headquarters from Astoria at the mouth of the river to Fort Vancouver, the state's oldest settlement. Columbia City, platted here in 1850, was renamed Vancouver in 1853 and became the county seat.

Most of the new arrivals to the area were Americans, so when the boundary dispute occurred with England in 1846 at the 49th parallel, the HBC moved operations north to Victoria. Initially, Clark County included all of Clark, Cowlitz, and Skamania counties and part of Lewis. Original emphasis on settlement in the area was south of the river in Portland, which saw much more rapid growth.

In 1848, Fort Vancouver became a U.S. Army post. Over the years, Sheridan, Grant, Bradley, Marshall, and other military notables were stationed here. Today, Vancouver's 300-acre Central Park, restored Fort Vancouver (now a national historic site), and homes on its Officers Row, just east of I-5 in the city, are a must stop for travels in the area. The George Marshall and Ulysses Grant houses on Officers Row have been restored and are open to the public.

The county is bounded on the north by the Lewis River and on the south and west by the Columbia River, which provides 41 miles of river frontage.

Forest and fish supported the early economy, with farming close behind. Railroads started arriving in the late 1800s. In February 1917, the first bridge over the Columbia opened between Vancouver and Portland, and ferry service ceased

Washington's first county

on opening day. In 1982, a second major bridge for I-205 to the east was completed, providing a bypass around the two cities.

The Columbia River Gorge National Scenic Area starts at the east end of the county, past Washougal. Near Woodland is the Cedar Creek Grist Mill, the only remaining mill of its type still operating in the state. A National Wildlife Refuge of more than 3,000 acres for deer, beaver, otter, and various bird species is near Ridgefield.

The economies of Vancouver and Portland have an interesting link. People decide where to live and shop based on no income tax in Washington and no sales tax in Oregon. (Those who work in Oregon but live in Washington do pay Oregon state income tax.) Vancouver's manufacturing base has expanded with high-tech companies and continued operations in paper and lumber products, aluminum smelting, and food processing. A deep-water port, interstate highways, and railroads are all major economic contributors.

Columbia County

	Amount	Rank
County Population	4,200	37
Dayton	2,558	
Density/mi²	5	36
Per capita income	$18,670	18
Area in mi²	869	31
Area in acres	554,900	31
Acreage of Public Lands	187,700	
Public land as % of Total	34	
Acreage of Federal Land	164,700	
Acreage of State Land	19,900	
Acreage of Indian Land	0	
Acreage of County Land	3,100	

The historic Dayton railroad depot, built in 1881. It is the centerpiece of the annual Depot Festival in August.

Although Columbia County was named after the river, the Columbia River is all the way across Walla Walla County to the west.

Nestled in the southeast part of the state, Columbia County has the Snake River for its northern border. The Little Goose Dam, near Starbuck (pop. 165) on the Snake, started producing power in 1970.

Columbia County's main source of livelihood is agriculture. Over 202,500 acres are under cultivation, of which 100,000 acres are in wheat, barley, and oats.

Dayton became a canning center in 1934, when the Pillsbury Green Giant Company built a plant and office facilities. Peas and asparagus are processed and canned in Dayton.

Fruits are grown here as well, and apple production amounts to 107,000 boxes annually.

Harvesting and processing timber is important in the county, with annual sales of forest products over $1 million. Other agricultural products produced in the county are cattle, poultry and eggs, sheep, and swine.

Most of the southeast portion of the county lies within the Umatilla National Forest (in the Blue Mountains). At 6,000 feet and 23 miles south of Dayton, Ski Bluewood has modern ski facilities. Excellent snowmobiling is also available. This region is bountiful in fish and game.

Before the arrival of Lewis and Clark and the white settlers, the Dayton vicinity was a common meeting place for the nomadic Indian tribes. The first permanent settlers arrived in the late 1850s. Dayton was originally homesteaded in 1859—and the plat registered in 1871—by Jesse Day, for whom the city is named. In 1875, Columbia County was created out

of the eastern portion of Walla Walla County, and Dayton was selected as the county seat.

Dayton and Columbia County are steeped in history. A Lewis and Clark campsite dating to 1805 is now Lewis and Clark Trail State Park. The first public school in Washington Territory was organized here in 1865. The original Dayton High School, organized in 1881, was the first public high school in the Territory. The courthouse was built in 1887 at a cost of $38,000—$2,000 under budget. (Things like that happened in those days.) It is the oldest courthouse in the state still in use. Recently restored, it is in the National Register of Historic Places. The cannons on the courthouse lawn are from the Civil War. They arrived in 1915.

The first government-built telegraph line was run from Dayton to Lewiston in 1879.

With a small population, about 300 days of sunshine, and plenty of opportunity for outdoor activity, Columbia County is a place to consider visiting to relax and reduce stress.

The Columbia County courthouse is the oldest in the state still in use.

Cowlitz County

	Amount	Rank
County Population	92,000	12
Kelso	12,000	
Longview	33,620	
Density/mi^2	81	9
Per capita income	$20,013	14
Area in mi^2	1,139	28
Area in acres	729,000	28
Acreage of Public Lands	109,000	
Public land as % of Total	15	
Acreage of Federal Land	22,000	
Acreage of State Land	82,400	
Acreage of Indian Land	0	
Acreage of County Land	4,600	

Some devastation from the Mount St. Helens eruption.

Created on April 21, 1854, by the Territorial Legislature, Cowlitz County is one of the oldest Washington counties. The name is the anglicized version of an Indian term that translates roughly as "creating the medicine spirit." The first county seat was in Montecello from 1854 to 1866. The territorial capital was also there for a short while until it moved to Olympia. Named for Jefferson's home, Montecello no longer exists; something to do with the high water of the river. The county seat moved to Freeport (1866–1873), on to Kalama (1873–1922) and finally to Kelso in 1922.

The county was working and resting peacefully until May 18, 1980, when Mount St. Helens, just over its eastern boundary, decided to erupt. Water from Spirit Lake and melting snow hurtled down the Toutle River, sweeping everything along, filling the Cowlitz River, and continued west into the town of Castle Rock. Damage from Mount St. Helens was extensive. Today, most of the thousands of people annually who visit the National Volcanic Monument also visit the county. One result of the event has been the building of immense berms along the river banks, some of which can be seen from I-5.

The main Mount St. Helens visitor centers and viewing sites are along SR 504, off I-5 at Castle Rock.

With the Columbia River as the county's southwest border, the Lewis River on the south, and the Cowlitz coming through the midsection from the north to join the Columbia, the initial economy centered on fish, fur, and forest. The fur trade met its demise in the mid 1800s from overharvesting. Large-scale fish-canning operations flourished in the late 1800s. Agriculture became more important as people moved in and needed food, including dairy products. Forests in this county and the surrounding areas provided the fuel for expanding businesses and plants, assisted by a deep-water port for oceangoing vessels at Longview.

Longview was built as a planned community in the 1920s, initiated by the Long-Bell Lumber Co. and named for the company's president, R. A. Long. Kelso, across the river, was named by Peter Crawford, its founder, for his native home in Scotland. There were various attempts to merge the two cities, but no agreement could be reached.

With water, rail, and roads converging in the Longview–Kelso area, the lumber companies have maintained their presence there and continue to upgrade their facilities.

Up the Lewis River from Woodland on State Route 503 is the village of Ariel. With only one store and tavern, it still is well known because this is the area where D. C. Cooper parachuted from an airliner with $200,000 after hijacking it in 1971. The search continues for Cooper, and each Thanksgiving weekend, Ariel holds a celebration called "The Cooper Capers."

Another annual event in the county is the smelt run during January and February. These small, silvery fish move up the Cowlitz river to spawn, and people line the river with nets for the catch. Kelso has become known as the "Smelt Capital of the World."

Adams
Ritzville

Asotin
Asotin

Benton
Prosser

Chelan
Wenatchee

Clallam
Port Angeles

Clark
Vancouver

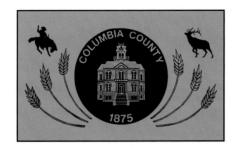 

Columbia
Dayton

Cowlitz
Kelso

Douglas
Waterville

Ferry
Republic

Franklin
Pasco

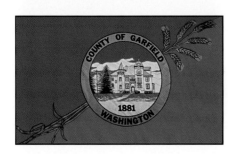 

Garfield
Pomeroy

Grant
Ephrata

Grays Harbor
Montesano

Island
Coupeville

Jefferson
Port Townsend

King
Seattle

Kitsap
Port Orchard

Kittitas
Ellensburg

Klickitat
Goldendale

Lewis
Chehalis

Lincoln
Davenport

Mason
Shelton

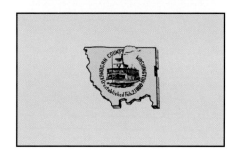

Okanogan
Okanogan

Pacific
South Bend

Pend Oreille
Newport

Pierce
Tacoma

San Juan
Friday Harbor

Skagit
Mount Vernon

Skamania
Stevenson

Snohomish
Everett

Spokane
Spokane

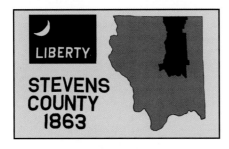

Stevens
Colville

Thurston
Olympia

Wahkiakum
Cathlamet

Walla Walla
Walla Walla

Whatcom
Bellingham

Whitman
Colfax

Yakima
Yakima

State Capitol & Flag

Ebey's Landing National Historical Reserve

Monuments around the State

Okanogan County World War I Memorial

Memorial to Washington State Medal of Honor Recipients

Washington State Korean War Memorial

Washington State Vietnam Veterans Memorial

Washington State World War I Memorial

Lady Washington (Grays Harbor)

Peace Arch (Whatcom)

Douglas County

	Amount	Rank
County Population	30,800	26
Waterville	1,100	
East Wenatchee	5,245	
Density/mi^2	17	26
Per capita income	$17,000	34
Area in mi^2	1,821	17
Area in acres	1,162,900	17
Acreage of Public Lands	161,000	
Public land as % of Total	14	37
Acreage of Federal Land	40,400	
Acreage of State Land	110,200	
Acreage of Indian Land	0	
Acreage of County Land	10,300	

Grand Coulee Dam

Indians of the Colville tribe and a few white trappers were the first known humans to journey across the land that was to become north-central Washington, following salmon and fur-bearing animals. In the 1870s, the first settlers were prospectors staking claims and looking for gold. Then, in 1883, cattle and sheep ranchers arrived.

On November 28, 1883, the Territorial Legislature created Douglas County, carving it out of Lincoln County and naming it after Senator Stephen Douglas of Illinois, chairman of the U.S. Commission of Territories when Washington became a territory. In its original form, the county encompassed both present-day Douglas and Grant Counties. The first county seat was in the city of Okanogan, but it was moved in 1886 to Waterville, which had a few more facilities.

Waterville was built on the fortunes of the livestock industry. Although prosperous trade and service industries emerged, they were largely dependent on the larger agricultural activity. In 1886, a range war commenced between the cattle and sheep ranchers. Eventually, the cattle ranchers won, but the winter of 1889–1890 was one of the harshest on record, and most of the cattle died from cold or starvation. In the spring of 1890, wheat seed was acquired, and the economic base shifted to grains. Later, fruit growing spread east to the fertile silt along the banks of the Columbia River.

From the west, State Route 2 parallels the river through acres of fruit trees and then ascends a 2600-foot plateau. After passing Waterville, it's wheat, wheat, and more wheat.

Nonagricultural industry—aluminum manufacturing, sporting apparel, gold mining, and lumber and wood products—is small compared with agriculture, which also supports food processing, trucking, warehousing, and wholesale trade. South of Waterville on Badger Mountain, a ski area is the nucleus for development of outdoor recreation and tourism. The museum in Waterville has an excellent mineral collection.

Fancher Field, across the Columbia from Wenatchee, was the airport where Clyde Pangborn and Hugh Herndon landed on October 5, 1931, after the first nonstop trans-Pacific flight.

Early in the Great Depression, the region and the state got a much-needed economic boost when dam building started on the Columbia. Eventually, five dams were constructed that directly affect the county. The first, Grand Coulee, is just outside its northeast corner. Downstream 60 miles is Chief Joseph Dam, and another 25 miles, Wells Dam. Then, 10 miles north of East Wenatchee is Rocky Reach Dam, and 25 miles south of that is Rock Island Dam. Maintenance and operation of the dams provide jobs and stability to the area. Grand Coulee is still the nation's premier producer of hydroelectric power, with a maximum capacity of nearly 6.5 gigawatts.

The first nonstop trans-Pacific flight ended successfully at Douglas County's Fancher Field.

Ferry County

	Amount	Rank
County Population	7,300	36
Republic	1,040	
Density/mi^2	3	39
Per capita income	$14,340	39
Area in mi^2	2,204	9
Area in acres	1,408,000	9
Acreage of Public Lands	1,177,700	
Public land as % of Total	84	
Acreage of Federal Land	532,500	
Acreage of State Land	38,200	
Acreage of Indian Land	602,500	
Acreage of County Land	4,400	

Sailboating on Lake Roosevelt

This is the place, if you like a lot of elbow room and want to get away. With fewer than three people per square mile, the county has the lowest population density in the state. The third county from the state's northeast corner, its origin and history are closely linked with Stevens County on the east.

Before white settlement, activity centered around Kettle Falls and fishing. In 1825, the Hudson Bay Company (HBC) established Fort Colville just south of the Falls. In the 1830s, missionaries arrived, and the Jesuit Fathers built Saint Paul's near Kettle Falls. In the late 1850s, gold was discovered at Rock Creek, which was just north of the poorly defined U.S./Canadian border. Soon after, a large tract of land was set aside for an Indian reservation, which included all of the present county. In 1896, the north half of the reservation was opened to allow prospectors to stake mining claims. The first claim was at the town of Eureka Creek. Later, the town name was changed to Republic, after one of the largest mines.

The Washington State Legislature formed the county on February 21, 1899, using land from the original Stevens County, and Republic became the county seat. The county was named for Elisha P. Ferry, the state's first governor. In 1900, logging restrictions on the reservation were lifted, and many sawmills soon commenced operations. The northern half was also opened for homesteading. The railroads came later.

The fortunes of the county have followed the times. At this writing, times are hard for Ferry County, which has the lowest per capita income in the state (see the economic discussion of the Tri-County area under Stevens County). The Grand Coulee Dam and Lake Roosevelt, which forms half of the county's southern border and most of its eastern border, provide jobs and electricity and attract tourists. The county is rich in minerals: gold, silver, lead, iron, and fluorite have been or are being mined.

There are known deposits of limestone, zinc, tungsten, pyrites, and silica sand. The county has three border crossings into Canada on the north, and two free ferries cross Lake Roosevelt on the east (Inchellium/Gifford) and south (Keller).

Sherman Pass, the highest pass in the state, at 5,575 feet, on SR 20 was named for the General Sherman of Civil War fame, who toured the area in 1883. On a clear day, the drive over Sherman Pass provides a grand view of the region.

Franklin County

	Amount	Rank
County Population	43,900	
Pasco	25,300	21
Density/mi²	35	19
Per capita income	$16,356	35
Area in mi²	1,242	27
Area in acres	795,500	27
Acreage of Public Lands	146,600	
Public land as % of Total	18	
Acreage of Federal Land	105,200	
Acreage of State Land	31,900	
Acreage of Indian Land	0	
Acreage of County Land	9,400	

Bridge across the Columbia from Pasco to Kennewick

Agriculture, trade, and transportation dominate the history of this county. At its south corner, the Snake River joins the Columbia where Lewis and Clark and their expedition arrived in 1805. Not until 1861 did the first settlers arrive and commence raising cattle.

The country was officially formed on November 28, 1883, by the Territorial Legislature and named for Ben Franklin. The city of Pasco became the county seat in 1885, although it did not incorporate until 1891. Virgil Bogue, a railroad engineer, named the city after another city—Cerro de Pasco—in the Andes mountains of Peru, where he previously worked. As in other southeastern Washington counties, agricultural activity soon shifted to raising crops. Some irrigation projects began in the 1890s with various schemes to pump water from the Snake River.

Pasco is the transportation hub for the area. First to arrive, because of the two rivers, was water traffic. Next, the railroads came to Ainsworth, now Ainsworth Junction, just east of Pasco. However, as Pasco grew, it gradually took over the siting of the railroad yards. Then, in 1910, the first airport west of the Mississippi was built nearby. The country's first airmail service began there in 1926. In World War II, the airport became a naval air station and is now known as the Tri-Cities Airport.

Prior to 1948, when the water from the Columbia Basin Irrigation Project arrived, the area was known for "wheat, heat, and rattlesnakes." Now, 160,000 acres (40% of the county)—mostly in the western part, is irrigated. The land rises somewhat from an elevation of 340 feet at Pasco to 1,000 feet in the northeast. Two Snake River dams are shared with Walla

The first airport west of the Mississippi River was built near Pasco. It is now the Tri-Cities Airport.

Walla County. The growing of grapes and their transformation into wine is now a notable component of the county's agriculture.

Sacajawea State Park is in the corner formed by the confluence of the Snake and the Columbia Rivers.

Other than Pasco, Connell, with 2,000+ people, is the only town with a population over 1,000.

To see the desert and its browns in the Evergreen State, visit the Juniper Dunes Wilderness, 8 miles northeast of Pasco. Get out of the car and walk through some of the 7,000 acres of sand dunes and juniper groves among desert wildlife and flowers. This wilderness provides unique habitat for mule deer, coyote, small rodents, and birds of prey. Summer and winter temperatures are extreme, and access is by permit only.

Garfield County

	Amount	Rank
County Population	2,400	39
Pomeroy	1,445	
Density/mi^2	3	38
Per capita income	$18,277	22
Area in mi^2	710	33
Area in acres	452,000	33
Acreage of Public Lands	118,000	
Public land as % of Total	26	
Acreage of Federal Land	101,000	
Acreage of State Land	14,350	
Acreage of Indian Land	0	
Acreage of County Land	2,700	

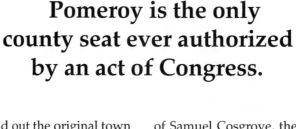

The natural path for the Nez Perce trail from the Columbia River to the Rocky Mountains was via the Snake and Clearwater (in Idaho) Rivers. However, to avoid the swift waters of the Snake in Garfield County, the trail followed Pataha Creek to the Tucannon River to the west. Lewis and Clark camped in what is now this county on their return trip in 1806.

Daniel Types, an Indian converted by the missionary Henry Spaulding, was the first permanent settler. Parson Quinn was the first non-Indian settler, making his home in the Pataha Valley, west of what is now Pomeroy, in 1861.

In 1864, J. M. Pomeroy's ranch became the site of the town of Pomeroy. He laid out the original town site and a year later erected the Pomeroy hotel.

The county was established by the territorial legislature in 1881, splitting from Columbia County after that county split from Walla Walla County in 1875. (Before 1875, Walla Walla County was one of the largest counties ever established in the United States.) It was named for President Garfield, who died the same year. Pataha was the temporary county seat. A bitter election decided Pomeroy to be the seat. A town called Mentor, charted on paper only, was created to split the Pataha vote. After more controversy, Congress validated several acts of the territorial government, including the election of Pomeroy, making it the only county seat ever authorized by Congress. The population of Pataha declined, and today it is only an unincorporated community 3 miles east of Pomeroy.

Shaped like an ice cream cone (or a mushroom cloud, depending on your Rorshachian proclivities), the county is bounded on the north by the Snake River and on the south by the Oregon border. The southern third is heavily forested, with 96,400 acres in the Umatilla National Forest. About 110,000 acres of cereal crops, mostly wheat and barley, are harvested each year from dryland farms. Another important crop is grass seed, including several varieties of blue grass that originate here, which is marketed around the world. Austrian winter peas are a seed crop on about 4,000 acres. The final important component of income from agriculture, beef cattle, amounts to about $20 million per year.

Lower Granite Dam, the last of the four dams built on the Snake, opened in 1975. It extends slack water upstream to Clarkston, in Asotin County, and to Lewiston, Idaho.

Annual precipitation ranges from 12 inches in the west to more than 20 inches in the east and up to 35 inches at higher elevations in the mountains. Many spring-fed creeks meander through valleys in the rolling farmland.

The present courthouse was built in 1901 to replace a frame structure that was destroyed in a fire in 1900 that destroyed the heart of the Pomeroy business district.

Pomeroy is the only county seat ever authorized by an act of Congress.

The bid for construction of the new courthouse must hold some sort of record for brevity in government circles. It was handwritten on a piece of hotel stationery.

The statue on the front lawn of the courthouse is of Samuel Cosgrove, the only resident of Garfield County to become a governor of Washington.

The first telegraph line built by the government, from Dayton to Lewiston, ran through Pomeroy.

The annual Garfield County Pioneer and Tumbleweed Celebration is held on the second Saturday in June.

Grant County

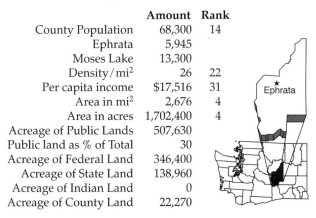

	Amount	Rank
County Population	68,300	14
Ephrata	5,945	
Moses Lake	13,300	
Density/mi^2	26	22
Per capita income	$17,516	31
Area in mi^2	2,676	4
Area in acres	1,702,400	4
Acreage of Public Lands	507,630	
Public land as % of Total	30	
Acreage of Federal Land	346,400	
Acreage of State Land	138,960	
Acreage of Indian Land	0	
Acreage of County Land	22,270	

At the arid center of the state, with annual rainfall of about 8 inches, Grant County is a prime example of what water can do.

Settlement of the area came late in the 1800s when, except for a few sites with good soil, most of the land was desert, covered with sagebrush. Wild horses roamed the countryside.

Where water existed, early settlers planted fruit orchards. Circa 1880, the railroads arrived. The first recorded deed in the Ephrata area was given by the Northern Pacific Railroad to an individual in 1882. The name Ephrata is the ancient name for Bethlehem, meaning "fruit region" or "fertile ground."

In 1909, when a bill arose in the State Legislature to divide Douglas County, a local group in control proposed a partitioning that kept the good wheatland on the plateau in Douglas County and cast off the desert lands in the southeast. Thus, Grant County, named for President Grant, was born on February 24, 1909, with Ephrata as the county seat.

After the depression and long periods of drought—when many had to abandon their land—the Grand Coulee Dam, authorized in 1933, eventually brought irrigation to the Columbia Basin, much of which is in Grant County. Irrigation districts were formed, but not until the 1950s did water actually start to flow in them.

From Grand Coulee, water is pumped into Banks Lake, a 31-mile reservoir for irrigation. Steamboat Rock, in Banks Lake, is a 700-foot-high butte with a hiking trail to the top, a popular landmark for travelers. Dry Falls, at the south end of Banks Lake, is 3.5 miles wide with a drop of over 400 feet. In comparison, Niagara Falls is only 1 mile wide with a 165-foot drop, so one can imagine how immense and spectacular Dry Falls was when the Columbia flowed in this channel.

Soap Lake is the last lake in the Grand Coulee chain. A heavy concentration of minerals in the water gives it a slick feeling, and many feel it eases rheumatic and skin conditions. An annual Greek festival is held there in late May.

The Quincy Valley has more than 200,000 acres of irrigated field and vegetable crops. Farther south is the town of George (there is no Martha), near which is the 15,000-seat Champs de Brionne Amphitheater, a popular spot for summer entertainment.

South of Vantage, where I-90 crosses the Columbia, are two dams: Wanapum and Priest Rapids. Wanapum's excellent interpretive center provides facts and lore about the Northwest. Eastward from there lie many new, irrigated fruit orchards. It's interesting to see apple trees grown as row crops.

Beyond the Saddle Mountains is the Columbia National Wildlife Refuge, much of which is off limits at various times to protect the wildlife. Ample water is provided by seepage from irrigation. O'Sullivan Dam, at the southern end of 23,000-acre-foot Potholes Reservoir, is the largest earthen dam in the United States.

Near the center of the county is Moses Lake, named for Chief Moses of the Sinkiuse (Columbia) tribe. The city is the county's largest, and it has 120 miles of shoreline around its 6,500-acre namesake lake. Just north of the city is Grant County Airport. Originally Larson Air Force Base, it was the testing site for Boeing's B-52 bombers and KC-135 tankers. It was decommissioned in 1965 and acquired by the county. Now, with a 13,500-foot runway in an area with more than 300 days of sunshine, it continues to be a primary Boeing test site and a pilot training site for more than 300 domestic and foreign carriers.

The Columbia River Basin Project intends to irrigate more than 1 million acres (60% of which lies in Grant County). More than 500,000 acres have water now, providing many oases and exceptional agricultural and recreational opportunities in what was once a cast-off wasteland.

Grays Harbor

	Amount	Rank
County Population	68,300	14
Montesano	3,610	
Aberdeen	16,690	
Density/mi^2	36	18
Per capita income	$18,529	19
Area in mi^2	1,917	15
Area in acres	1,227,500	15
Acreage of Public Lands	379,900	
Public land as % of Total	31	
Acreage of Federal Land	161,000	
Acreage of State Land	81,900	
Acreage of Indian Land	129,500	
Acreage of County Land	7,400	

In 1792, Captain Robert Gray explored the only deep harbor on the Pacific coast of what is now Washington, naming it Bullfinch Harbor after one of his ship's owners. He then continued south to the Columbia River. In 1843, William O'Leary established the area's first homestead. On April 14, 1854, Chehalis County was carved out of Lewis County by the Territorial Legislature. In 1915, it and its harbor were renamed Grays Harbor (no apostrophe).

Because of the ocean and its flat geography, the county initially depended on fishing, canning, lumber, and agriculture. Rivers provided an excellent means to float logs to the harbor, where several mills were built. During World War I, wooden steamships were constructed in Grays Harbor. The Depression devastated the area, especially the timber industry.

Montesano, meaning "healthy mountain," has been the county seat since the county was first formed, surviving several attempts to move it. The community of Wishkah ("where two rivers merge"), renamed Aberdeen after the city in Scotland, and its twin, Hoquiam ("hungry for wood"), along with Cosmopolis ("city of the world"), were established in the late 1800s.

In 1855, Governor Stevens drew up a treaty with the Indians, creating the Quinault Indian Reservation (over 100,000 acres) in the northwest corner of the county.

Grays Harbor has long seen commercial vessels, and now a few cruise ships call there as well. Home ported here is the Lady Washington, a tall ship built in 1989 for the Washington State Centennial. A 112-foot replica of the namesake 18th-century vessel that explored the area, it sails Northwest waters on educational and recreational voyages.

South of the harbor is Markham, where a plant processes all the commercial cranberries grown on the coast. At Westport, where the southwest corner of the harbor meets the ocean, is a marina with a large charter and commercial fishing fleet. Anyone entering the ocean from here (and also Ilwaco) must be prepared for large breakers with considerable rolling and pitching.

The road north of the harbor leads to Ocean Shores, a planned resort community with a convention center and homes on its canals and five miles of sandy beach. Besides numerous festivals during the year, digging for clams, kite flying, and beachcombing are favorite activities. During the summer, a passenger-only ferry runs from there to Westport.

On the north is Olympic National Forest and Lake Quinault, with an excellent resort and a trail head for hiking into the surrounding temperate rain forest, with some of the largest trees in the world.

Overlooking the Satsop Valley in mid-county are two huge towers of an ill-fated program to build nuclear power plants. Sited on 1,600 acres, one cooling tower is 80% complete and the other 30%, plus other improvements. The estimated $50 million cost to level the towers appears unacceptable, so other options are being explored for future use.

In 1988, the Grays Harbor National Wildlife Refuge was established around Bowerman Basin in the northeast part of the harbor. This is one of four major staging areas for shorebirds in North America and the West Coast's largest. More than a million birds gather here in the spring, normally late April, to rest and eat before beginning their last nonstop leg of a migration that may exceed 15,000 miles round trip. There is no large gathering in the fall, because they arrive at different times.

This basin covers only 2% of the intertidal mudflats of the harbor estuary, but up to 50% of the birds gather here because, as the highest elevation in the tidal flats, it is the last to flood at high tide and the first to reappear at ebb and expose the food the birds like.

Island County

	Amount	Rank
County Population	71,60	13
Coupeville	1,610	
Oak Harbor	20,190	
Density/mi^2	343	5
Per capita income	$19,839	16
Area in mi^2	209	38
Area in acres	133,120	38
Acreage of Public Lands	19,100	
Public land as % of Total	14	
Acreage of Federal Land	8,300	
Acreage of State Land	6,700	
Acreage of Indian Land	0	
Acreage of County Land	4,100	

Island County, where the Strait of Juan de Fuca meets Puget Sound, encompasses eight islands, but only two—Camano and Whidbey—are significant. Whidbey Island is 45 miles long, the longest island in the contiguous 48 states. (The U.S. Supreme Court ruled that Long Island, New York, is a peninsula.)

Because of its convenient location and 148 miles of shoreline on Whidbey and 52 miles on 16-mile-long Camano, Island County is a magnet for tourists and weekenders looking for saltwater fishing, art galleries, nature trails, scuba diving, and bird watching. Whidbey is only 27 miles north of Seattle via the Mukilteo-Clinton ferry and is also accessible via SR 20 from the mainland across Fidalgo Island, a commuter airline, and another ferry from Port Townsend on the Olympic Peninsula.

The Deception Pass Bridge, connecting Whidbey to Fidalgo Island, is a scenic attraction that draws visitors from around the world. Deception Pass is Washington's "favorite state park" and just one of seven state parks on Whidbey.

Camano Island, home of popular Camano Island State Park, is an unincorporated, rural residential area with a population of 10,000. It is easily reached by a bridge from the mainland a short distance from Interstate 5, and is about a 50-mile drive from Seattle.

A Camano resident can see the county seat of Coupeville, across the Saratoga Passage on Whidbey, but to conduct business there requires at least a half-day, round trip via Skagit County and the bridge or via Snohomish County and the ferry. Every election year, candidates for county offices promise to work out an intercounty exchange of Camano for Fidalgo to facilitate intracounty business.

One consolation for the Camano resident is that Coupeville is nice. Founded by Captain Thomas Coupe in 1852, it claims to be the second oldest town in the state and has more than 100 buildings listed in the National Historic Register. It lies within Ebey's

Landing National Historical Reserve, the nation's first, dedicated to protecting historic farm lands and buildings from development. To the west are magnificent views of the Strait of Juan de Fuca, Puget Sound, and the Olympic Mountains. To the east are Penn Cove, its famous mussels, and sweeping views of the Cascades from Mount Baker to Mount Rainier.

Just south of Ebey's Landing is another favorite state park, Fort Casey, one of three forts constructed at the turn of the century to protect Seattle from naval invasion. Of interest there are 10-inch "disappearing" guns, the Admiralty Head Lighthouse, the spectacular Admiralty Inlet, and adjacent Keystone Underwater State Park, a scuba divers' mecca.

On Whidbey's north end is the county's largest city and commercial center, Oak Harbor, home of Naval Air Station Whidbey Island, a favorite Navy duty location and the county's largest employer. Retired military personnel comprise a significant part of the area's large retiree population. Situated in the Olympic Mountains' "rain shadow" (see Geography & Climate), the north end gets less than 20 inches of rain annually. From Coupeville south, rainfall increases steadily to about 38 inches in Seattle.

On Whidbey's south end is picturesque, romantic Langley and the villages of Freeland and Clinton. Because of its proximity to Seattle and Everett's Boeing plant, the south end's commuters and visitors contribute heavily to one of the Washington State Ferry System's busiest runs.

Jefferson County

	Amount	Rank
County Population	26,300	27
Port Townsend	8,330	
Density/mi^2	15	29
Per capita income	$21,100	10
Area in mi^2	1,809	18
Area in acres	1,155,200	18
Acreage of Public Lands	910,700	
Public land as % of Total	79	
Acreage of Federal Land	704,200	
Acreage of State Land	199,000	
Acreage of Indian Land	3,700	
Acreage of County Land	3,750	

Travel by land directly across Jefferson County in any direction is difficult, if not impossible. The Olympic Mountains and dense forests are right in the middle, and no roads cross the county. Residents on the Pacific Ocean side must cross over into Clallam County on the north or Grays Harbor and Mason Counties on the south to get to the county seat of Port Townsend (PT) on Puget Sound. The easiest route is via U.S. Highway 101, which connects the two ends of the county across the top of the Olympic Peninsula and provides access from the south on both sides. The principal entry from the east is the Hood Canal floating bridge from the Kitsap Peninsula. Another scenic route is via ferry to PT from Keystone on Whidbey Island.

In 1851, Alfred Plummer built a cabin in what is now downtown PT. At the entry to Puget Sound, it soon became a shipping port and the customs station. In 1852, the Oregon Territorial Legislature conferred county status and named it after President Jefferson. Initially, it included Clallam County, which was separated later. Early on, PT was called the "Key City of Puget Sound." The economy boomed with seaport activity and the possibility of the railroad coming to the area, but a bust came in 1890 when the railroad changed to Seattle.

Fort Wilson was built in 1855 for protection from Indians, but it was abandoned when hostilities ended. Then, in 1897, construction started on Fort Worden on Point Wilson as part of a "Triangle of Fire" to provide protection for Puget Sound cities and the naval shipyard at Bremerton. It was named for Admiral Worden, commander of the ironclad U.S.S. Monitor in the Civil War, and is the only Army post ever named for a Navy man. At the same time, another Triangle component, Fort Flagler, was built on Marrowstone Island. On the way to Marrowstone Island, Indian Island has a naval ordnance station.

When the Army left in 1953, Ft. Worden became a state juvenile treatment center, and in 1973, a state park and conference center. Through all these changes, the buildings remained intact, and it is now a National Historic Landmark and Historic District.

Crown Zellerbach built a paper mill in 1928, which brought employment stability to the area. To the south in Hood Canal are Dabob and Quilcene Bays, home to the Quilcene oysters, which resulted from importing Japanese oysters in 1940 to protect the bays. One hatchery is the largest in the world.

At the entrance to Discovery Bay is Protection Island, a National Wildlife Refuge—no people allowed.

Port Ludlow was founded by Andrew Pope and William Talbot in the 1870s as a site for their lumber mill. Today it is a recreational and residential community, with excellent moorage and one of the best golf courses in the region.

All along the east edge of the county, streams cascade from and trails head up into the mountains. On the west side are the Hoh Indian Reservation, the Quillayute National Wildlife Refuge, the Olympic National Park Beaches, and, along the Hoh River, a principal entry into the Olympic rain forest. All are must sees for anyone visiting the area. At the end of the road into the forest is a trailhead for hiking up Mount Olympus. Kalaloch, on the ocean, is a fine place to pick up colorful rocks that are worn smooth by the action of the water.

Before the industrial tide shifted to Seattle and Tacoma, many Victorian homes were built in PT. Most are still in fine condition and in use as private homes, B&Bs, and professional buildings. They are the best examples of such architecture north of San Francisco, and the whole town has been designated a National Historic District. A Victorian homes tour every year is one of many events that draw visitors to PT.

At the Northwest School of Wooden Boat Building, students learn the craft of building wooden boats using traditional tools and methods.

King County

	Amount	Rank
County Population	1,646,200	1
Seattle	536,600	
Density/mi^2	774	1
Per capita income	$31,248	1
Area in mi^2	2,126	11
Area in acres	1,361,900	11
Acreage of Public Lands	440,900	
Public land as % of Total	32	
Acreage of Federal Land	341,100	
Acreage of State Land	73,500	
Acreage of Indian Land	1,490	
Acreage of County Land	24,700	

When the first settlers arrived in 1850, the Suquamish and Duwamish Indians lived near the water and the Snoqualmie inland. John Holgate, the first settler, set up his residence on Elliot Bay, now Seattle's waterfront. In 1851, a group of 22—including the famous names Denny, Boren, and Bell—changed course from the Willamette Valley in Oregon and landed at Alki Point, now West Seattle. Other early arrivals were Doc Maynard and Henry Yesler. The county was formed on December 22, 1852, by the Oregon Territorial Legislature and named for Vice President-elect William King, who died en route to taking office. In 1986, the county council voted to link the county's name to the late Martin Luther King, Jr.

In 1853, Yesler began a log mill in what is now downtown Seattle and furnished logs needed for San Francisco. The ships that carried logs returned with merchandise, and soon Arthur Denny had a store to handle these items. Later, Denny and Dexter Horton opened a bank, which became Seafirst Bank. Now, alas, it has been absorbed by the huge NationsBank.

Crops grown inland floated down the Green River to Puget Sound. Coal was discovered in the Renton area in 1853 and later in Newcastle and Black Diamond. In 1893, the Great Northern Railroad arrived.

In 1889, most of downtown was destroyed by fire, but it was rebuilt atop the old city. The Alaska Gold Rush made Seattle a major trade center in 1897. Part of the gold found in the north later returned to Seattle. Further putting the area on the map was the 1909 Alaska-Yukon-Pacific Exposition, at the University of Washington (founded in the 1860s). Several Exposition buildings became part of the UW.

In 1906, the Moran Shipyard built the battleship Nebraska. When the state legislature authorized independent port districts in 1911, the Port of Seattle was formed. In World War I, many more naval ships were built, and planes started rolling out at what later became Boeing. In WW II, shipbuilding employed 140,000 and Boeing's payroll rose to 44,000.

In 1950, the county's population soared past 730,000. Then, the jet age arrived with the Boeing 707—the first jet airliner. In the port, cargo volume increased. The Seattle World's Fair, Expo '62, was a success and left the city with its signature Space Needle. Then, in 1970, Boeing's employment dropped from 100,000 to 38,000 almost overnight. Many still remember the famous billboard, "Will the last person leaving Seattle please turn out the lights." Many did leave, but most stayed and waited until the economy improved. Today, the county's economy is one of the strongest in the country.

Because the Sound and Lake Washington arrest Seattle's growth, most growth lately has taken place elsewhere in the county. In the middle of the lake is Mercer Island, an affluent residential city of 20,000. On the east side, Bellevue, once a bedroom community, now has its own identity. To the northeast is Redmond, home of well-known Microsoft. Farther east is the residential Sammamish plateau and the Sahalee golf course. Issaquah and North Bend, rising into the Cascade Mountains along the I-90 corridor, are growing. Visitors to this area make a point to see Snoqualmie Falls, with a drop of over 200 feet.

South of Seattle is Renton, with Boeing plants, Boeing Field, and Seattle-Tacoma International Airport. The valley south of Renton to Auburn, not long ago acres of produce and dairy farms, is now mostly industrialized. Vashon and Maury Islands, in the Sound to the southwest and accessible only by ferry, provide a rural lifestyle.

Home of many various companies large and small and the regional headquarters of others, King County is a key element of transportation and trade to the Far East and Alaska. Growth may have reached a point where more is not the best. Property values are soaring, and congestion is a problem in both commuting and just getting around during the day. Major efforts are underway to solve these growth problems.

Kitsap County

	Amount	Rank
County Population	229,400	6
Port Orchard	6,965	
Bremerton	38,600	
Density/mi^2	579	2
Per capita income	$20,004	15
Area in mi^2	396	36
Area in acres	251,500	36
Acreage of Public Lands	41,500	
Public land as % of Total	16	
Acreage of Federal Land	9,600	
Acreage of State Land	18,500	
Acreage of Indian Land	4,100	
Acreage of County Land	9,200	

Vancouver and his party first charted the Kitsap Peninsula in 1792. Helping them to a safe anchorage off Restoration Point on Bainbridge Island was an Indian named Chief Kitsap. In 1841, Lt. Charles Wilkes charted Puget Sound for the U.S. Navy, noting that the harbor (now Sinclair Inlet) had a "bold shore and good anchorage" suitable for large ships.

Logging was the first industry, in the early 1850s. One mill was built at Teekalet (Port Gamble) by Andrew Pope and William Talbot, who arrived from Maine via San Francisco. The "company town" was patterned after their native town of West Macheas, Maine. The mill ceased operating in 1995, but its Victorian-era buildings still stand and are well maintained. The town was named for Lt. Robert Gamble, who was wounded in the War of 1812.

Created by the Territorial Legislature on January 16, 1857, the county was named Slaughter County after Lt. William Slaughter, victim of an Indian uprising. In July 1857, county citizens voted to change the name to Kitsap, Indian for "good" and "brave" and, ironically, the name of the chief who led the uprising that killed Slaughter.

In 1888, the Navy decided to locate a drydock on Sinclair Inlet and purchased 190.25 acres of waterfront forest and marsh for $50 an acre in September 1891. The drydock was completed in 1896 for $744,636. By 1900, employment exceeded 600, an economic stimulus that pulled the area out of a timber industry slump. A second drydock, finished in 1913 for $2,300,000, was then the largest drydock in the Navy. Next, a hospital was added, and the facility became the Puget Sound Naval Shipyard. During World War I, more than 6,000 employees built scores of vessels, and in World War II, the number of workers soared past 34,000. Five of the eight battleships damaged at Pearl Harbor were repaired here. Many mothballed naval vessels, the Bremerton Naval Museum, and the Naval Undersea Museum are open to the public.

The county's other naval facilities are the Naval Undersea Warfare Engineering Station (NUWES) at Keyport, a Trident nuclear submarine base at Bangor, and Camp Wesley Harris Naval Station (a rifle range). With more than 30,000 military and civilian personnel, the Navy is the county's biggest employer.

Bainbridge Island, named for a commodore who commanded the USS Constitution (Old Ironsides), was first inhabited by the Suquamish, whose leader during the late 1800s was Chief Sealth (a.k.a. Chief Seattle). His grave is on the Suquamish Reservation, just across the Agate Pass bridge on the peninsula. Today, there are two Indian reservations, Port Madison in two large parcels and Port Gamble.

The Point No Point Lighthouse, at Hansville on the northern tip of the Kitsap Peninsula, marks a popular salmon fishing hole. Nearby, a hike up Foul Weather Bluff, provides a view of Whidbey Island.

Poulsbo ("Little Norway") was settled in 1892 by Norwegian fisherman and loggers who felt that the Liberty Bay area compared favorably with their native fjords.

The original county seat was at Port Madison, on the north end of Bainbridge Island. In 1893, the county government moved to Port Orchard, named for one of Vancouver's officers.

Four ferry routes link Kitsap County and Seattle: Kingston to Edmonds, Winslow (the only town on Bainbridge Island) to Seattle, Bremerton to Seattle, and Southworth to Fauntleroy (West Seattle), with a stop on Vashon Island. One passenger-only ferry connects Port Orchard and Bremerton. Many travelers use these ferries to avoid traffic congestion around Tacoma and Olympia to reach the Olympic Peninsula (Jefferson County) via the Hood Canal bridge or the Hood Canal and Shelton area (Mason County).

Just south of the Hood Canal bridge is a ferry site at Lofall. When the bridge sank in a 1979 storm, this ferry was activated until the bridge was rebuilt.

Kittitas County

	Amount	Rank
County Population	31,500	25
Ellensburg	13,600	
Density/mi^2	14	30
Per capita income	$17,652	29
Area in mi^2	2,297	8
Area in acres	1,477,100	8
Acreage of Public Lands	836,900	
Public land as % of Total	57	
Acreage of Federal Land	546,600	
Acreage of State Land	286,300	
Acreage of Indian Land	240	
Acreage of County Land	3,700	

Most travelers going from Seattle to Spokane go through Kittitas County on I-90 through Snoqualmie Pass to Vantage, where a bridge crosses the Columbia River. Going from Wenatchee to Yakima, travelers cross the county from Cle Elum to Ellensburg.

The county is named for the K'tatas Indians, but the original meaning of the name is uncertain. One in favor is "gray gravel bank." As early as the 1700s, Indians occupied the entire stretch of land along the Yakima River, including the Kittitas Valley. As white settlement blossomed, the once formidable tribes were dislocated and finally moved onto the Yakima Indian Reservation.

White settlers started moving into the area in the 1860s and founded the first community in 1870. The first store was acquired by John Shoudy in 1872, who platted 160 acres as a townsite, which he named Ellensburg, for his wife Mary Ellen. When the Territorial Legislature created the county on November 24, 1883, Ellensburg became the county seat. Later, when the territory petitioned for statehood, Ellensburg, because of its central location and explosive growth, was a prime candidate for the state capital. In speculation, a governor's mansion was actually built, but a fire on July 4, 1889, destroyed that aspiration along with most of the town. When Washington became the 42nd state, Ellensburg (rebuilt in brick, this time) was chosen as the site for the Normal School for the Preparation of Teachers, now Central Washington University.

Cattle ranching, the early principal economic activity, has had its peaks and valleys. The downs have resulted from overgrazing, harsh winters, and overproduction. Cattle were wintered here before being driven north to the mining areas in The Okanogan, spanning the border between Washington and Canada. After that demand diminished, drives continued over the Cascades to the cities around Puget Sound.

A related cash crop, then and now, is hay for both cattle and horses. After a low period in the 1920s when the internal combustion engine replaced horsepower, the return of horse racing in the 1930s and pleasure horses in the 1950s revived the demand for hay. Today, Kittitas County hay is marketed to many other states, including Kentucky, and to Pacific Rim and European nations. Thanks to irrigation and long, warm growing seasons, the valley produces some of the best timothy hay in the country.

Coal, discovered around Cle Elum in 1883, became a viable industry once the railroads arrived. Logging, lumber, and wheat are other major contributors to the economy. Now, large orchards are planted on the high ground around the valley.

Even before coal was discovered, prospectors flocked to the region, mostly searching for gold, but silver, copper, lead, iron, chromium, mercury, manganese, molybdenum, nickel, and antimony were also present. Interest in mining has waxed and waned over the years. Some gravel surface mining continues today on private lands, and the National Forest Service issues permits for exploratory precious metal mining.

Modern Ellensburg still has an aura of tradition even as it hums with activity. At the crossroads of I-90 and I-82, it is a hub for travelers and truckers bound for Puget Sound, Spokane, the Inland Empire, the Tri-Cities, and the rest of the Northwest.

Visitors know it well as the site of two annual events. In May is the National Western Art Show and auction, featuring the finest talents in western art. During the Labor Day weekend is the Ellensburg Rodeo and Kittitas County Fair, complete with a parade. The rodeo is one of the top ten in the country.

The county's outdoor recreation includes rafting down the Yakima river on a warm, sunny day or boating or water skiing on one of several lakes.

Klickitat County

	Amount	Rank
County Population	19,000	30
Goldendale	3,520	
Density/mi²	10	31
Per capita income	$17,164	32
Area in mi²	1,872	16
Area in acres	1,203,200	16
Acreage of Public Lands	247,400	
Public land as % of Total	21	
Acreage of Federal Land	39,800	
Acreage of State Land	125,800	
Acreage of Indian Land	73,800	
Acreage of County Land	7,900	

Long, narrow Klickitat County lies on the Columbia River. Going eastward from White Salmon, the first 30 miles or so is part of the Columbia River Gorge National Scenic Area. In that distance, the climate changes from wet to dry. A line drawn from the southwest to the northeast corners of the county divides it roughly into timber (upper) and open agricultural area (lower).

Before settlers arrived, the Klickitat (Chinook for "beyond") Indians were trading intermediaries between the coastal and inland tribes, especially during the fishing season. Lewis and Clark camped near present-day Wishram in October 1805. The Oregon Trail intersected the Columbia just across from the county's middle.

The first white settlers were Erastus Joslyn and his wife, who crossed the river in 1853 and homesteaded where Bingen is now. The county was partitioned from Skamania County by the Territorial Legislature on December 20, 1859. The first county seat at Rockport was moved to its present site, Goldendale, in 1879.

The first settlers raised cattle and drove them to market in the mining camps of The Okanogan and British Columbia. Bad winters in the late 1800s decimated most herds and forced a shift to agriculture because hay and grain were needed to feed the animals. By the 1880s, logging and lumber industries were well established. The railroad arrived in 1908 with the completion of the North Bank line from Pasco to Portland. Little changed in the economy until the 1950s, when the John Day and The Dalles Dams were built, providing additional employment and another major resource.

Samuel Hill, a wealthy financier and lawyer who built the Peace Arch in Blaine at the Canadian border, created two of the county's attractions. In 1907, he bought 7,000 acres overlooking the Columbia to establish a Quaker community. He began building what was to be his home and named it Maryhill for his daughter, but he never moved into it. In 1926, Queen Marie of Romania dedicated the unfinished structure as the Maryhill Museum. Completed under the supervision of Alma Spreckels (of sugar and San Francisco fame), it was opened after Hill's death in 1940.

Just east of Maryhill is Stonehenge, a replica of the one in England and the first monument in the U.S. to honor our World War I dead. Hill, a pacifist, believed the original Stonehenge had been a sacrificial site, and the replica was to remind everyone that "humanity is still being sacrificed to the god of war." The community Hill built later burned and was never replaced.

North of Goldendale is Goldendale Observatory State Park, with a 24½-inch reflecting telescope.

Mount Adams, up north in Yakima County, is best reached from Klickitat County via Trout Lake, where the Mount Adams District Ranger Station is located.

At the county's east end is Bickleton, where scores of bird houses sit atop fence posts. Started by one family, maintaining the houses is now a community project. The views and scenery along the southern rim of the county overlooking the Columbia and parts of northern Oregon are well worth a trip.

The Roosevelt Regional Landfill, east of Goldendale, serves the area from British Columbia to California's Napa Valley. Designed to last 40 years, it has a capacity of 3 million tons/year of waste streams, incinerator ash, wood wastes, sewage sludge, and petroleum-contaminated soils.

The 2,545-acre site was designed with state-of-the-art technology and meets or exceeds all present-day standards. In a natural, bowl-shaped depression, the site is not visible from roads. It sits atop a virtually impermeable 340-foot-deep layer of natural clay.

The county receives several million dollars a year from disposal fees and electricity generated from the methane gas recovered from the site. As each section is filled, it will be covered with topsoil and recovered for agricultural use.

Lewis County

	Amount	Rank
County Population	68,300	14
Chehalis	7,035	
Centralia	13,480	
Density/mi²	28	21
Per capita income	$18,241	24
Area in mi²	2,408	6
Area in acres	1,541,760	6
Acreage of Public Lands	592,000	
Public land as % of Total	38	
Acreage of Federal Land	470,400	
Acreage of State Land	113,500	
Acreage of Indian Land	630	
Acreage of County Land	7,600	

Created by the Oregon Provisional Government on December 21, 1845, and named for Captain Meriwether Lewis, Lewis County is the second oldest in the state and is called the "mother of all Washington counties." It originally included all territory west of the Cowlitz River and north to 54°40', the boundary with the Russian territory that later became Alaska. But boundaries changed, its size decreased, and the present lines were essentially in place by 1861.

The first settler was John Jackson, who lived on land called the Jackson Prairie, about ten miles south of the present site of Chehalis, named after an Indian tribe whose name meant "sand." The Jackson courthouse has been preserved. Soon, Toledo was established at the head of the navigable part the Cowlitz River.

The "mother of all Washington counties"

In the early days, the county seat moved around. From 1862 to 1872, it was in Claquato, near Chehalis, which became the county seat in 1872. The site of Chehalis was originally a 640 acre donation land claim taken by Schuyler Saunders in 1852, when it was called "Saunders Bottom" due to considerable low ground. The name Chehalis is derived from an Indian word meaning "shifting sands."

Chehalis's "twin city," Centralia, was founded in 1852 by a man named George Washington, who staked a squatter's claim where the Chehalis and Skookumchuck Rivers join. He operated a ferry there, which he called Cochran's Landing because, being black, he was afraid that public exposure of his name would interfere with his holding title to the land. In 1872, when the railroad came through, Washington donated land and started building a town, calling it Centerville. In 1885, the name changed to Centralia.

To the east, Packwood was established, and coal discovered in the area. Around 1900, coal mining became profitable. Agricultural businesses in the form of dairy, berry, poultry, and hops farms were started. And there were the trees, especially in the eastern end of the county. Railroads helped in all areas of the economy. The 1920s and the Great Depression took a toll. During World War II, employment improved as many people commuted to Tacoma for work in the shipyards. After the war, State Route 12 was completed over the Cascades via White Pass, and U.S. Highway 99, later I-5, became the main north-south road. In 1971, the Centralia steam plant opened, using nearby coal for its energy source. Dams on the Cowlitz create electricity.

Light manufacturing is gaining a foothold. With the twin cities of Centralia and Chehalis halfway between Seattle and Vancouver or Olympia and Longview/Kelso, it will be interesting to watch their expansion and resulting infill toward a small-scale megalopolis.

Most of the eastern county is in national forest and wilderness. The southern edge of Mount Rainier National Park is in the northeast corner. One entrance to the park is just off SR 12 east of Packwood.

West of the turn-off to Rainier, at the town of Randle, Forest Service Road 26 leads south to Mount St. Helens National Volcanic Monument. There, at Windy Ridge, is an excellent view of the results of the 1980 eruption. This route leads through tall trees on the north side of a ridge and then suddenly, around a bend to the south side, all the trees lie flat, pointing away from the mountain.

Life is coming back to the area as elk move in to graze in the now treeless meadows and birds follow insects to the new wetlands formed by landslides.

Lincoln County

	Amount	Rank
County Population	9,800	35
Davenport	1,764	
Density/mi^2	4	37
Per capita income	$21,410	9
Area in mi^2	2,311	7
Area in acres	1,478,400	7
Acreage of Public Lands	111,500	
Public land as % of Total	8	
Acreage of Federal Land	47,900	
Acreage of State Land	50,310	
Acreage of Indian Land	0	
Acreage of County Land	13,200	

Lincoln County was formed on November 24, 1883, from a portion of Spokane County, but only four days later, it lost a large amount of territory when Douglas County was partitioned off.

Naming the county and the county seat created some amusing times. The residents of the town of Sprague expected the county to be named for the town and the town to be the county seat. However, the county was named for President Lincoln, and Davenport was designated the temporary seat. In the next election, Davenport, Sprague, and Harrington vied for the seat. The number of votes cast in both Davenport and Sprague exceeded their populations. Regardless, Sprague was designated the winner. In 1890, another vote was cast, and Sprague won again. In a third and final contest in 1896, Davenport was victorious.

Settlement began in the late 1860s, when some of those who had passed through returned. Most started raising cattle on the bunch grass that grew in the bottomlands. The number of cattle increased until a severe winter in '80–'81 wiped out almost 90% of the herds. The ranchers rebuilt, but another killing winter came in '89–'90.

Although wheat growing had commenced, this crop also suffered during the winter, and it was realized that more feed was needed to keep cattle alive during the winter months. Soon, wheat became more profitable than cattle, landowners converted, and it became the principal industry.

The railroads arrived in the 1880s, and with them more settlers and transportation to ship cattle and grain to the East.

The topography of the county is mostly channeled scablands on what is known as the Big Bend Plateau. The western part of the northern county boundary is the Columbia River and Lake Roosevelt. As the river flows south, it makes a big bend to the west, hence the name. The Spokane River is the eastern portion of the northern boundary.

The presence of Coulee Dam National Recreation Area provides excellent water-related recreation for residents and tourists. The dam itself is near the very northwest corner of the county. The Keller ferry crosses the lake north of the town of Wilbur.

Some local residents commute to jobs only 30 to 40 miles east in Spokane County. The basic attributes of Lincoln remain the soil, sun, wheat, and only four people per square mile.

Since 1897, the Lincoln County courthouse has served as a focal point of county government. On December 21, 1995, an arson-caused fire heavily damaged it.

However, triumph arose from tragedy. The "Grand Old Lady" was carefully reconstructed and restored to its original character within one year of the tragic fire.

Using a "fast track" format, the contractor performed selective demolition and construction on the structure's interior as the architect completed the final design work.

First, photos taken throughout the building documented existing features, including interior trim and woodwork. Architects drew as-built plans, along with full-scale details of all the structure's woodwork, to restore its historic features. A millwork shop duplicated the interior trim and moldings.

The rebuilt cupola, placed atop the roof by crane in a "topping off" ceremony on June 26, 1996, features a pre-aged copper roof and has custom-made windows to protect the interior from weather-related damage.

Now, fully refurbished inside and out and conforming to present building, life, and safety codes, the Lincoln County courthouse stands ready to meet the needs of its second century of citizens. It was formally reopened in a ceremony that took place on December 20, 1996.

Mason County

	Amount	Rank
County Population	47,900	20
Shelton	7,770	
Density/mi^2	50	14
Per capita income	$17,133	33
Area in mi^2	961	30
Area in acres	615,000	30
Acreage of Public Lands	236,000	
Public land as % of Total	39	
Acreage of Federal Land	165,000	
Acreage of State Land	62,600	
Acreage of Indian Land	3,910	
Acreage of County Land	5,470	

Exploration of the southwest reaches of Puget Sound took place circa 1840, when Lt. Charles Wilkes, USN, and his party were mapping the Sound. Settlement was slow because of the dense forests and higher elevations. The principal tribes living there were the Skokomish and Squaxin, whose reservations today are a result of the Medicine Creek Treaty of 1855.

When the Washington Territory was formed in 1853, Thurston County included the present Mason County. However, because communication with and travel to Olympia, the county seat, were difficult, the Territorial Legislature partitioned off Sawamish County on March 13, 1854. In 1864, the county was renamed Mason for Charles Mason, the first secretary to Governor Stevens and the Legislature and the acting governor during Stevens' absence.

Mount Olive was the first county seat, for a year. The next was Oakland, which was near Shelton but no longer exists. The last move, to Shelton, occurred in 1888, allegedly because Oakland refused to allow a saloon in town. Shelton sits at the end of Hammersley Inlet, which provides access to Puget Sound.

Logging was the early economic foundation of the county. In 1887, Solomon Simpson arrived to supervise the construction of a railroad. In 1895, he formed the Simpson Logging Company. By 1905, it had a payroll of more than 500 people. Clear cutting by all the loggers created open land for agricultural enterprises.

Shelton is frequently called "Christmas Town, USA," because of the area's large Christmas tree industry. Many companies and hundreds of small landowners cut more than 3 million trees each year from over 70,000 acres and ship them all over the United States and beyond.

With changes in forest management, another forest-related industry—specialty forest products—has become a vital part of the economic mix. Four categories of crops are involved: native landscape plants, floral greens, medicinal plants, and wild edibles. Floral greens are harvested throughout the year and sold worldwide. Wild edibles include mushrooms, of which the county produces 35% of the state's output, over $8 million annually. Medicinal plants include Pacific yew, used in cancer research; devil's club, used in a tonic drink; cascara, a laxative; and foxglove, a heart medication.

Many workers in the state capital, Olympia, commute from Mason County. The Rayonier Company—one of the world's largest producers of specialized wood pulps used in rayon fabrics, tire cord, cellophane, and many other items—has a research center in Shelton. The main buildings have over 100,000 ft^2 of lab and office space.

The southeast entrance to the Olympic Peninsula can be reached via Shelton and other towns along the Hood Canal. The miles of saltwater shoreline along the canal and scores of freshwater lakes support many vacation homes and recreational activities, which include gathering shellfish.

Early commercial harvesting of oysters was so intense that the beds were almost all depleted by 1887. As a result, the Puget Sound Oyster Association was formed, and seeding of the beds was initiated.

The availability of the famed Olympic oyster, small but succulent, has declined, being replaced in many beds by the Pacific oyster, the seed for which was originally imported from Japan but is now produced locally.

At the county fairgrounds each year in early October is the West Coast Oyster Shucking Championship and the Washington State Seafood Festival. The winner of the shucking contest (about 24 oysters in less than 3 minutes) goes on to the nationals in Maryland. The food includes oysters on the half shell and in stews, fritters, cocktails, sandwiches, and more. Partaking of this unlimited variety of oyster dishes, plus clams, crabs, salmon, chowder, and local wines and microbrews is a great way to taste and see the harvest of the county and northwest Washington.

Okanogan County

	Amount	Rank
County Population	38,400	23
Okanogan	2,415	
Omak	4,495	
Density/mi²	7	34
Per capita income	$18,253	23
Area in mi²	5,268	1
Area in acres	3,379,800	1
Acreage of Public Lands	2,372,000	
Public land as % of Total	70	37
Acreage of Federal Land	1,591,400	
Acreage of State Land	346,900	
Acreage of Indian Land	424,300	
Acreage of County Land	9,380	

The largest of the 39 counties also has the most acreage in the public domain and Indian lands. Situated in the north central part of the state on the border with Canada, the county can be accessed in winter months only from a southerly direction. State Route 20, over the North Cascades, closes in the late fall and reopens in the spring when the drifts are dug out.

The original natives were the Okanogans, Nesplelems, Methows, and San Poils. These are now part of the Colville Federation of Tribes, with headquarters in Nespelem. In July 1811, David Thompson and his fur traders were the first white men into The Okanogan, as the area was, and is, called. Later that summer, Astor's Pacific Fur Company built a trading post on the Okanogan River at the point where it joins the Columbia. This was the first site to fly the American flag in Washington State. In 1821, ownership of the post changed to the Hudson's Bay Company (HBC). Furs were gathered from the whole region, including western Canada, and placed on boats there for transport to Vancouver and on to England. By the 1860s, the fur business dwindled to insignificance.

During 1857–1858, a stampede of prospectors moved north through the area, headed for the Cariboo gold fields in British Columbia. Food followed in the form of cattle on drives from the south that reached 800 miles. It was reported that these cattle drives were more difficult than those from Texas to Kansas.

The first permanent resident was Herman Smith, who settled by Osoyoos Lake and planted the first fruit orchards. The Colville Reservation was established in 1872, and the portion west of the Okanogan River was opened for miners and homesteaders in 1886.

The county, the last formed by the Washington Territorial Legislature, was carved out of the western part of Stevens County on February 8, 1888. It derives its name from the Indian tribe and word meaning "rendezvous." The first county seat was Ruby, but it was changed the next year, by a heated election, to Conconully. Then, in 1914, it was moved to Okanogan.

The economy has always depended on livestock, orchards, mining, and timber to varying degrees. The building of the Grand Coulee and Chief Joseph Dams later boosted employment and provided water.

The North Cascades National Park is a plus in tourism and recreation. Harts Pass in the Kettle Mountains is the highest road in the state. In the two mountain ranges are many miles of cross-country ski and snowmobile trails. Activity and development is focused along the Okanogan, Methow, and Columbia Rivers and the valleys through which they flow. A drive along any of them when the orchards are in bloom reveal the breathtaking harmony that man and nature can accomplish.

The largest of the 39 counties, with the most acreage in the public domain and Indian lands

The town of Winthrop has an old western town theme. Omak, the largest town and a sister to Okanogan, hosts the Omak Stampede and its infamous Suicide Race during the second weekend in August. This horse race comes down a steep bank, across the river, and into the rodeo grounds. Another highlight of this event is the Omak Indian Encampment, with dancing and stick games. This is a must see for visitors.

Pacific County

	Amount	Rank
County Population	21,300	28
South Bend	1,670	
Raymoond	2,971	
Density/mi²	22	23
Per capita income	$17,601	30
Area in mi²	975	29
Area in acres	581,100	29
Acreage of Public Lands	107,600	
Public land as % of Total	19	
Acreage of Federal Land	11,000	
Acreage of State Land	93,500	
Acreage of Indian Land	340	
Acreage of County Land	2,780	

Located in the southwest corner with the Pacific Ocean on the west and the Columbia River on the south, Pacific County has beautiful sunsets and a pristine environment compared to other growth areas. It was home to bands of Chinook Indians before the explorers and settlers came.

In 1788, an English Captain Meares mistook the mouth of the Columbia for part of the ocean and named the jetty Cape Disappointment. Then, in 1792, U.S. Captain Gray (see Grays Harbor) sailed into the Columbia River and named it for his ship. This was a large factor in the United States' claim to the area. Lewis and Clark reinforced this claim in 1805 when they reached Cape Disappointment and camped in the area for a short time.

Settlement of the county was limited in the early 1800s by rain, fog, ocean exposure, swamps, and flooding, but it was sufficient for a nucleus of the county, which was created on February 4, 1851—the third in the state and the first by the Oregon Territorial Legislature. Initially, the county seat was in Chinook. In 1861, it moved to Oysterville. Then, as South Bend grew, its residents requested a vote to move the seat there. They won, but a suit was filed, and the move was delayed. Tired of waiting, South Benders took two steamers to Oysterville and "kidnapped" the records on February 5, 1893. In June 1911, the county had a beautiful new courthouse. Costing $132,000, it was once called "The Gilded Palace of Reckless Extravagance" for its grand dome.

For the first century, the existing natural resources anchored the economy. Most of the virgin forests were harvested, so now only limited second or third growth trees are available. The first cannery was built in 1864 to meet the demand for salmon. By 1900, canning of oysters and clams followed. About 800 people were employed in canning operations as late as the 1930s. Now, new oyster beds have had to be created, and salmon runs are much reduced, thus limiting the

charter fishing business that had been a mainstay of Ilwaco, at the mouth of the Columbia.

Almost the entire county is one watershed (680,000 acres) in the Willapa Bay ecosystem, one of the cleanest estuaries in the nation because of extensive tidal cleansing. Saltwater combines with nutrients coming down the streams to provide a rich food source for certain plants and animals. The Willapa National Wildlife Refuge, established in 1937, includes Long Island, which is being kept in its natural state and is accessible by small craft. The island's 274-acre Cedar Grove, one of few forests left along the whole coast, has some 1,000-year-old trees. The Refuge is a stopover for migrating shore and sea fowl. Lowlands around the bay support cranberry farms.

Long Beach Peninsula's 28-mile beach is believed to be the longest in the world. At the south end is Ilwaco, where the Cape Disappointment lighthouse began operation in 1856 and is now the oldest operating lighthouse on the West Coast. At Fort Canby is the U.S. Coast Guard Lifeboat Station and Surf School. The oyster is the mainstay of Oysterville, Nahcotta, and restaurants all along the peninsula.

Just above where the Willapa River flows into the bay is South Bend, and before that is Raymond. Lumber mills, oyster farms, government, and retail trade are the main economic activities. The Port of Willapa Harbor has barge-handling facilities. Near Tokeland is the Shoalwater Indian reservation.

In 1992, an informal group called the Willapa Alliance formed to see what could be done to improve the county. Included were conservation groups, local business people, other citizens, and Weyerhaeuser (the timber company). Because of this diversity, the major question was could everyone work together? In 1998, they are still functioning, learning from each other, and starting to make progress toward continuing and improving a wonderful ecosystem.

Pend Oreille County

	Amount	Rank
County Population	11,200	33
Newport	1,940	
Density/mi^2	8	33
Per capita income	$15,560	37
Area in mi^2	1,400	25
Area in acres	896,000	25
Acreage of Public Lands	575,700	
Public land as % of Total	64	23
Acreage of Federal Land	529,500	
Acreage of State Land	34,500	
Acreage of Indian Land	4,560	
Acreage of County Land	7,080	

*An occasional moose is seen in
Pend Oreille County's back country.*

The correct pronunciation of the county's name is "Pon-der-ay." The French traders used the term *pendand d'oreille*, meaning "earbobs," to describe the local Indians, who wore shell ornaments on their ears. Some purists still use an apostrophe before the O.

The settlers who arrived in this northeast corner of the state in 1885 were cattlemen who liked the wild hay in the Kalispel valley. Soon, the south and central areas were opened for homesteading, and mining and timber operations commenced. The northern part around Metaline was isolated until 1906, when a channel at Box Canyon on the Pend Oreille River was cleared, making the river navigable to Metaline Falls. This enabled commercial mining to take place, with one desirable ore being limestone. With this, the county's cement industry flourished.

The residents in this part of what was then Stevens County tired of traveling four days over or around the mountains to get to the county seat of Colville. So, on March 1, 1911, the State Legislature created this county, the last of the 39 counties in the state. The town of Newport, the county seat, was for a short time in Idaho. Now, the portion of the city in Idaho is called Old Town.

A large portion of the county in the Selkirk Mountains was placed in the public domain in the Colville and Kaniksu National Forests. The Kalispel Indian Reservation was established in 1914 and is the smallest one in the United States. Kalispel means "eater of camas," a blue flower that grows along the river banks. Buffalo are raised by the Kalispels. From the mountain peaks, some exceeding 6,700 feet, can be seen parts of Canada, Washington, Idaho, and Montana.

The last of the 39 counties, created on March 1, 1911

The Pend Oreille River is one of only seven in the world that flow north. After crossing the border into Canada, it joins the Columbia, and the waters find their way back into the state. Within the borders of the county, it has two dams : Boundary and Box Canyon (see Dams).

This is a sportsman's paradise, with 55 lakes and 48 streams providing fishing year round. The river is the natural habitat of the osprey and nesting ground for geese, ducks, and cranes. In the timber live deer, elk, bear, cougars, moose, goat, and a few grizzly bears.

This so-called Panorama Country is north of and convenient to the metropolitan area of Spokane. A visitor entering the valley of the Pend Oreille River can easily become transfixed with its beauty and serene surroundings.

Pierce County

	Amount	Rank
County Population	674,300	2
Tacoma	185,600	
Density/mi²	40	4
Per capita income	$20,945	11
Area in mi²	1,675	23
Area in acres	1,072,000	23
Acreage of Public Lands	471,900	
Public land as % of Total	44	
Acreage of Federal Land	411,100	
Acreage of State Land	42,330	
Acreage of Indian Land	70	
Acreage of County Land	18,390	

An ocean port facility (in Commencement Bay), a major urban area, open fields and farms, Mount Rainier National Park—Pierce County has it all. Mount Rainier's Indian name is "Tahoma," whence the name of Tacoma, the third largest city in the state.

In 1833, Fort Nisqually, a fur trading post of the Hudson's Bay Company, was built on or very near the border between Pierce and Thurston Counties. The first settlers (circa 1850) were involved in the lumber business, shipping their product out via Commencement Bay. On December 22, 1852, the county was created by the Oregon Territorial Legislature and named after President-elect Franklin Pierce. Steilacoom was the original county seat until 1880, when it moved to Tacoma. "Old Tacoma," the area now called Old Town, was settled in 1865. Then, in 1873, Tacoma was selected as the site for the western terminus of the Great Northern Railroad, and a "New Tacoma" sprang up along with the railroad linking the state to the east. The link-up was completed in 1883, and in 1884, the two Tacomas merged into one and adopted the nickname, "City of Destiny." By 1892, the city had a population of 50,000. The population declined with the financial depression of 1893, but rebounded around the turn of the century.

About 1900, Frederick Weyerhaeuser started the Weyerhaeuser Timber Company with a purchase of 900,000 acres at $6 per acre. Another 1 million acres was soon added, and in 1914, the company built its headquarters in downtown Tacoma. Its present headquarters is located in a campus-like setting north of the city. During World War I, the Army established Camp (now Fort) Lewis south of the city, and in 1938, McChord Field (now Air Force Base) was added nearby. Both of these installations have survived the military cutbacks of recent years and are major staging sites for U.S. power projection to worldwide hot spots.

In the northwest part of the county are Anderson (residential) and McNeil (a prison) Islands, which are reached only by ferry. A bit of the Kitsap peninsula is also part of the county and is reached via the Tacoma Narrows bridge. The original bridge, known as "Galloping Gertie" for the way it moved, collapsed in a wind storm only four months after it opened in 1940. It was rebuilt in 1950 after a lot had been learned about aerodynamic flutter.

In 1983, the Tacoma Dome, maybe the world's largest wood-domed arena, was completed for sporting events, exhibitions, and other public entertainment. The Washington State Historical Museum is located in a restored Union Station in the downtown.

Competing with "The Mountain" and its park as attractions are Tacoma's 700-acre Point Defiance Park, with recreational facilities, a zoo and an aquarium; Northwest Trek Wildlife Park, a 600-acre nature preserve an hour south of Tacoma, where various wild animals can be viewed in a natural environment; and the Puyallup (say "Pew-al-up") Fairgrounds, located in and named for the city where the Western Washington State Fair is held every September and the home of many other events during the year, such as the Daffodil Festival in the spring with a large floral parade.

Located on I-5 only a few miles south of Seattle-Tacoma (Sea–Tac) International Airport, Tacoma is a major transportation center for the Northwest and the nation. Higher education is available in Tacoma at Pacific Lutheran University and The University of Puget Sound.

San Juan County

	Amount	Rank
County Population	12,500	32
Friday Harbor	1,875	
Density/mi²	72	12
Per capita income	$29,837	2
Area in mi²	175	39
Area in acres	114,560	39
Acreage of Public Lands	14,100	
Public land as % of Total	12	23
Acreage of Federal Land	3,000	
Acreage of State Land	9,230	
Acreage of Indian Land	0	
Acreage of County Land	1,870	

Friday
Harbor

Sitting in an inland sea is one of the most beautiful, rural, and unique counties in the state. With no land connection (except by underwater power and communication lines) and away from the major urban areas, the pace is slow, and the population and speed limits are low. The islands are really the tops of a mountain range that lies between the Straits of Georgia, Puget Sound, and the Strait of Juan de Fuca. The name was given by an early Spanish explorer, Francisco Eliza, in honor of the Viceroy of Mexico, Señor Don Juan Vincent Aquay.

The San Juan Archipelago (which includes the Gulf Islands of British Columbia) consists of about 786 islands and reefs at low tide and 457 at high tide. Only 175 have names. The islands' various geological characteristics depend on what the glaciers did as they receded. The channels of water surrounding the islands are quite deep—600 to 1,000 feet—and the water temperature stays within a small range of 45 to 52°F. The cool water and continuous tidal changes of several feet result in very clear water. With only 179 square miles of land, San Juan County has 375 miles of saltwater shoreline—more than all of Washington state's Pacific Ocean waterfront.

Captain Vancouver explored the San Juans along with the surrounding area in the 1700s and provided many of the names. In the early 1800s, both British and American settlers homesteaded, and both countries claimed ownership. Even the treaty of 1846, which established the northern U.S. boundary, did not settle the issue, for it said the boundary in this immediate area was "between the channel that separates the continent from Vancouver Island." The problem was that there are two channels—Haro and Rosario—with the San Juans in between.

In 1851, the British established a salmon-curing station and, two years later, a sheep ranch. At the same time, the Oregon Territorial Legislature (whose territory included Washington) declared San Juan

part of its territory and incorporated it into Island County. In 1853, Washington (then a separate territory) attached it to Whatcom County.

In 1859, Lyman Cutlar, an American settler, shot and killed a pig belonging to the Hudson's Bay Company because the pig was rooting in his garden. Both sides escalated the incident and started sending troops. (One U.S. troop commander was Captain George Pickett, later of Civil War fame.) Soon, several hundred troops arrived from each side and established positions at Garrison Bay (the English Camp) and Cattle Point (the American Camp). After a 12-year standoff, the Treaty of Washington was signed, with the question of the San Juans referred to Kaiser Wilhelm I of Germany, who ruled in favor of the U.S.

During those years, known as "The Pig War," no shots were fired (except at the pig, the only casualty), and the two sides frequently socialized. The camps now are part of San Juan National Historical Park.

The Territorial Legislature officially created the county on October 31, 1873, with Friday Harbor, its only city, the county seat. Four islands contain most of the people and have ferry service: San Juan, Orcas, Lopez, and Shaw. On San Juan (57 mi²) is Roche Harbor, a well-known boating resort. Orcas, slightly larger at 58 mi², has Mount Constitution—the county's highest point at 2,400 feet—and Rosario Resort, originally a palatial private residence. Lopez, with 47 mi², is rather flat, and its people always wave as they pass on its 25 miles of paved roads. The smallest of the four, 4,900-acre Shaw, is really quiet. It has only one small store, run by Franciscan nuns, at the ferry landing.

Tourism and retirement are the two principal sources of income, and many residents are involved with arts and crafts in some form. Public beaches, private beaches, access to them, and tidelands are active public issues—along with growth management. The people are relaxed and friendly, but they do want to maintain the special character of their beautiful, rustic, and serene surroundings.

Skagit County

	Amount	Rank
County Population	96,900	11
Mount Vernon	22,280	
Density/mi^2	56	13
Per capita income	$21,535	8
Area in mi^2	1,735	21
Area in acres	1,110,400	21
Acreage of Public Lands	642,000	
Public land as % of Total	58	
Acreage of Federal Land	492,000	
Acreage of State Land	137,000	
Acreage of Indian Land	4,900	
Acreage of County Land	7,500	

A traveler on Interstate 5 (I-5) through the western part of Skagit County has some options upon reaching State Route 20 (SR 20) at Burlington. Heading east, the road runs along the Skagit River into the mountains and is known as the North Cascades Highway (closed in winter above Newhalem) leading to Okanogan County. Going west, the SR 20 Spur ends at the ferry terminal in Anacortes on Fidalgo Island for a journey through the San Juan Islands to Sydney, B.C. The main branch of SR 20 West turns south toward Deception Pass and Whidbey Island (see Island County), the Keystone ferry to Port Townsend, or the ferry to Mukilteo to complete a loop back to I-5.

From salt water to the mountain crest, the county has variety and a calm, rural beauty less than two hours from busy Seattle and Everett. Settlement came in the mid 1800s, and the name derived from a local Indian tribe. It became a county on November 28, 1883, by approval of the Washington Territorial Legislature. The first county seat was La Conner, but by vote changed to Mount Vernon in 1884.

How Mount Vernon was established is interesting. Because of a massive log jam on the Skagit River, boats had to stop and unload. At that spot, the community of Mount Vernon started and grew. In October 1997, a statistical analysis showed Mount Vernon to be the "best small city" in the nation.

The second-largest river (after the Columbia) in the western United States, the Skagit has always been the lifeline of the county. With more than 2,900 streams contributing to its flow, it is the largest watershed in the Puget Sound region, provides 20% of its fresh water, and has the largest concentration of wintering bald eagles in the contiguous 48 states.

The Skagit begins in Canada and fills Ross Lake (Whatcom County) and two other lakes, where three dams help control the flow and provide cheap hydroelectric power. Leaving the hills, it feeds the allu-

vial farmlands of the delta, where dikes and sloughs provide additional control. However, the river is still prone to flooding because rainfall and runoff from winter snows often overwhelm all the controls. Near Puget Sound, the river's North and South Forks create Fir Island, actually a delta with fertile farmland and a wildlife recreation area that is a winter home for snow geese and trumpeter swans.

Out in the Sound, the county has several "real" islands. Across the Swinomish Channel to the west lies Fidalgo and the city of Anacortes, with a large oil refinery and the ferry terminal. Just north of Anacortes is Guemes, known for relaxed living. Cypress is large, but is mostly a national resource conservation area. Hat and Saddlebag are great for crabbing. Samish, really a peninsula, is residential. Sinclair and about six others have no significant population.

The ethnic mix is diverse. Native Americans come from the Swinomish, Samish, Sauk-Suiattle and Upper Skagit tribes. Anacortes has a large Croatian community. Other communities have German, Dutch, and Scandinavian heritage. Many loggers of various cultures came west from North Carolina.

A big event is the spring Skagit Valley Tulip Festival. More than 2,000 acres of tulips, daffodils, and irises bloom just west of Mount Vernon with a blaze of colors that can be appreciated only by seeing them in person. This bulb industry is one of the largest anywhere.

The economy is mixed. Fishing and marine-related activity, logging, and farming are still core businesses. Mount Vernon and Burlington, separated only by the Skagit River, are a focal point for retail trade and, of course, government. Education, primarily at Skagit Valley College, and health care employ many. In addition to the Tulip Festival, tourism is strong, supported by scenic La Conner and eagle watching on the Skagit. Light industry is slowly moving into the county as it seeks a haven outside the greater Seattle area.

Skamania County

	Amount	Rank
County Population	9,900	34
Stevenson	1,210	
Density/mi²	6	35
Per capita income	$18,036	26
Area in mi²	1,656	24
Area in acres	1,071,000	24
Acreage of Public Lands	908,900	
Public land as % of Total	85	1
Acreage of Federal Land	817,500	
Acreage of State Land	88,800	
Acreage of Indian Land	0	
Acreage of County Land	2,700	

An elk near Mount St. Helens

Skamania (from an Indian term meaning "swift water") County is bisected by the Cascade Mountain Range. On its southern border, the Pacific Crest Trail exits the state at the Bridge of the Gods across the Columbia River into Oregon. Of all Washington counties, it has the largest percentage of public land—over 85%. Most of it is in the Gifford Pinchot National Forest and is primarily wilderness area.

After Mount St. Helens erupted in 1980 (elev. 9,677 feet before, 8,365 feet after), it was designated the first National Volcanic Monument. Although the volcano itself is in the northwest corner of Skamania County, the main approaches to view the results of the blast are through either Cowlitz County on the west or Lewis County on the north.

Wildlife is coming back to the area devastated by the eruption in surprising ways. Elk are more numerous now than before the eruption. Because they are grazing animals, they now find the meadows more inviting than the forests that were destroyed. Insects have swarmed to the new lakes and wetlands formed by landslides and other river blockages, bringing a larger variety of birds.

Commerce and development in the county have always centered in the Columbia River Gorge, which is now a national scenic area. Long before Lewis and Clark passed through, Native Americans harvested enough salmon from the river to provide plenty of food for themselves plus extra to trade. Fur trading flourished in the early 1800s. Then, in the mid-19th century, some of the pioneers migrating west over the Oregon Trail decided to stop and settle here rather than struggle more miles down the river. Because of this increased settlement, the Territorial Legislature conferred county status on March 9, 1854. The town of Cascades (now North Bonneville) was the county seat until 1893, when it moved to Stevenson.

Logging, providing wood for the steamboats, and fishing were major components of the early economy.

One item developed for catching salmon was a fish wheel, which scooped the fish from the river. It proved to be too effective, however, and it was finally outlawed in 1934. The railroad arrived on the Oregon side in 1880 and on the north bank in 1908. This track is now part of the Burlington Northern.

In 1933, President Roosevelt authorized the building of the Bonneville Dam, which was completed in 1937 for only $31 million. Its purposes were to create jobs, generate electricity, and make the Columbia River more navigable.

Now, the economy is mostly tied to federal employment in support of the national forest, fish and wildlife matters, and the dam. Logging still has a place in the county's economy, along with light manufacturing and recreation. Some of the best windsurfing anywhere is here on the Columbia River.

Even though it is unremarkable in size and economic clout, Skamania County has several assets that are well known. Many people who may not know the county by name are aware of the volcano, the forest, the river, the gorge, and the dam.

Snohomish County

	Amount	Rank
County Population	551,200	3
Everett	84,130	
Density/mi^2	264	7
Per capita income	$22,495	4
Area in mi^2	2,090	13
Area in acres	1,342,800	13
Acreage of Public Lands	807,900	
Public land as % of Total	60	
Acreage of Federal Land	634,800	
Acreage of State Land	148,500	
Acreage of Indian Land	10,200	
Acreage of County Land	14,600	

Snohomish is one of 12 counties that border on Puget Sound. Its eastern boundary is the crest of the Cascade Mountains, including nearby Glacier Peak at 10,541 feet. With 60% of its land in the public domain as forest and wilderness to the east, development is limited to the western lowlands and the I-5 corridor.

Two major river systems flow from the higher elevations, resulting in productive agricultural lands. In the north is the Stillaguamish, with its North and South Forks, and in the south the Snoqualmie and Skykomish come together and form the Snohomish.

Although some of the area was charted as early as 1792 by Captain Vancouver, who named Port Gardner Bay at Everett and Port Susan Bay to the north, only a few trappers and traders traversed the area during the next 50 years. When the Washington Territory was formed in 1853, Snohomish County was part of Island County. In 1855, the Treaty of Point Elliot was signed, and 22 local Indian tribes were granted land that is now the Tulalip Indian Resveration. With the treaty in place, the pace of settlement increased. Logging and lumber milling, with plenty of water to transport the logs, were the main industries, and Everett was called the "Lumber Capital of the World" circa 1900.

The present county officially was formed on January 14, 1861. The county seat was at Mukilteo (Indian word for "union of men" or "warriors") for a short time. It then moved to Snohomish until 1897, and finally to its present site, Everett.

The first rail into the county arrived in 1888. In 1893, the Great Northern Railroad arrived from the east. As land was cleared by logging, agriculture,

including dairy, increased in scope. In 1917, the Snohomish County Dairymen's Association was started and is now the Darigold Company.

The economy had its ups and downs until World War II, when construction began on Paine Field to train military pilots. In the 1960s, it became the site of Boeing's new 747 plant. Boeing has continued to increase its plane building at Paine Field and now produces the 747, 767, and 777 there. Boeing's assembly plant in Everett is the largest building, by volume, in the world.

The tremendous growth of the county has come from three sources. In addition to Boeing, many high-technology businesses populate a high-tech corridor along I-405 and I-5. The third element is the U.S. Navy, which built a homeport for an aircraft carrier battle group in Everett.

The border with King County on the south has essentially disappeared in the county's built-up western portion. The cities of Edmonds, Lynnwood, Mukilteo, and Everett flow together and form a megalopolis that extends from Marysville, just north of Everett, all the way south through Seattle and Tacoma to Olympia. State Route 2 to eastern Washington via Stevens Pass (in King County) is heavily traveled and is experiencing considerable growth. On this route, Monroe is the home of one of the state's correctional institutions.

In the northwest corner

The Boeing 747 assembly plant in Everett is the largest building, by volume, in the world.

of the county is Stanwood and the only land access to residential Camano Island, which is part of Island County.

Plenty of trees and countryside still exist around Darrington, where an annual Bluegrass festival is held, but vacant lowlands are fast disappearing as industry and population continue to spread north toward Bellingham.

Spokane County

	Amount	Rank
County Population	409,900	4
Spokane	188,300	
Density/mi^2	232	8
Per capita income	$20,575	13
Area in mi^2	1,764	19
Area in acres	1,129,000	19
Acreage of Public Lands	100,500	
Public land as % of Total	9	
Acreage of Federal Land	21,400	
Acreage of State Land	51,400	
Acreage of Indian Land	10,200	
Acreage of County Land	27,700	

Spokane River

The economic heart of the Inland Northwest (formerly called "The Inland Empire") is in Spokane County, centering on its namesake city (and county seat). Bordering on Idaho and midway between Canada and Oregon, the rural landscape of the county has patches of desert, forests, lakes, rivers, and rolling wheat fields.

The city of Spokane is the eastern anchor of the state, 280 miles from Seattle, the western anchor. It is the trade and medical center of the 36 counties of eastern Washington, adjacent northern Idaho, western Montana, and even parts of Oregon, British Columbia, and Alberta.

Before settlement by pioneers, the area was home to the Spokane Indians, who traded dried salmon from the coast for buffalo hides east of the mountains and then traded these hides for items from the coast. In the early 1800s, fur traders of John Jacob Astor's Pacific Fur Company established a trading center, the Spokane House, on the Spokane River. Later, missionaries arrived, and full settlement of the region was underway in the 1850s. Trouble between Indians and the settlers erupted after the 1855 treaties, and war continued between the groups until 1858.

The Territorial Legislature created Spokane County on January 29, 1858. The county area at that time consisted of much of the eastern part of the territory and included part of what is now Idaho. The name Spokane is derived from an Indian word meaning "sun" and finally "children of the sun."

In 1873, James Glover constructed a mill and general store at Spokane Falls, later shortened to just Spokane. In 1881, the Northern Pacific Railroad arrived, followed by the Great Northern in 1901 and the Union Pacific in 1911. This made Spokane a major railroad city, but rates were high because of the railroad monopoly and the lack of competition by water transportation.

Spokane has always been the county seat, except for the period from 1881 to 1886, when it was at nearby Cheney. In 1889, a fire destroyed much of Spokane, but it was rebuilt with many buildings in classic European style. The courthouse is a magnificent example.

The area emerged from the 1929 depression during World War II. Military facilities built during the war are still military, such as Fairchild Air Force Base, or converted to civilian use, such as Geiger Field, now Spokane International Airport.

The World's Fair in 1974 was a success, drawing more than 5 million visitors. It gave a long-lasting boost to the economy, leaving Riverside Park and buildings for permanent use and revealing the city and the Northwest to newcomers.

Several two- and four-year schools are situated here, including Gonzaga University (in Spokane) and Eastern Washington University (in Cheney).

In addition to financial and retail economic activity, the county is a major source of agricultural support for the region.

An athletic event of note is the annual Bloomsday Run in May, which attracts more than 50,000 runners.

Stevens County

	Amount	Rank
County Population	37,400	24
Colville	4,690	
Density/mi²	15	27
Per capita income	$15,201	38
Area in mi²	2,478	5
Area in acres	1,579,500	5
Acreage of Public Lands	656,700	
Public land as % of Total	42	
Acreage of Federal Land	353,000	
Acreage of State Land	162,600	
Acreage of Indian Land	131,400	
Acreage of County Land	9,600	

At the time it was established in 1858, Stevens County covered what are now 13 counties in eastern Washington, all of northern Idaho, and much of western Montana. It was named after Isaac I. Stevens, the first governor of Washington Territory, who rested at Fort Colville in 1853 before continuing on his way to Olympia to assume administration of the new territory.

Before settlement, Kettle Falls on the Columbia River was a gathering place for many tribes who fished there for salmon. These falls, the highest on the whole river, would later be covered with water backed up from the Grand Coulee Dam. In 1811, explorers continued downriver from Kettle Falls to what would become the site of the Fort Colville trading post. Established in 1825, it was the principal outpost for Hudson's Bay Company operations in the entire area from the Mississippi River to the Cascade Mountains. Today, Colville is the principal market and shopping place north of Spokane.

Early trappers were aware that gold and silver existed, but fearing that such news would be destructive to the fur trade, they kept it secret. Thus, gold and silver were not "officially" discovered in Stevens County until 1854 and 1883, respectively. Precious metals such as magnesite were also discovered, making Stevens one of the notable mineral producing areas in the state and nation.

With development of the mining industry came rail systems to transport the ores. Today, the major land-use activities for the three northeast Washington counties (Ferry, Stevens, and Pend Oreille) are forestry, mining, recreation, and agriculture. Mining and timber constitute the economic backbone of the so-called Tri-County region, and both have suffered

Stevens County once covered what are now 13 Washington counties, northern Idaho, and much of Montana.

fluctuations in recent years. The prices of gold and silver plummeted in the 1970s and again in the 1990s, but the value of zinc has buoyed the local mining industry.

As in the mining industry, prosperity in the region's lumber and wood products industry depends more on economic events than on the availability of raw resources. Consequently, interest rates, trading of the U.S. dollar in foreign exchange markets, efficiency measures, and competitiveness will continue to play key roles in determining the future of the lumber industry in the Tri-Counties.

The labor situation also is an issue. Because of new technology and other efficiency measures, traditional industries operate with fewer employees. Consequently, there is no guarantee that a return to past production levels will mean re-employment for all previously dislocated workers.

The number of younger workers in the Tri-Counties is shrinking due to a lower birth rate and a net out-migration. Many young adults leave for college and do not return. The overall result has devastated the region's economy, as demonstrated by the county's next-to-last position in the state's per capita income.

The economy has improved somewhat with that of the whole country. With the building of the Grand Coulee Dam and the creation of Lake Roosevelt, at the western boundary of the county, outdoor recreational activity has increased.

The Spokane Indian Reservation contains more than 100,000 acres in the southern part of the county, and the Colville National Forest occupies over 300,000 acres in the Selkirk Mountains. The higher elevations and cool, dry weather provide excellent skiing in the winter. The county has two border crossings into Canada.

Thurston County

	Amount	Rank
County Population	197,600	8
Olympia	38,650	
Density/mi^2	272	6
Per capita income	$22,258	5
Area in mi^2	727	32
Area in acres	465,300	32
Acreage of Public Lands	103,700	
Public land as % of Total	22	
Acreage of Federal Land	23,800	
Acreage of State Land	67,400	
Acreage of Indian Land	1,050	
Acreage of County Land	11,400	

In 1792, Lieutenant Peter Puget of Captain Vancouver's party put longboats ashore in what is now south Puget Sound. Explorers returned in the 1820s, when Hudson's Bay Company (HBC) people searched the area for fur sources and a possible location for a base for their operations in the Sound. In 1833, Dr. McLoughlin, chief factor for the HBC, directed that a trading post be established at Nisqually. Colonel Michael Simmons led the first group of Americans to settle in 1846 and staked a claim by the waterfalls of the DesChutes River near Budd Inlet. There, a sawmill and a grist mill were built, and the settlement was named New Market, which later became Tumwater.

Levi Smith and Edmond Sylvester established a claim on a small peninsula jutting into Budd Inlet just north of Tumwater. First named Smithfield, it later became Olympia. The county was created by the Oregon Territorial Legislature on January 12, 1852, and named after Oregon's first Congressional delegate, Samuel Thurston. Isaac Stevens, the first governor of the Washington Territory, established the capital at Olympia in 1853. Over the next three decades, other cities vied to be the capital, but after statehood was granted in 1889, a referendum confirmed Olympia as the capital in 1890. Today, Olympia, Tumwater, and Lacey have essentially flowed together into one metropolitan area, which, in turn, is the southern terminus of a megalopolis that stretches all the way to Marysville in Snohomish County.

Initially, timber was the county's main industry, but getting the product to market was a problem because massive mud flats appeared offshore at low tide. By the time dredging provided a chan-

The Thurston County seat, Olympia, is also Washington's capital.

nel, the cities to the north had surpassed Olympia in size and industry. Hopes for a major rail terminal faded in 1873, when the Northern Pacific chose Tacoma, partly because of Commencement Bay's deep water. In the south part of the county near Tenino, coal mining and sandstone quarrying were undertaken. The market for sandstone faded as concrete use increased after WW I. The county is also home to the small, succulent Olympia oyster, although the number harvested today is very small.

Except during Prohibition, the Olympia Brewery has been a stabilizing part of the economy throughout this century. It was founded in 1894 as the Capital Brewing Company by Leopold Schmidt, who heard about the area's good water. Declines in the timber industry were offset by the increase in state government, which is now the focus of the economy.

The present Capitol was completed in 1927. Its dome was modeled after the one in the "other Washington." The campus of the Capitol contains memorials to the veterans of several conflicts.

Since 1974, the Nisqually National Wildlife Refuge, in the northeast corner of the county, has protected many fish and wildlife habitats and is a stopping place for migratory birds in the Pacific Flyway. The Nisqually River, along with McAllister and Red Salmon Creeks, form one of the largest remaining undisturbed estuaries in the state. Visitors are welcome in the area, and trails and observation decks have been provided. Higher education in the county is provided by South Puget Sound Community College, St. Martin's College, and The Evergreen State College.

Wahkiakum County

	Amount	Rank
County Population	3,900	38
Cathlamet	545	
Density/mi^2	15	28
Per capita income	$17,893	27
Area in mi^2	264	37
Area in acres	167,000	37
Acreage of Public Lands	44,500	
Public land as % of Total	27	
Acreage of Federal Land	2,600	
Acreage of State Land	41,000	
Acreage of Indian Land	0	
Acreage of County Land	870	

The Wahkiakum, the last ferry on the lower Columbia

Wahkiakum (Wuh-key'-uh-kum) County is small in size and population, but because of its location, it was involved in much of the state's early history. It has 55 miles of shoreline on the north bank of the Columbia River, and it is only a short distance from the river's mouth on the Pacific. Its early inhabitants witnessed Captain Gray's discovery of the river in 1792, and then Lt. Broughton sailed his British ship Chatam upriver and discovered and named Puget Island. Next was the arrival of the Lewis and Clark party in 1805.

Upriver at Vancouver, Washington, was the Hudson's Bay Company (HBC), established in the 1820s. The first settler in the area was James Birnie, a retired HBC employee. His trading post, "Birnie's Retreat," is now the county seat, Cathlamet. The county was established on April 25, 1854, shortly after Washington became a territory.

Columbia white-tailed deer at the Julia Butler Hansen Wildlife Refuge

Wahkiakum means "tall timber" in Chinook. Cathlamet takes its name from the Chinook word for "stone." Lewis and Clark found the Cathlamet (or Kathlamet) and Wahkiakum tribes living along a stretch of the Columbia's rocky bed.

Skamokawa (Skum-mah-kuh-way), meaning "smoke on the water," was the site of a 2,000-year-old Indian village once known as "Little Venice." It is now a National Historic District.

With more than 80 percent of the land in forest, the logging and lumber industries join fishing as the main supporters of the local economy. As land was cleared, dairy farming took root.

Must sees are Meserve Park and the popular Grays River Bridge, the last covered bridge remaining over a public road in Washington.

Puget Island, which belongs to Wahkiakum County, is connected to Cathlamet by a bridge. The south side of the island connects to Oregon by ferry, the only one remaining on the lower Columbia.

The Julia Butler Hansen National Wildlife Refuge provides a home for the endangered Columbia White Tail Deer and an area for waterfowl on the Pacific Flyway.

Walla Walla County

	Amount	Rank
County Population	54,000	19
Walla Walla	29,100	
Density/mi^2	43	16
Per capita income	$18,122	25
Area in mi^2	1,270	26
Area in acres	1,579,500	26
Acreage of Public Lands	55,200	
Public land as % of Total	7	
Acreage of Federal Land	21,100	
Acreage of State Land	21,600	
Acreage of Indian Land	0	
Acreage of County Land	7,400	

Walla Walla is a rough translation of an Indian term meaning "many waters." Frequently called The Cradle of Northwest History, this county was one of the first regions between the Rockies and the Cascades to be settled. As early as 1818, a Hudson's Bay Company post was built in the area. Then, in 1836, Marcus and Narcissa Whitman arrived and founded their famous mission among the Cayuse Indians. It was located at Waiilatpu ("place of the people of the rye grass").

Marcus Whitman was born in New York state in 1802 and became both a physician and a missionary. Narcissa and Eliza Spaulding, wife of the Rev. Henry Spaulding, were the first white women to cross the continent. The Spauldings' mission was established about 100 miles east of Waiilatpu at Lapwai among the Nez Perce.

Because of Whitman's medical and blacksmithing abilities, his mission drew many travelers from the main route of the Oregon Trail, about 50 miles south. However, their missionary objective to convert the Indians was doomed. The Whitmans and many others were massacred by the Cayuse in 1847 after an epidemic of measles decimated the tribe.

Afterward, trouble with the Cayuse and other tribes continued, and Territorial Governor Isaac Stevens convened meetings with the Indians to negotiate treaties. In 1855, one of the main gatherings in the peace process was the Walla Walla Council. The next year, Lt. Col. Steptoe had temporary quarters for peacekeeping troops built at the site where the trail forded Mill Creek. This was the start of the city of Walla Walla. The temporary became permanent in 1858 with the establishment of Fort Walla Walla. The county had already been formed on April 25, 1854, by the Territorial Legislature. Only a few years later (1863), the Whitman Seminary—the first college in the state—was established. We know it today as Whitman College, a liberal arts institution. There were not many people in the whole territory, and as late as 1880, Walla Walla—the most populated city—had just over 1000 residents.

Agriculture flourished and still is a major part of the economy. Along with wheat and green peas, the area is known for the Walla Walla Sweet Onion—juicy, low in sulfur, and sweet—the result of a unique combination of soil and climate. In 1995, the U.S. Department of Agriculture issued Marketing Order 956, which designates that only onions grown in this area of Washington and Oregon may be called Walla Walla Sweet Onions. The onions do not keep long, so people rush to acquire them during the July harvest.

Today, the county is similar to others in the region, with emphasis on agriculture, water, and sunshine. The city of Walla Walla is an oasis, its streets lined with deciduous trees planted years ago. Its basic economy revolves around education, government, retail trade, and tourism. There are two four-year colleges, Whitman and Walla Walla, and a community college. The state penitentiary here has been making auto license plates since 1905.

The Whitman Mission National Historic Site features a monument and a common grave for the victims of the massacre. National Park Service historians provide a balanced picture of the events that took place there circa 1847. A section of the diverted Oregon trail still shows the ruts from narrow wagon wheels.

The Fort Walla Walla museum and park complex features a pioneer village and a large grain combine with a team of 33 life-sized fiberglass mules. In the western corner of the county, at the confluence of the Snake and Columbia Rivers, is the McNary National Wildlife Refuge. Besides the Onion Harvest Fest in July, visitors flock to the Hot Air Balloon Stampede in May, the Walla Walla Fair & Frontier Days over the Labor Day weekend, and Wings Over Walla Walla in October.

Walla Walla, the Cradle of Northwest history

Whatcom County

	Amount	Rank
County Population	156,200	9
Bellingham	61,240	
Density/mi²	74	11
Per capita income	$19,775	17
Area in mi²	2,120	12
Area in acres	1,360,000	12
Acreage of Public Lands	962,880	
Public land as % of Total	71	23
Acreage of Federal Land	861,930	
Acreage of State Land	79,850	
Acreage of Indian Land	9,890	
Acreage of County Land	11,210	

Anthropologists say the Whatcom County area was inhabited by the ancestors of the Lummi, Nooksack, and Semiahmoo tribes 10,000 years before white explorers arrived. Captain Vancouver charted the area in 1792 and named Bellingham Bay for a British official who provisioned his expedition.

Settlers arrived in 1852 looking for a site with water for a sawmill. They found one on the shores of Bellingham Bay near a waterfall the natives called Whatcom, or "noisy water." Coal was found in 1853 near what is now Bellingham. On March 9, 1854, the county was created by the Territorial Legislature.

In 1858, the discovery of gold in Canada's Fraser Valley created short-lived boom towns near Bellingham Bay as miners headed north. In 1883, the community of Fairhaven was created and thrived when James Hill promised to put a railroad terminal there. That boom ended in 1898 with the Alaska gold rush and the diversion of the terminal to Seattle.

Fairhaven, Sehome, Whatcom, and New Whatcom merged in 1903 to form Bellingham. Timber, fishing, and farming were the main industries through most of the 1900s, but recently have declined in importance.

Of Washington's 13 international border crossings, 5 are in Whatcom County. The busiest is at the 67-foot-high Peace Arch on I-5 at Blaine. Given by railroad builder Samuel Hill, it sits right on the international boundary, half in each country, surrounded by well-kept gardens. It was dedicated in 1921 to commemorate lasting peace between the two nations.

Establishment of the 49th parallel as the international boundary left the resort community of Point Roberts on a small peninsula at the northwestern end of the county. Travel between it and the main part of the county requires going through customs twice.

Water supports recreation and industry in the western end of the county: fishing, boat building, dry docks, shipping, marinas, and whale watching tours to the San Juan Islands. The southern terminal of the Alaska Marine Highway ferry system is at Fairhaven. A twice-hourly ferry provides service to Lummi Island.

From I-5 in Bellingham, a 58-mile drive east along the Mount Baker Highway leads to Artist Point (elev. 5,140 ft). The last 24 miles is a National Scenic Byway, and all of the highway is a State Scenic and Recreation Highway. Dominating the whole area are 10,778-foot Mount Baker (named for one of Captain Vancouver's junior officers) and 9,038-foot Mount Shuksan. Mount Baker, which can be seen from Seattle on clear days, has the longest ski season in the state.

The county is home to the North Cascades and Mount Baker National Parks, the Snoqualmie National Forest, and the Mt. Baker, Noisy-Diosbud, and Pasayten Wildernesses. Although most of this area is inaccessible, State Route 20 brings visitors to the Ross Lake National Recreation Area. The Ross and Diablo Dams supply power to Seattle and the region.

The Lummi reservation, 13,000 acres on a peninsula just north of Bellingham, is supported by a large fishing fleet and an aquaculture program. The Lummi heritage continues via teachings at the Northwest Indian College. In contrast, the Nooksacks were a river-dwelling people who subsisted by hunting and harvesting. About 1,500 members of this tribe reside in the area.

Lynden, a town in the fertile Nooksack Valley with a rich Dutch heritage, holds the Northwest Washington fair in August. The town is surrounded by well-managed dairy farms. The county is ranked among the top dairy producers in the nation.

Loggers assemble in June at the Deming Logging Show. Large portions of food are a trademark, and a new "Bull of the Woods" is crowned each year.

During the Memorial Day weekend is the Ski-to-Sea race, an 82.5-mile relay from Mt. Baker to the shore.

Western Washington University, founded in 1893 as a state normal school, was incorporated into the State University system in 1977.

Whitman County

	Amount	Rank
County Population	41,200	22
Colfax	2,830	
Pullman	24,970	
Density/mi²	19	8
Per capita income	$16,154	36
Area in mi²	2,159	10
Area in acres	1,376,340	10
Acreage of Public Lands	58,370	
Public land as % of Total	4	39
Acreage of Federal Land	12,090	
Acreage of State Land	32,290	
Acreage of Indian Land	30	
Acreage of County Land	12,960	

Whitman County is a land of rolling hills and grain fields that glisten golden in the summer sun. Part of the eastern boundary of the state, it is a major segment of the area called the Palouse (Spanish for "grassy plain," and the name of an indigenous Indian tribe). Less than 5 percent of the land is in the public domain—the lowest of any county in the state.

Settlers began arriving to the area in 1868. The early ones engaged mostly in livestock grazing, taking full advantage of the abundant grasslands. Soon, the productivity of the soil became apparent, and the land was converted to growing field crops of wheat, oats, and barley. Fruits and vegetables were also started wherever there was ample water, specifically along the Snake River, which forms the southern boundary of the county. This conversion to growing crops was essentially completed in the 1880s.

Colfax, the pioneer city of the Palouse, was founded in 1870, when James Perkins arrived at the confluence of the North and South Forks of the Palouse River. The town was named for Schuyler Colfax, vice president in the first administration of President Grant. Today, it is the county seat.

The county was organized by the Territorial Legislature on November 29, 1871, by partitioning Stevens County, which then covered most of eastern Washington. Later, in 1883, the new county itself would be partitioned to spin off Franklin and Adams Counties. It is named in honor of Marcus Whitman, the unfortunate missionary to the Cayuse Indians (see Walla Walla).

Pullman, the largest city, was settled in 1876 by Bolin Farr. It was first called Three Forks because of the coming together here of Dry Fork Creek, Missouri Flat Creek, and the Palouse River. It was renamed for the designer of the Pullman railroad car in hopes of attracting railroads and more business to the area.

Washington State University (WSU), a Land Grant institution and the source of most of the city's population, was born in 1890 as the State Agricultural College of Washington. It has broad academic scope with excellence and renown in all aspects of agriculture. From its experiment station have come many of the advancements that keep agriculture a major player in the economy of the state. It maintains cooperative extension facilities throughout the state and now has upwards of 20,000 students and 4,000 staff and faculty. The term "Cougar Gold" refers to a cheese, well known in the region and state, made and sold by WSU.

Just east of Pullman is the national headquarters for the spotted horse known as the Appaloosa. The county has many times been ranked as the number-one producer of wheat and the center of the largest region producing dry peas and lentils in the United States. The Port of Whitman County has several sites on the Snake River, which carries large amounts of grain and other products for export.

Some notable landmarks: Steptoe Butte rises 1,000 feet above the surrounding area, providing a great panoramic view. Palouse Falls, in a state park, has a drop of 198 feet. Codger Pole in Colfax, said to be the largest chainsaw sculpture in the world, was erected in honor of a 1988 football game that was a rematch, by the same players on the same field, of one in 1938.

Colfax, the pioneer city of the Palouse, was founded in 1870.

Yakima County

	Amount	Rank
County Population	208,700	7
Yakima	63,510	
Density/mi²	49	15
Per capita income	$18,427	20
Area in mi²	4,296	2
Area in acres	2,743,700	2
Acreage of Public Lands	2,018,600	
Public land as % of Total	74	3
Acreage of Federal Land	713,100	
Acreage of State Land	226,700	
Acreage of Indian Land	1,066,600	
Acreage of County Land	12,110	

All along the Yakima River from Naches southeast through Selah, Yakima, Union Gap, Toppenish, Zillah, Granger, Sunnyside, and Grandview are orchards, vineyards, and fields of hops, mint, asparagus, and others. This county is one of the richest growing areas in the nation.

Before the settlers arrived, this was the land of the Yakima Indians. A Catholic mission was established in 1847 southeast of Yakima. In 1855, Chief Kamiakin signed a peace treaty with Governor Stevens that gave more than 45,000 square miles to the newcomers in exchange for a 1.3-million-acre reservation for the 14 tribes in the area.

However, Indian uprisings occurred the following year, and the Army arrived and established a garrison at Fort Simcoe, 38 miles southeast of Yakima. Within a couple of years, peace was restored. Fielding Thorp was the first permanent settler in 1860, bringing a cattle herd with him.

The county was officially established on January 21, 1865, with the city of Yakima as the county seat. The name is given to mean "people of the narrow river." A census in 1870 showed only 432 pioneers in the county. Ten years later, there were nearly 3,000.

In 1884, the Northern Pacific Railroad came into the valley. When the city would not give it sufficient concessions, the railroad moved its terminal four miles north to a new site, which it named North Yakima. It then offered to move the buildings of any cooperative citizens to the new community. Most people accepted the offer, and rollers were placed under their buildings and moved north. Business was carried on during the move.

On January 27, 1886, North Yakima was incorporated and named the county seat. In 1918, the name reverted to Yakima, and the old site was referred to as either Old Town or Union Gap, and the latter finally was officially adopted as the name.

One of the richest agricultural areas in the nation

Irrigation in the Yakima Valley is part of its history. The first ditch was probably that of Kamiakin in 1853. The first trench dug by settlers came in 1886, carrying water from the Yakima River, a mile south of the city, to a small wheat field. This was soon followed by many more canals. In 1902, with passage of the Reclamation Act, the government got into the business of moving water. In 1910, the first of several reservoirs was completed at Bumping Lake, which opened up a regulated supply of water. Today, agriculture flourishes, nurtured by ample sun and water. With apples leading the way, the top 20 crops gross about $1 billion annually.

Many factors influence land use in the county. Almost 75% is in the public domain, the largest sector being the Yakima Indian Reservation, with over a million acres in the south. In the northeast corner is part of the U.S. Army's Yakima Training Center (160,000+ acres). The west contains the Mount Baker/Snoqualmie National Forest, within which are several wilderness areas, including one named for former Supreme Court Justice William O. Douglas. Mount Adams, at 12,276 feet, resides in the southwest corner in a wilderness area of the same name.

Two Cascade mountain passes provide access from the west: White and Chinook (closed in winter). One of the state's major alpine ski areas is at White Pass.

In Union Gap, the Central Washington Agricultural Museum has an extensive collection of farm machinery. Yakima's Sun Dome houses sporting events and other entertainment.

During winter months, the State Game Department feeds hundreds of elk at the Oak Creek Wildlife Recreation Area near the junction of State Routes 12 and 410. Rafting down the Yakima River during warm summer days is popular.

Tours of the wine country and wine tasting bring the most visitors. At least 25 wineries are available to visit. Pick up a map at the first one you see.

Facts & Fun

Here are some notes on miscellaneous facts, fun activities and places, and the associated rules and regulations in and around the Evergreen State. Some toll-free phone numbers are contained in the appendices.

Airfields

More than 400 airports dot the state, the two principal international airports being Sea-Tac, between Seattle and Tacoma, and Spokane. Vancouver (WA) and the southwest area use Portland International just over the Columbia River. Other major fields are Paine Field (Snohomish County Airport) next to the Boeing Everett plant, Boeing Field (King County Airport) in Seattle, Renton Field, and Grant County Airport near Moses Lake. Military airfields are Fairchild Air Force Base near Spokane, McChord Air Force Base near Tacoma, and Naval Air Station Whidbey Island near Oak Harbor. In addition to all these airfields are numerous lakes and Puget Sound, where float planes can operate. At the north end of Seattle's Lake Washington is Kenmore Air, which offers scheduled float plane service around Puget Sound and into the coastal area of British Columbia. These planes fly at just a few thousand feet and provide excellent views of the American and Canadian San Juan Islands and all the surrounding waters.

Air Shows

During the summer, first-rate air shows are held in Yakima, at NAS Whidbey Island, and elsewhere. In conjunction with the Gold Cup Hydro races on Lake Washington during Seattle's Seafair, the Navy's Blue Angels normally perform over the race course, with 300,000 or more spectators watching from boats and the shore. The state's military bases hold annual open houses, usually with air shows that often include the U.S. Air Force Thunderbirds and other top-notch exhibition flying.

A flight of AT-6 Texans

Alaska

Although many miles of Canada separate Alaska and Washington, the two states are closely tied economically and culturally. Seattle is about 600 air miles from Ketchikan, in the lower Alaska panhandle, and 1,400 air miles from Anchorage. A large percentage of the supplies for the north are processed through Puget Sound. Ocean barges load up at piers in Seattle and head north in the summer, some going all the way to the oil fields at Prudhoe Bay. Puget Sound is home to many vessels that fish Alaskan waters. Bellingham is the southern terminus of the Alaska Marine Highway System (ferries). Some of our more adventurous boaters cruise all the way to Glacier Bay in the summer. In turn, Alaskans come south for business, special medical treatment, and entertainment.

Antiques

The state has scores of antique stores, many of which specialize in particular categories. Some accept items on consignment and/or hold estate sales. In many areas, you can obtain maps showing their locations.

Archery

Frequently referred to as "the world's first sport," archery has a very active following in the state. The lead organization is the Washington State Archery Association, which has many chapters all over the state. During spring and summer, frequent events are held at various locations. Bow-and-arrow hunting seasons are established for selected game. *The Quiver* is the publication of the WSAA.

Arts

The vitality and variety in all forms of art throughout the state mirror the many diverse life styles and cultures of the people. The Washington State Arts Commission was created to support promotion, growth, development, and preservation of the arts, foster artistic merit, and ensure that the arts are accessible to all citizens within the state. Several programs contribute to this mission.

Art In Public Places (AIPP) legislation, passed in 1974, allocates 1/2 of 1% from capital funding for state buildings to purchase or commission works of art to be displayed in schools and various institutions. The law was revised in 1983 to allow pooling of artwork allocations. The state was the second in the nation, after Hawaii, to pass such a program. Of the 28 or more states with such programs now, only three include public schools. Presently, the value of the more than 3,500 artworks funded by AIPP state wide in the State Art Collection is about $10 million.

Folk Arts Program—Created in 1991, the program preserves, presents, and protects the traditional arts of the many cultures represented in Washington.

- **WoodWorks** celebrates the heritage of the Pacific Northwest timber communities. Its events feature logger poets, singers, and storytellers and also explores both sides of the timber resource issue.

- **Asian Traditional Festivals** supports special events of minority cultures: Hmong New Year of Laos, Diwali Festival of Lights of India, and Cherry Blossom Festival of Japan.

- **The Washington Grange Hall Project** explores the importance of music, past and present, in the Grange movement and to better understand the importance of the Grange in the lives of the people.

- **The Spirit of the First People** project researches, records, and keeps alive the songs and the musical traditions of the Coast, Sound, and Plateau Native Americans.

- **Gritos del Alma** is a similar program for Mexican Americans in the state.

Community Arts Development Program—This assists people in local communities in various components of the arts, providing technical assistance, leadership, financial support, and information.

Arts in Education promotes contributions to arts education by artists and arts organizations, offers arts curriculum grants to public schools, and supports other activities that promote the arts as basic education in mainly grades K-12.

Performing Arts

Dance—The Pacific Northwest Ballet (PNB) is widely acclaimed for its varied repertoire as well as its wide range of performance styles. In a typical season, the PNB showcases both classical ballet and modern dance, and its annual production of "The Nutcracker" has even been immortalized in a major motion picture. No fewer than six contemporary dance companies bring the best of modern choreography to fans across the state, and touring groups feature the traditional dances of many cultures.

Tacoma, Spokane, and other communities also boast excellent dance companies.

Music—No matter what one's musical tastes may be, there is plenty to please, including the 90-year old Seattle Symphony, the Northwest Chamber Orchestra, numerous brass and string ensembles, choirs and other vocal groups, and musical theater. The Seattle Symphony has just played its first concert in its fabulous new "home," Benaroya Hall. Many communities have either light or classical opera companies (or both). The Seattle Opera Association is recognized as the leading Wagnerian Company in the United States, and its productions of Wagner's four-opera Ring Cycle have drawn worldwide acclaim. Modern music abounds, from classic jazz, to country and western, to rock and roll.

Theater—Almost every town of any size has a theater group. (There are more than 30 professional and semiprofessional theaters in the Puget Sound area alone.) Seattle is the state's theater hub, with more than ten professional theater groups to satisfy every conceivable taste and age range. Seattle's highly praised Children's Theater, for instance, caters exclusively to younger audiences. Each year, more theatrical performances are available in Seattle than in any other U.S. city outside of New York.

Visual Arts

The kaleidoscope of Northwest art includes thousands of pieces on display in Washington's museums, private collections, and public spaces. Public art is everywhere. Of particular interest are the many exhibits featuring the art of the Northwest Coast Indians and Alaska Natives, and Russian-American and Asian-American pieces also attract many viewers. There are scores of galleries in which to browse for top-notch paintings, glasswork, photos, and sculpture. Seattle has a new Art Museum.

Arts and Crafts

Outdoors throughout the summer and indoors at other times, the state's arts and crafts shows and many festivals are staples in the diet of the lookers and buyers in most communities. Artisans travel many miles: witness the carver of wooden shoes from Michigan exhibits his skill at the Holland Happening in Oak Harbor on Whidbey Island in April. One of the state's biggest fairs is in Bellevue each July, and it rarely, if ever, has "rained on their parade."

Backyard Sanctuary Program

Want to be a wildlife habitat manager on your own property? Contact the Washington Department of

Fish and Wildlife for a sanctuary packet that has suggestions on how to attract birds and other wildlife.

Bed & Breakfasts

A significant number of B&Bs are situated throughout all regions of the state, but not the numbers that you will find in, say, Ireland or England. Several associations, such as AAA and chambers of commerce, can help the traveler find suitable B&B accommodations.

Basketball

Basketball is played at all academic and professional levels by both men and women. Washington State University and the University of Washington are in the Pac-10 conference. Seattle has hosted both the National Collegiate Athletic Association regionals and the "Final Four." The Seattle Supersonics were the NBA champions for the 1978–1979 season and are frequently in the playoffs. Their home court is the Key Arena in the Seattle Center.

Baseball

Baseball is found all over Washington, from little league to major league. The majors are represented by the Seattle Mariners, who presently play in the Kingdome. A new stadium designed for baseball is being built just south of the Kingdome. It will have a retractable roof to let the sun in and keep the rain out.

Beaches

Many miles of both salt- and freshwater beaches are magnets for various activities, such as walking, clamming, fishing, swimming, kite flying, beach combing for driftwood and rocks, just sitting and listening to the waves, and taking in the fresh air. The longest beach in the nation (28 miles) is Long Beach (Pacific), which hosts an annual kite-flying festival. At Kalaloch (pronounced "Clay-lock") on the Pacific coast (Jefferson), people look for "Kalaloch Rocks," which are rounded and smoothed by the tides—Nature's own lapidary. Take care on the ocean beaches, where tidal changes of 10 to 12 feet are not uncommon and can surprise and surround the unwary visitor. Some beaches are privately owned and do not permit free and unlimited access.

Bicycling

Little of the terrain in Washington is flat, but that has not diminished an intense interest in bicycling.

Bike trails and suitable paths are available in most communities, and many streets in urban areas have special bike lanes. Biking is allowed in most state parks, which offer campsites for bikers in addition to those for motor vehicles.

Bikers and foot passengers are first on and off the state ferries and have first priority in loading, whereas vehicles with more than two wheels may have to wait for the next ferry run in the busy summer months. This helps make the San Juan Islands popular with tour-bikers. In some areas, buses have bike racks to further assist bikers in both urban areas and the countryside, notably the islands.

Bicycle clubs sponsor frequent tours and races. One major event each summer is the Seattle-to-Portland ride of about 200 miles. Both Spokane and Seattle host major championship races. Redmond is a center for both road and velodrome racing. All regions have specific tours, and several publications provide local and more general information.

Birding

The climate, vegetation, terrain, and location on the ocean and in the Pacific Flyway invite huge numbers of birds and people active in various aspects of birding. Watching, feeding, building backyard sanctuaries, hunting, and protecting are all programs with intensive interest.

Many birds stop over during their annual migrations to feed and rest. Grays Harbor (see Counties) is one special place where tidal action provides excellent feeding. Several hundred bald eagles come to the banks of the Skagit River near Rockport (see Skagit County), where they winter and feed on migrating salmon. Eastern Washington—with its grain fields, lakes, and streams—is a hunter's paradise. Several wildlife refuges on the coast and inland provide shelter and privacy for many species.

A continuing focus of the news media and government is the spotted owl as an endangered species and its interface with the timber industry.

Boating

The state has long been known as the "boating capital" of the world, and with good reason. Large bodies of water abound—Puget Sound, Lake Washington, Lake Roosevelt, the Columbia River, and hundreds of lesser ones. In the sheltered Sound and Canadian waters between Vancouver Island and the mainland, enthusiasts can experience the beauty and excitement of saltwater boating without the dangers of the open ocean. Even these waters can be danger-

Opening Day of boating season in Seattle.

ous at times, but the prudent boater keeps an eye and ear on the weather, and anchorages are plentiful if it turns foul.

The area teems with both sail and power craft, some over 100 feet long. Yacht clubs are available throughout the state, and joining them is not usually difficult. Desirable moorage is another matter, and it can take months or years to get a slip in a prime location.

Boating is a year-round activity because few of the waters freeze, but the first Saturday in May marks the official start of the "boating season." In Seattle, this is the occasion for a parade of boats from Portage Bay through the Montlake Cut and into Lake Washington. Many boats are decorated, and prizes are awarded for various categories. Crew racing is another part of the day's activities, and thousands of spectators afloat and ashore line the course. For many oar pullers, this will be the largest crowd who will ever see them race. Boaters wanting a good place on the log boom to watch the festivities typically tie up two days in advance.

Several locations in the state park system provide permanent buoys for tying up craft. By early afternoon in the summer, most are already in use, so an early arrival is necessary.

Taking a boat through locks is an interesting adventure. All the dams on the Columbia and Snake Rivers except Grand Coulee have locks. However, those ashore will have the most fun at the Hiram Chittenden Locks in Seattle's Ballard District, through which boats move between the Sound and the Ship Canal and on into Lake Washington. On the last day of a long summer weekend, the spectacle of hundreds of pleasure craft returning from the saltwater with their captains and crew attempting to follow the shouted directions of the lock masters is a whole show in itself—and all for free. Beware of dive-bombing seagulls, however.

Almost all boats 16 feet and longer require registration and titling and are subject to an annual excise tax (license). Those who do not desire to own may choose a suitable craft—and crew, if needed, from among many charter and rental businesses. In general, boating is expensive. Some say the two happiest days in a boater's life are the day the boat is acquired and then, after pouring many dollars into this "hole in the water," the day it's sold.

Breweries

The Olympia Brewing Company, in Tumwater since 1894, and Rainier, in Seattle, are long time regional and national beer companies. And then came the brewpubs and microbreweries: for example, Yakima Brewing and Malting (one of the oldest), Kemper in Poulsbo, and Hart in Kalama. Red Hook, in the Ballard district in Seattle, has expanded from the "micro" classification into a regional brewery.

British Columbia (B.C.)

Canada's westernmost province and Washington's northern neighbor is much like a sister state. It is more than five times as large (359,000 mi^2) as Washington but has only half as many residents. British Columbia's southern border runs along all of Washington and Idaho plus part of Montana. To reach the northwestern corner of Whatcom County, Point Roberts, land travelers must go through B.C. to get there.

Vancouver is B.C.'s principal city and the southern terminus of most cruises up the Inside Passage to Alaska. Victoria, on Vancouver Island, is the capital of the province and is frequently referred to as a "little bit of Olde England." Tea is served daily in many of Victoria's establishments, perhaps the most famous of which is the Empress Hotel, overlooking the Inner Harbour. Excellent museums and the Provincial Parliament are nearby, and about 17 miles north of the city are the beautiful Butchart Gardens.

The ferry system serving all the province's islands and the mainland is one of the largest in the world. Washington boaters look upon the Canadian San Juan Islands and the Desolation Sound area near Campbell River as an extension of Puget Sound. Many spend several weeks in the summer there and, if necessary, commute by float plane.

There are several border crossings, the busiest being at Blaine, between Vancouver and Bellingham. During peak periods, expect considerable delays at customs. One way to speed things up is to obtain a PACE (Peace Arch Crossing Entry) permit. Permit holders use a special lane where only spot checks are made.

Downtown Vancouver, B.C.

Camping

Camping is a favorite activity of both residents and visitors. Scores of facilities are available in state and national parks, national recreation areas, and private campgrounds for hikers, bikers, trailers, RVs, and boaters. These are located throughout the state by water, in flatlands, and in the mountains. Some sites have cabins. Various summer camps for young people are available. There is high demand in the summer for good sites, and most are available on a first come, first-serve basis. Reservations (if possible) well in advance and early arrival are recommended.

Climbing

World-class about sums it up. A climb (with guides) up Mount Rainier, where many climbers train for Mount Everest, normally takes three days—one to get acclimated and two to make the climb and return. Many other peaks and climbing areas in the Cascades, Olympics, and other mountain areas offer a variety of difficulty. There are manmade rock surfaces for practice and testing equipment at the

Mount Rainier

University of Washington and inside the REI sporting goods store in Seattle. Always remember, "The Mountain is King."

Community Property

Washington in a community property state. This system of property ownership is based on the theory that ". . . all property acquired during marriage by the industry and labor of either spouse (or both spouses), together with the produce and increase thereof, belongs beneficially to both, and they should share equally in property acquired by them through their joint efforts during marriage."

Curling

Originated in Scotland, curling is a popular sport across the northern tier of states and in Canada. The Northwest has only one club, Granite Curling in Seattle, but B.C. has more than 100. Guided by the team's "skip," or boss, one player slides, or "curls," a granite stone down a 10-foot-wide lane of smooth ice to the "house," or target circle, more than 100 feet away. Using brooms, the team's two remaining players brush the ice in front of the moving stone to guide it toward the center of the circle. Curling became an official competitive sport in the Winter Olympics in 1998.

Fairs and Festivals

Every month, some sort of celebration takes place around the state. Since upward of 1,000 events are scheduled each year, several events usually compete for visitors each week. Among the favorites are county and state fairs, rodeos, and arts and crafts gatherings. Here are some of the notables:

Jan Seattle International Boat Show; Mid-Columbia Circuit Rodeo Finals, Yakima; Wrangler Pro Rodeo Classic, Spokane; Snow Days Outhouse Races, Concully (Okanogan).

Feb Fasching, Leavenworth (Chelan); USA Motor Spectacular, Spokane; Celebration of Chocolate & Red Wine, Yakima.

Mar Victorian Festival, Port Townsend (Jefferson); Indoor Pro Rodeo, Grays Harbor; U.S. Team Roping Championships, Pasco.

Apr Daffodil Festival, Tacoma; Tulip Festival, Mount Vernon (Skagit); Holland Happening, Oak Harbor (Island); Apple Blossom Festival, Wenatchee (Chelan).

May Boating Season Opening Day, Seattle; Walla Walla Balloon Stampede; Greek Festival, Soap

Lake (Grant); Muzzle-Loader Rendezvous, Asotin; Bloomsday Run, Spokane.

Jun Okanogan Days; Strawberry Festival, Marysville (Snohomish); Yakima Air Fair; Deming Logging Show (Whatcom).

Jul Sea 'N' Sky Fest and Race Week, Oak Harbor (Island); Darrington Bluegrass Festival (Snohomish); Columbia Hydroplane Races, Tri-Cities; Port Townsend Jazz Festival (Jefferson).

Aug Seafair, Seattle; Omak Stampede and Suicide Race (Okanogan); Steelhead Days, Sedro Woolley (Skagit); Clallam County Fair, PA.

Sep Labor Day Rodeo, Ellensburg; Western Washington State Fair, Puyallup; Lake Chelan Hydrofest; regional and county fairs all over.

Oct Autumn Leaves, Leavenworth (Chelan); Wings Over Walla Walla; Salmon Days Festival, Issaquah (King); Apple Days, Cashmere (Chelan); Heritage Days, Forks (Clallam); Cranberry Harvest Festival, Grayland (Grays Harbor); Oktoberfests and harvest festivals all over.

Nov Guy Fawkes Day, Snohomish; Yakima Nation's Veterans' Day Celebration, White Swan (Yakima); Festival of Trees, Bremerton (Kitsap); Christmas Kickoff, Dayton (Columbia); Northwest Wine Festival, Tri-Cities (Benton/Franklin).

Dec Zoolights, Tacoma's Point Defiance Zoo; Victorian Country Christmas, Puyallup (Pierce); Christmas tree lightings, ethnic holiday celebrations, and New Year's Eve parties, all over.

Fall Foliage

It's not New England, but the state has plenty of color for enchantment during early October in the mountain passes and late October in the lowlands. Especially pretty is Stevens Pass above Leavenworth (Chelan) along State Route 2.

Ferries

A ferry is as much a symbol of the state as the Space Needle is. An integral part of the state's transportation network, ferries are a lifeline to many islands. Most of the attention is focused on the Washington State Ferries (WSF) system, which operates around Puget Sound. However, but there are more than a dozen other ferry runs around the state, several of which are essential (see table).

The beginning of WSF was the Mosquito Fleet, which started soon after the area was settled. This consisted of hundreds of small, independently owned steamers crossing the Sound over many routes carrying freight and passengers.

The first double-ended vessel was built in 1888, which saved time by not having to turn around to unload and load at each end of its run between Seattle and West Seattle.

Competition was fierce, and various consolidations of ownership took place. The one that finally

Ferries other than WSF

Between or Name	Location (Counties)	Notes
Gooseberry Point & Lummi Is.	Whatcom	Only transportation available
Port Angeles & Victoria, B.C.	Clallam	International
Seattle & Victoria, B.C.	King	International
Port Orchard & Bremerton	Kitsap	Passenger only
Annapolis & Bremerton	Kitsap	Passenger only
Steilacoom & Anderson/McNeil Islands	Pierce	Only transportation available
Hartstene Is. & Graham	Mason	
Westport & Ocean Shores	Grays Harbor	Summer, passengers only
Puget Is. & Westport, OR	Wahkiakum	Crosses Columbia River
Inchellium/Gifford	Ferry & Stevens	Crosses Lake Roosevelt
Keller	Ferry & Stevens	Crosses Lake Roosevelt
Chelan & Stehekin	Chelan	Only transportation available
Anacortes & Guemes Is.	Skagit	Only transportation available
Bellingham & Alaska	Whatcom	Alaska Marine Highway

surfaced was the Puget Sound Navigation Company, also known as The Black Ball Line. In 1930, it had 25 boats running on 17 routes.

The fleet was enlarged in the 1930s with several vessels purchased from the Southern Pacific–Golden Gate Ferries, which no longer needed them after the Golden Gate Bridge opened. Four of these vessels are still in operation: Nisqually, Quinault, Illahee, and Klickitat.

A combination of labor unrest, rising costs, and a perceived growing monopoly led to the State of Washington stepping into the business. In December 1950, it purchased the Black Ball Line for $4.95 million. Included were 16 ferries, 20 terminals, one destroyer escort, and various supplies and equipment. The official start of state operations was July 1, 1951.

Today, WSF operates 25 vessels (3 passenger-only) on 10 routes with 20 terminals. The smallest car-carrying ferry is the Hiyu, which carries 40 cars and 200 passengers within the San Juan Islands. In 1996, MV Tacoma, the first of three new jumbo vessels, was launched. These are about 460 feet long and carry 218 cars and 2,500 passengers at speeds to 18 knots on the high-density Seattle runs. The system has about 600 departures a day and carries 25 million people a year. Its longest run is international (40 miles) from Anacortes to Sidney, B.C., on Vancouver Island.

In 1979, one WSF route was reactivated for a couple of years at Lofall on the Hood Canal while the Hood Canal floating bridge was repaired after sinking in a storm.

Besides providing basic transportation for residents and commerce, ferries are a great tourist attraction. Many people board just to ride and view the sights and scenery. A trip through the San Juan Islands, across the Sound from Seattle to Bremerton or Winslow, or to Victoria can be a memorable journey.

Hydrofoil ferry

Husky Stadium from Lake Washington

Football

Football is a major sport in the state, with Seattle's Seahawks being the Northwest's only National Football League team. The Kingdome, where they currently play, will be torn down and replaced with a new stadium. The Cougars of Washington State University and the Huskies of the University of Washington, both Pac-10 teams, maintain a fierce cross-state rivalry, culminating in the annual Apple Cup game each November. Going to UW games by boat and mooring beside Husky Stadium on Lake Washington is a long-standing tradition for boat people. State playoffs for high school teams are held in major stadiums.

Free Rides

Some counties and other jusrisdictions have free bus service: downtown Seattle, Island County, and Skagit County, to name a few. Many buses in those areas have racks on the front for hauling bikes. Check it out, and leave the driving to somebody else.

Fruit and Vegetable Picking

Washington's abundant fruits and vegetables are "there for the picking" in many places. You can pick just enough for your own needs, or, if you want to put your back into it, you can even make a few dollars. Many teenagers earn pocket money by working in the fields and orchards. Some large orchards provide camper hookups. You can take a vacation, get come exercise, eat fine fruit, and maybe make enough to pay for the trip.

Local classified ads or chambers of commerce will help locate these growers. Many small vegetable and berry farms are close to the cities, and plenty of roadside stands are available in season. The overall picking season lasts from June to September.

Gaming

Ample opportunity exists to play games of chance in card rooms and casinos on Indian reservations throughout the state. Bingo is popular, and some fraternal organizations have specially authorized sites for gaming. Almost all games are played, except that pull-tabs currently take the place of slot machines. The state currently says no to slots, but the matter is under constant discussion. Frequent flying trips are available to Reno and Las Vegas, and driving time to those cities is two days, at most.

Gardens

The region offers several famous gardens: Ohme Gardens in Wenatchee, on a hill with a wonderful view of the Columbia River; the Arboretum in Seattle, with its serenely beautiful Japanese garden and teahouse; and Butchart Gardens near Victoria, B.C., painstakingly crafted from what was once an old quarry.

An interesting garden in Seattle is Freeway Park, built over Interstate 5 next to the convention center. Many other excellent gardens are scattered through out the state.

Want to be a "master gardener?" Washington State University, in an excellent program through its cooperative extension, trains individuals to be gardeners who then volunteer their time to work with the public.

Ohme Gardens, Wenatchee

Glass

In 1971, the Pilchuck Glass School was born near Stanwood (Snohomish) in an impromptu array of tents, teepees, scrap-wood cabins, and even a hollowed-out cedar stump. In the early 90s, glass art was sufficiently established in Washington that the Glass Art Society moved its headquarters from Corning, NY, to Seattle, now acknowledged as the glass art center of the nation. Several galleries in Seattle and elsewhere hold glass shows virtually every month, and the Seattle Art Museum has held glass art exhibits and seminars. This art form is prominent at arts & crafts shows throughout the state.

Gold Rush

Three places in Seattle tell the story of the Gold Rush and depict the role Seattle played in it: Klondike Gold Rush National Historical Park in Pioneer Square, the Museum of History and Industry in the Montlake area, and the Children's Museum in Seattle Center.

Golf

Public and private courses abound in all regions, with more continually being constructed. Widely varying terrain offers many different kinds of links— some hilly, with narrow, tree-lined fairways; others relatively open and level. Most courses can be played year round, but on the wet side, you may have trouble finding your ball in the fairway if it's really wet and the ball plugs after a high, arcing drive. Sahalee, in Redmond (King), is the top-ranked private course according to one golf publication, and the top eight public courses are as follows:

Desert Canyon, Orondo (Douglas)

McCormick Woods, Port Orchard (Kitsap)

Semiahmoo, Blaine (Whatcom)

Apple Tree, Yakima (Yakima)

Port Ludlow, Port Ludlow (Jefferson)

Indian Canyon, Spokane (Spokane)

Merriwood, Lacey (Thurston)

Kayak Point, Stanwood (Snohomish)

Grange

The Grange, an agricultural family fraternity begun nationally in 1867, is alive and well in Washington. The first Washington chapter was formed in 1889, the year Washington became a state. It has been active in family farm water rights, vocational agriculture, community recreation, and other issues especially relating to the rural environment.

Gunkholing

Gunkholing is the Northwest pastime of scouring tide flats looking for small crabs, starfish, worms, or whatever else may be found in tidal pools or under rocks at low tide. Depending on the temperature of the water, boots or tennis shoes are highly recommended.

Hang Gliding

Wherever updrafts (thermals) occur, such as along the east side of the Cascades, hang gliding is popular. Lake Chelan is a mecca for this sport.

Hiking

Such a multitude of hiking areas and trails exists in the state that a complete inventory probably has never been attempted of even the formally designated locations. Places range from the long, flat beaches on the coast to steep, difficult paths in the mountains. Hikes are possible from north to south along the Pacific Crest Trail, or east to west from the Idaho border to the coast. Endless trails honeycomb Olympic National Park. Especially rewarding is the trail through the rain forest along the Hoh River and up to the Blue Glacier on Mount Olympus. This one 40-mile trek offers a sampling of the best that the park has to offer.

Hockey

Three teams comprise the Western Hockey League (WHL): Spokane Chiefs, Tri-Cities Americans, and Seattle Thunderbirds. There is youth hockey in a few locations. The possibility of bringing a National Hockey League (NHL) team to the Puget Sound area has been discussed, but there is nothing concrete so far. For now, major league hockey fans can find NHL games in Vancouver, B.C.

Horseback Riding

From the home built on a "horse acre" (about 35,000 ft^2) as part of a development featuring riding trails, to the destination resort or "dude ranch," horses and riders are everywhere in Washington.

Horse Racing

Thoroughbred racing is popular in the region: September to November at Playfair in Spokane; April to September at Emerald Downs in Auburn (King); October to April at Yakima Meadows; and October to April at Portland (Oregon) Downs. Several other cities have race meets of two to three days. Off-track betting is authorized.

Hydroplane Racing

For a day to remember, attend a hydro race either in the Tri-Cities on the Columbia River or on Lake

Hydroplane race on Lake Washington, Seattle

Washington in Seattle. The Seattle races, part of the city's Seafair activities, normally take place on the first Sunday in August. Upward of 300,000 fans line the shores or occupy pleasure craft along the log boom and take part in one big party while watching the "thunder boats." Usually, an added attraction is the Navy's Blue Angels, who perform aerobatic routines over the race course and the surrounding area.

Maybe a surprise attraction will appear. In the 1950s, test pilot Tex Johnson flew over the crowd and did a roll in a Boeing 707. Nobody else ever did that, and probably never will again.

International Customs and Taxes

Crossing the border to or from Canada normally is not difficult, but delays can occur on busy weekends and all summer. Some identification should be carried, but a U.S. citizen does not need a visa or passport. Proof of residence, such as a driver's license, may be required. Naturalized U.S. citizens should carry a naturalization certificate or some other evidence of citizenship. Other items of interest:

- Each country accepts valid driver's licenses of the other country. Proof of insurance is required in case of an accident. (Some U.S. insurance companies issue a certificate for Canada.) Carry your vehicle registration. Buckle all seat belts.

- Cats and dogs in good health are welcome in Canada. If over 3 months old, they must have current rabies certificates. Check for other animals.

- Handguns may not be brought into Canada. Hunting rifles and shotguns are allowed without a permit, but they must be declared.

- It is best to exchange money at a bank or money exchange before going into Canada. However, most businesses close to the border will accept "U.S. Green." However, get rid of Canadian currency before returning to the U.S. Merchants on this side of the border are not likely to honor any foreign currency. For purchases within any foreign country, credit cards automatically provide the most accurate (and usually best) exchange rate. For cash within a foreign country, ATM withdrawals and credit card cash advances are also at prevailing exchange rates and thus are usually less expensive than currency-exchange booths, but check the transaction fees involved.

- U.S. citizens returning from Canada may bring back limited amounts of goods, liquor, and tobacco duty free, but the amounts depend on the length of time spent in Canada. Check for current allowances.

- Canadian excise tax is refundable on hotel rooms and other purchases. However, the total of all purchases must be at least C$200 to qualify for this refund, and no single sales receipt used to reach the total may be less than C$50. Therefore, purchases should be carefully structured to ensure that they qualify.

Islands

Some Washington islands have significant human populations, and others have only birds and other wildlife. Puget Sound has hundreds of small to large outcrops of land; some connected by ferries or bridges. Two counties, Island and San Juan, are nothing but islands. Mercer Island is a city of over 20,000 with some very expensive waterfront homes in the middle of Lake Washington. The lower Columbia River also contains several, notably Puget Island, which is connected to Wahkiakum County by bridge and to Oregon by ferry.

What is interesting about island living is the detachment most island residents feel. Even if the island is just a short distance over a bridge, there is a sense of being able to put aside the worries connected with the mainland. A ferry adds to this feeling of freedom and solitude. Each island takes on a personality and customs of its own. To fully under stand the phenomenon requires becoming "one of them."

Kite Flying

Where there are strong breezes, kite flying is very popular, especially on ocean beaches such as Long Beach (Pacific).

Lighthouses

More than 20 lighthouses serve as aids to navigation in the Pacific Ocean and waters around Puget Sound. The majority were constructed in the late

Point Wilson Lighthouse (Jefferson)

1800s. Most, if not all, are now automatic. The towers are locked, but a few have caretakers who may have time to show visitors around. Some are accessible by car and others by boat. They are excellent subjects for photographers and artists.

Liquor, Beer, and Wine Sales

Liquor stores are run by the state, meaning no liquor purchases on Sundays or holidays (or late at night). Repeated attempts to shift this particular retail business into the private sector have proven unsuccessful. Beer and wine, however, are available in grocery and convenience stores.

Llamas

Tired of carrying your own pack? Visit one of the many outdoor facilities that provide this pack animal on their camping journeys.

Logging Shows

The number of working loggers is declining, but many still develop the traditional logging skills—axe throwing, sawing, pole climbing, topping, and log rolling—and they put on good shows. Modern technology has become part of the act in the form of high-powered chainsaws that cut through a 3-foot log in 5 to 8 seconds. An excellent two-day event is in Deming (Whatcom) in June. Each year, a new "Bull of the Woods" is selected from loggers who have made notable contributions to the business.

Lottery

There is a daily numbers game (three numbers), a twice-weekly Lotto (six of 49 numbers), and twice weekly Quinto, which starts at $100,000. The minimum prize for Lotto is $1 million, and occasionally the jackpot goes over $10 million. Scratch tickets are available in many stores.

Lutefisk & Lefsa

These are Scandinavian delicacies that are often served together. Lutefisk is codfish that emerges from a lye bath as a sort of paste. Lefsa is a Norwegian tortilla made from rolled potatoes. Good-natured fun is often made of lutefisk, so it's easy to overlook the fact that many people actually relish its unique flavor, especially in Scandinavian enclaves such as Ballard (King) and Poulsbo (Kitsap).

Markets

New markets featuring homegrown or organic produce continue to appear every growing season. Throughout the state during harvest time, roadside stands offer freshly picked fruits and veggies. For those in Seattle and surrounding communities, the famous Pike Place Market features seafood and many nonfood items. In Vancouver, B.C., Granville Island has a large food market and a variety of shops and restaurants.

Museums, General

Art, history, wooden boats, agriculture, airplanes children, ships, military, nuclear power—scores of museums and interpretive centers are devoted to them. Almost all counties have historical museums, and several are devoted to the culture and life of Native Americans. Life of the pioneer settlers is well documented.

Museum of Flight

At the south end of Boeing Field in Seattle is a unique museum where visitors can reach out and touch aviation history. Many smaller planes are suspended from the ceiling of the six-story building. Outside, larger aircraft sit for examination. The Red Barn, where much of the early Boeing engineering took place, has been preserved within the museum, with many of the old drawings available for viewing. Air shows are held here, which use the airstrip for live flying and staging for exhibition flights all over the state. It is not uncommon to see formations of World War II-vintage aircraft flying around the coastal communities during these shows. Aviation pioneers frequently are invited to give talks in the museum's auditorium.

National Parks and Scenic Areas

Columbia River Gorge National Scenic Area

The Columbia River created the gorge over millions of years. The latest geological event, about 12,000 years ago, was the great Missoula flood that changed much of the eastern Washington landscape, creating the channeled scablands and other features.

Human presence dates back at least 10,000 years. Large salmon runs sustained early Indian tribes. Then, its natural passage through the mountains provided a transportation corridor for fur trappers and settlers heading for Oregon. Later, sternwheelers, then railroads, and now highways have continued to increase its importance as a major transportation corridor. Dams came to alter the landscape, submerging the falls and creating lakes, fishladders, and locks for big barges to ply the waters.

With completion of the dams, more people became concerned with the future of the gorge. It is considered a national treasure, with its combination of scenery, geology, plants, wildlife, and history. Its natural scenic resources include waterfalls and geological formations, such as monolithic Beacon Rock, America's own Rock of Gibraltar.

In the 1950s, both Oregon and Washington created commissions to determine what to do. In 1980, a National Park Service study concluded that further land development threatened the resources of the gorge. Congress then became involved and, in 1986, passed the Columbia River Gorge National Scenic Area Act, designating the gorge America's first National Scenic Area. On the Washington side, it spans 83 miles of river and shoreline from Gibbons Creek in Clark County, east through Skamania County, to a line 4 miles east of Wishram in Klickitat County. Management responsibility for the Scenic Area lies with the U.S. Forest Service and the Columbia River Gorge Commission, which includes members from the involved Washington and Oregon counties.

For management purposes, the area is divided into three categories: urban, special management (SMA) and general management (GMA). There are 13 cities designated urban: 10 in Washington and 3 in Oregon. In the SMAs, mostly in the west, new homes must be on parcels 40 acres or larger, and forest practices are regulated. The GMA, in the east, is mostly agricultural with scattered residential areas.

Stability has come to the gorge since the Act was passed, but there will still be some change. Stop, relax, and enjoy the scenery.

Mount Rainier National Park

"Of all the fire mountains which, like beacons, once blazed along the Pacific Coast, Mount Rainier is the noblest."
John Muir

Mount Rainier is the highest peak in the Cascades, a mountain range that stretches from Mount

Mount Rainier

Although volcanic activity built Rainier, glaciers continue to shape it. More than 34 square miles of glaciers radiate from the summit, the largest collection of glaciers on one peak in the contiguous 48 states. Only time will tell if it will erupt again or the glaciers will erode it away.

North Cascades National Park

North Cascades National Park is a wild, alpine region of high, jagged peaks, glaciers, waterfalls, forests, meadows, and valleys embracing 505,000 acres in north central Washington. Its northern and southern sections, separated by Ross Lake National Recreation Area, are bordered by Okanogan National Forest to the east, Lake Chelan National Recreation Area to the southeast, Wenatchee National Forest to the south, and Mount Baker–Snoqualmie National Forest to the west.

More than 315 active glaciers continue to mold the character of the park's terrain, which includes sheer canyons and many rivers and lakes.

Mountain goats, deer, and black and grizzly bears are among the most common animals in the park. Rarely visible but present are cougars and wolverines. Smaller mammals and a host of birds, including white-tailed ptarmigans, also inhabit the area. Several varieties of trout live in park waters.

The park can be reached off SR 20 (The North Cascades Highway), from Marblemount on the west side and from Mazama through Okanogan National Forest on the east side. The highway is closed between Diablo Lake and Mazama from the first snowfall until late spring or early summer. From Marblemount, Cascade River Road runs east for 22 miles and is the only accessible road into the park. The park can also be reached by boat via Lake Chelan or from Canada via Ross Lake.

Visitor centers have interpretive exhibits. Mule and horse rentals, professional guides, and pack-train service are available. Activities include fishing, hiking, and mountain climbing. There are five campgrounds. Back country use permits may be required for certain activities. Hunting is prohibited.

The park is open daily 24 hours year round, but highway access is nonexistent in winter. Hiking access and roadside views of the northwest corner of the park are offered from SR 542 east from Bellingham. A passenger ferry provides round-trip service between Stehekin, in Lake Chelan National Recreation Area, and Chelan, at the southern end of Lake Chelan (see Chelan County). Shuttle bus service transports visitors from Stehekin to High Bridge and Cottonwood in the remote southeast portion of the park, mid-May through September.

Garibaldi in British Columbia to Lassen Peak in northern California. Formed by volcanic activity over a period of many years, it is an active volcano.

Scientists think Rainier's volcanic activity occurs in a 3,000-year cycle. Its last big eruption, 2,500 years ago, created a second volcanic crater that overlaps the original crater at its 14,411-foot summit. Its last eruption was in the early to mid-1800s, and it may continue to spew ash and steam intermittently during the next century, causing floods and mudflows.

Tahoma News, the park newspaper, with seasonal information on naturalists' talks, programs, and other activities, is available at park entrances and visitor centers. Be sure to stop at a visitor center first. Park rangers can answer your questions, and you can see slide presentations and exhibits for a preview of the wonders you will encounter.

It is said that Mount Rainier creates its own weather, so prepare for a variety of conditions. Dress in layers and carry a sweater and rain gear. Temperatures average in the mid-70s in summer and the mid-20s in winter, with frequent snowstorms.

Climbing Rainier offers challenges and a well-deserved sense of danger. Many Mount Everest climbers use Rainier as a training ground.

You can glimpse the many moods of the mountain most easily by traversing the south and east sides of the park. Start from the Nisqually (west) entrance on SR 706. At the Longmire Museum, look at exhibits and walk down the self-guided Trail of the Shadows. Drive on to Paradise, where summer meadows blaze with wildflowers. Continue to the Stevens Canyon entrance, then head north to White River and Sunrise. The 80-mile trip winds through forests of cedar, fir, and hemlock and provides views of four dormant volcanoes, including Mounts Baker and Adams. At Sunrise, the highest point accessible by car, telescopes provide close-up views of Rainier's glacier-packed northeast flank.

North Cascades panorama

Trails suitable for hiking and climbing wind through the back country. Primitive campsites are available by permit issued at most ranger stations. The most-developed sites are off SR 20 in the Ross Lake National Recreation Area. Summer naturalist activities, including evening programs and guided walks, are featured at campgrounds in both recreation areas.

An information center on SR 20 in Sedro Woolley is open daily, mid-June through Labor Day, on weekdays the rest of the year. Weather forecasts, trail conditions, and permits for back-country camping are available at the Chelan, Marblemount, Newhalem, and Stehekin ranger stations.

Olympic National Park

In 1938, President Franklin D. Roosevelt signed legislation creating Olympic National Park, 922,651 acres of incomparable beauty, incredible variety, and (being only a couple of hours' drive from Seattle) unusual accessibility. Although the National Park Service claims more than 3 million visitors a year, few ever venture far into the park. U.S. Highway 101 almost encircles it, offering visitors many opportunities to drive into the fringes, but hardier souls who follow one of the numerous trails into the interior feel utterly isolated after the first mile.

And such splendid isolation it is! Much of the park's low-lying interior is temperate rain forest, with annual rainfall reaching about 180 inches (yep, 15 feet). Here, towering firs and cedars filter the sunlight down to giant ferns and spongy carpets of moss. Fallen trees abound because their roots, made lazy by the abundant rainfall, extend only inches into the ground and provide little support during occasional high winds. These fallen trees then nurture the roots of new trees that spring up, straight as fence rows, in colonnades on the decaying trunks. The total effect is not unlike a cathedral, with subdued light-

ing, impressive architecture, and lush tapestries. Indeed, a feeling of mind and soul refreshment approaching spiritual revival is not unheard of among visitors to the area. The rain forest along the Hoh River is especially notable and is accessible from Highway 101.

On the park's central Olympic Mountains, the highest of which is 7,965-foot Mount Olympus, the gods dump more than 200 feet of snow each year, sustaining more glaciers than exist in Glacier National Park. In magnificent alpine meadows, a hiker's solitude is rarely interrupted by more than a marmot's whistle or the sight of a herd of Roosevelt Elk (named for T.R., not F.D.R.). A trek of 20 miles up the Hoh brings the serious hiker to the Blue Glacier on Mount Olympus. A bear or two might be seen along the way.

The visitor who prefers not to venture far from the comfort of a vehicle can appreciate many of the park's wonders with a 10-mile drive from Port Angeles to Hurricane Ridge on the park's north side. At Hurricane Ridge is a visitor center that offers refreshment and tours hosted by naturalists during the summer and doubles as a ski lodge (no overnight

Marymere Falls, Olympic National Park

accommodations) for day and night skiing during the winter. The panorama of snow-clad peaks and alpine meadows seen here is otherwise available to visitors only with some fairly strenuous hiking.

To soothe the aches and pains from hiking or prolonged driving, Sol Duc (or Soleduck) Hot Springs Resort, a short drive from Highway 101, may be just the ticket. Just past the springs is a trailhead, with ample parking and a hitching post for horses, for long trips into the interior or just a short hike along the river to Sol Duc Falls.

Adjacent to the highway, pristine Lake Crescent offers amenities ranging from campgrounds to cozy resorts with fine dining. Short trails from Lake Crescent give the casual visitor access to moss-laden, old-growth forest and picturesque waterfalls.

Completely separate, both geographically and esthetically, from the main park are Olympic National Park's gloriously wild Pacific Ocean beaches— simply numbered 1 through 4. Perhaps the mind is sufficiently boggled by their beauty that no descriptive names are really adequate. As proof of this hypothesis, First Beach is also known as Rialto Beach, and Third is Ruby. Within this 57-mile strip lies the most primitive coastline in the U.S. outside of Alaska and Hawaii. Some beaches are accessible only by a lengthy hike or horseback, but others are only steps from paved roads and parking lots.

Whatever the visitor's stamina, any energy expended to enjoy the many inspiring wonders of Olympic National Park will be generously rewarded. Because it is 95% protected wilderness, its magical tranquillity is guaranteed for future generations.

Coulee Dam National Recreation Area

(See Upper Columbia Dams and Lake Roosevelt under Environment.)

Ebey's Landing National Historical Reserve

(See Island County.)

Fort Vancouver National Historic Site

(See Clark County.)

Lake Chelan National Recreation Area

(See Chelan County and North Cascades National Park.)

Mount St. Helens National Volcanic Monument

(See Cowlitz and Skamania Counties.)

Ebey's Landing from Fort Casey State Park

Ross Lake National Recreation Area

(See Whatcom County and North Cascades National Park.)

San Juan Island National Historical Park

(See San Juan County.)

Parks—State, County, and Local

Parks abound throughout the state from sea level to the mountain tops and offer something for everyone. They range from a few square yards to several thousand acres in size. Facilities and services vary from full hookups for RVs to places for pitching tents or buoys for tying up boats. Visiting parks has become so popular that reservations are often recommended weeks in advance. If reservations are not offered, it is best to arrive early in the day. Many city parks offer golf. Parks frequently require fees for entrance or use. A comprehensive listing of parks and their amenities would require a sizable publication of its own. For information on state parks, call the toll-free number or look up the web site: www.parks.wa.gov.

Restaurants

There are so many places to take nourishment throughout the state that it would not be advisable to mention only a few specific places by name.

There is excellent seafood all along the coast, with many of the menu items fresh. The metro areas around the Sound have numerous places featuring ethnic foods, especially from Pacific Rim countries. On the dry side, Mexican food is popular. One or more vegetarian items, Washington State wines, and fresh local produce are normally available.

It's especially enjoyable to take a boat to a restaurant with docking facilities and sit at a table overlooking the water. Another unique experience is to attend a classic Indian salmon bake, where fillets are mounted on wooden planks and cooked by the heat of an alderwood fire.

River Rafting

A popular experience is to get into a rubber raft or special boat and take a trip down a river that generally has some whitewater (rapids). Some trips are short—3 to 4 hours—while others may take a day or two and involve camping overnight. Although this is normally a summer activity, a few trips go in the winter. (Wear a wetsuit.) Most rafting rivers originate in the mountains, and trips are offered in both the eastern and western parts of the state.

Rodeos

Most counties have rodeos, usually in connection with annual county fairs. Many are connected with the Professional Rodeo Cowboys Association. Asotin County claims that its event in April is the first in each calendar year. Each August is the Omak Stampede and world-famous Suicide Race (see Okanogan County). On Labor Day in Ellensburg (Kittitas) is one of the top rodeos in the country. There are still many people who will take their chances riding the horses or bulls or trying for the best time in calf roping or steer wrestling.

Okanagan Stampede

Rowing

Led by the University of Washington, which is a frequent contender for the #1 boat in the country, several colleges and high schools feature this sport. On occasion, even yacht clubs round up a few able bodies, put them in

Crew race on Lake Washington, Seattle

a shell, and hope there are no heart attacks. The Montlake Cut course, off Lake Washington, is well sheltered and excellent for viewing races.

Seaplanes

One of the few, and maybe only, scheduled seaplane operations is that of Kenmore Air, at the north end of Lake Washington. Its routes are mostly north and into Canada. They will even land near your boat, where you can transfer to a dingy. A few folks use their own private float planes to commute from their waterfront homes, and others are available for charter.

Scuba Diving

The self-contained underwater breathing apparatus (scuba) way of diving is a fast-growing sport that is thriving in Washington, especially in Puget Sound.

Just about every sizable community has a dive shop that offers scuba gear for sale or rent, diving instruction, information on local sites and conditions, and guided tours to local and far-flung sites.

Divers at Keystone Underwater State Park (Island)

The waters provide an underwater garden of animal and plant life and a whole new world of adventure. Because water temperatures don't fluctuate as much as on land, diving with a wetsuit is possible year round, and the waters are actually less cloudy in the fall and winter months, after the landlubbers have gone home.

Seniors

Considerable attention is given to the large elder segment of the state's population. Many retirement facilities are available, ranging from basic apartments to communities providing full continuing care. Several guides are published, and many of those are free. Most communities have "senior centers" and senior programs run by the local parks and recreation units. Elderhostel offers several programs, both on land and afloat.

Skiing

About a dozen alpine and Nordic skiing locations dot the state, and some provide both types. Everyone in Washington lives within 2 to 3 hours of a slope, and most residents around the Sound can make it to a ski lift in an hour.

The season normally starts in November and can last well into April—even May at Mount Baker. Lighting for night skiing is common. In addition, Idaho, Oregon, and British Columbia add many more ski areas close by. Rates for lift tickets vary, with season passes available.

The Summit at Snoqualmie (King) is a combination of four ski areas now under one management. Most Nordic areas have groomed trails. Methow Valley (Okanogan) has more than 120 miles of trails.

While most of the slopes are in the Cascades (Mount Baker, Stevens Pass, Crystal, White Pass), the east has Bluewood (Columbia), Mount Spokane (Spokane), Sitzmark for Nordic near Tonasket (Okanogan), and Mission Ridge near Wenatchee (Chelan).

Skydiving

For those who fancy jumping out of perfectly good airplanes, the opportunity is available for free-fall, tandem, and static jumps. The minimum age is 18, with a weight limit of 230 lb for men and 200 lb for women.

Snow

With the abundance of rain, one naturally expects snow in the winter and almost year round at the higher elevations, but it depends mostly on the region. Around Puget Sound, some winters come and go with no snowfall or just a "light dusting."

On ski slopes in the Cascades, it is common to have a 100-inch base. Each winter, Cascade peaks get several hundred inches of heavy (i.e., high-water-content) snow. In the east, the snow is much lighter, but 30 to 40 inches in most areas is the norm. This "powder snow" is ideal for Nordic skiing.

The large accumulations in the Cascades frequently cause avalanches, which can close highways and make it necessary for those who go into the back country to be especially careful.

Snowmobiling

The Washington State Snowmobile Association (WSSA) works with State Parks and others to provide more than 2,400 miles of groomed trails, much of which is in the east. All snowmobiles must be registered with the Department of Licensing (DOL) annually. Included with the registration is a Snopark permit. Individuals under 12 are not allowed to operate a snowmobile, and those between 12 and 16 must pass a safety course. Snowmobiles are not permitted in wilderness areas, but boundaries of these areas are not well marked, so care needs to be exercised to avoid trespassing.

Snoparks

Snoparks is a State Parks program to provide cleared parking areas for winter recreation. More than 50 areas for nonmotorized use and an equal number for multiple use (i.e., snowmobiling allowed) are spread throughout the state, many with groomed trails. Permits are required for one or three days or for the season, and the money is used to remove the snow and maintain and improve the facilities. Idaho and Oregon honor Washington permits. Leave the dog(s) at home.

Soccer

This popular sport has plenty of teams and leagues for girls and boys throughout the state. There are a few leagues for adults as well. The Tacoma Stars, a major league indoor soccer team, plays in the Tacoma Dome.

State Symbols

Animal (official). The Roosevelt Elk, named for Teddy Roosevelt.

Animal (unofficial). The banana slug.

Bird. The willow goldfinch (a.k.a. the wild canary), a delicate little bird with a yellow body and black wings, was adopted the Legislature as the state bird in 1951.

Dance. When the pioneers came west, they brought with them a dance called the quadrille ("square" in French). The pioneer liked the simpler term, and so the square dance was born. On April 17, 1979, it became the official state dance.

Fish. The steelhead trout is an anadromous fish—meaning a saltwater fish that returns to freshwater rivers to spawn (see Environment). One of the most popular prizes in sport fishing, it was adopted by the Legislature as a state symbol in 1969.

Flower. In 1892, before they had the right to vote, Washington women, who wanted an official flower to enter in a floral exhibit at the 1893 World's Fair in Chicago, selected the Coast Rhododendron as the state flower.

State flower: Coast Rhododendron

Fruit. No surprise here—the apple was named a state symbol in 1989, the Centennial Year.

Gem. Centuries ago, the interior of Washington was swampy and mild, covered with trees such as cypress, oak, elm, and ginkgo. A layer of logs was created and preserved with each new lava flow from volcanic vents, and over time, water seeped through the lava and permeated the wood with silica. Eventually, the wood was completely replaced by silica, thus petrifying the logs, exact in form and detail to the original wood. In 1975, petrified wood was adopted as the state gem. The best place to see petrified wood is in the Ginkgo Petrified State Park at Vantage (Kittitas).

Grass. A state symbol unique to eastern Washington, Bluebunch Wheatgrass was a blessing to Washington's pioneer farmers and continues to play a major role in our agriculture today. It was adopted by the 1989 Centennial Year Legislature as the official state grass.

Motto. *Alki* is an Indian word meaning "bye and bye." This motto first appeared on the Territorial seal designed by Lt. J. K. Duncan of Governor Stevens' surveying expedition.

Nickname. Washington was nicknamed "The Evergreen State" by C. T. Conover, pioneer, Seattle Realtor, and historian, for its abundant evergreen forests. The nickname was adopted by the Legislature in 1893.

Ship. In 1983, the S.S. President Washington was proclaimed the official state ship and is the first container ship to be adopted by a state. The 86-foot vessel is one of the largest container ships ever built in the U.S. It has a 43,000-horsepower diesel engine, and its 23-foot propeller weighs 98,000 pounds.

Song. "Washington Beloved" (lyrics by historian Edmond Meany and music by Reginald de Koven) was adopted as the state song by the Legislature in 1909 but was never formalized in a bill, so it never was official. In 1959, a bill was introduced to make "Washington, My Home," by Helen Davis, our state song. It was approved unanimously.

Tree. In 1946, the *Portland Oregonian* teased Washington for not having a state tree and picked out the Western Hemlock for us. However, Washington newspapers decided to choose their own and selected the popular Western Red Cedar. State Representative George Adams of Mason County pleaded with the Legislature to adopt the Western Hemlock, which, he said, would become "the backbone of this state's forest industry." Adams' bill passed the Legislature and was signed into law in 1947.

Trails/Cascadia Marine Trail

Nearly every State Park and National Park and Reserve has trails to increase enjoyment of its natural wonders (see Hiking and National Parks). In addition, a new trail deserves special mention—the Cascadia Marine Trail. Created by the Washington Water Trails Association in 1993, it stretches more than 400 miles from Budd Inlet through Admiralty Inlet, into the San Juans, all the way to the Canadian border. Along the way are campsites acccessible only by human-powered, beachable watercraft (e.g., kayaks). What a way to intimately investigate the places and history that define the region!

Trapping

One of the principal occupations of the original settlers in the 1800s, trapping is now licensed, regulated, and a part of wildlife management. Anyone obtaining a trapping license for the first time must complete a course in proper trapping procedures or pass an examination that demonstrates the requisite knowledge. Muskrat and beaver, which burrow and weaken canals and ditches on irrigated lands, and coyotes, which prey on young livestock, are some of the animals of interest to trappers. The Carnivore Plague Surveillance Program of the Department of Social and Health Services (DSHS) uses trapping as a source of specimens..

Travel Tips

Always listen to weather and road reports, especially in the winter when planning to head over the mountain passes.

Missing a ferry happens to everyone eventually, so learn to relax and enjoy the wait. Keep reading material in the car.

On pleasure boats, wear soft-soled shoes with good traction to save both the deck and your neck. Except in midsummer, take a jacket or sweater. Before throwing a line, check to see that it is attached to a cleat.

If there is only one person in the car, stay out of the HOV lanes.

Be careful about speeding. The State Patrol uses unmarked cars, motorcycles, radar, and spotter planes.

Don't look for a lot of special airfares to and from Seattle.

Commuting in the Puget Sound area can be very time-consuming. Consider that when deciding where to work and live.

Veterans' Memorials

On the State Capitol campus in Olympia, and elsewhere, are veterans memorials for World War I, Vietnam, Korea, POW/MIAs, and Medal of Honor recipients (see color pages). During a visit to the Capitol, it takes just a few minutes to view these memorials, which are all within a short walk of each other. A World War II memorial is being created.

Videos

There are several good videos about the state. One that gives a great view from above is "Over Washington," which is one hour long and was created by KCTS, Seattle's PBS television channel. Call the toll-free number or visit its web site: www.kcts.org.

Volkssports

These are "people's sports" that include walking, swimming, etc. The name comes from Europe, where the idea originated. Most popular is the Volksmarch, a noncompetitive 6-mile (10-kilometer) walk. The group, of any size, goes anywhere there is something interesting to see. The Evergreen State Volkssport Association has many chapters, and their publication is called *The Pathfinder*.

Whale Watching

Pacific Gray Whales pass along the coast during annual migrations and frequently show up in coastal harbors and even parts of the Sound. Pods of Orcas ("killer whales") inhabit the Sound and the Strait year round. Whale watching cruises are available from ports in the Sound and along the coast.

Windsurfing

Wherever there is water and wind, windsurfers will appear. This is a popular sport even in the winter because wetsuits are used year round, and the water temperature in the Sound and the ocean really doesn't change all that much. One of the best surfing places anywhere is the Columbia River Gorge, where the east wind and current often complement each other and enable surfers to reach 40 mph or better.

Wooden Boats

Many boaters are purists and prefer wood to fiberglass. To this end, there is the Center for Wooden Boats in Seattle and a school in Port Townsend (Jefferson) where the art of building of wooden boats is taught.

You Can't Get There from Here!

Staying within the boundaries of the county or state is not always possible when going from A to B. Check your map.

Going to Point Roberts by land from the rest of Whatcom County requires crossing the border into Canada and then back across the border. Point Roberts is a peninsula that is severed from the rest of the state by the international boundary (the 49th parallel). Even busloads of school children who live there must go through customs twice a day.

Although it is possible to stay within the state when traveling from Pullman (Whitman) to

Clarkston (Asotin), the main road goes through Idaho.

No roads cross the Olympic Mountains, so travel across Jefferson County requires going through Clallam County or Grays Harbor and Mason Counties.

A resident of Camano Island who needs to go to the (Island) county seat in Coupeville on Whidbey Island and can't travel by boat must go through Snohomish and Skagit Counties and across the Deception Pass bridge or through Snohomish to the Mukilteo ferry.

Zoos

The state has several zoos/wildlife parks. Notable are Spokane's Walk in the Wild, Eatonville's Northwest Trek (Pierce), Tenino's Wolf Haven (Thurston), Tacoma's Point Defiance Zoo (Pierce), Sequim's Olympic Game Farm (Clallam), and Seattle's Woodland Park Zoo. Resident animals of the Olympic Game Farm have been featured in many movies, and they can be viewed from the comfort of private vehicles. Portland (OR) and Vancouver (B.C.) also have excellent zoos and aquariums.

Finally,

Here are some pictures of neat places that we wouldn't want to leave out, but we didn't have room to put them anywhere else. A few words were written about each of these scenic delights in the discussions of their counties. Now, go out and explore the Evergreen State. As one of the slogans used by the Washington tourism folks says,

"It's a Constant State of Wonder."

Snoqualmie Falls (King)

Rosario Resort, Orcas Island (San Juan)

Admiralty Head Light, Fort Casey State Park (Island)

Appendix A—Relocation

For many people, it might be more appropriate for relocation to be called "dislocation," even if the move is within the state. It can be very hard to tear self and family away from a familiar environment and start a new life among strange people, surroundings, and circumstances. Whether relocation is viewed as an adventure or a traumatic upheaval depends on the attitude of the relocatee and the quality of information available about the new home.

As far as attitude is concerned, relocation is naturally stressful, but understanding the stresses involved is the first step in overcoming them. This is where the second element—information—plays a key role. With advance knowledge, it is easier to offset the frustration, fear, and concerns about the future that can accompany the decision to move—a principal reason for this book!

The relocation process consists of four distinct and easily definable periods of stress: decision, preparation, movement, and settling in.

Decision Period

Whether you are considering a move on your own, or your company (including Uncle Sam) has asked (or told) you to relocate, a scouting trip to your prospective new location is a must, unless you're already familiar with the area. If the move will involve changing jobs, this will give you a chance to scout employment opportunities. If your company is relocating you, your employer may pay for you (and perhaps your entire family) to make the trip, which will reduce the expense of seeing what sort of lifestyle you can expect. Once the decision to move has been made, you can increase your advance information by working with a real estate agent experienced in relocations. Depending on the area and your personal finances, whether to buy or rent may be another major decision. Even if government housing is offered, there may be a waiting period for it, during which a short-term rental may be necessary.

Preparation Period

Preparation may be the period of greatest long-term stress, since it involves both the sale of your old home and the selection of your new one. Considerable apprehension can arise when the old home just doesn't seem to be selling. This is especially true if you're moving to an area with higher housing costs, which may mean choosing a smaller home or one with fewer features. A good idea is to have the agent in the new area coordinate efforts with your listing broker to make sure the sale and purchase are reasonably in sync, especially when it comes to having funds available from the sale for the down payment on your new residence. If the trailing spouse is planning to seek employment in the new location, it's never to early to start looking.

Movement Period

During the move itself is where intense, short-term stress occurs, starting with the packing and the almost endless decisions that go with it: what to take and what to leave, what to dispose of and what to replace at the other end, and which moving company to select. It's important to choose a reliable mover who will keep you informed about the location of your goods while they're in transit. Once you and your goods are on the way, stressful situations can still arise, such as when you have an empty house awaiting furnishings and the van is still two days away.

Settling-in Period

Once you have found and purchased a new home (we hope the old one has sold) and are starting to get settled, it is time to get acquainted with the new neighbors and local businesses, take care of school registration, license your vehicles, open a bank account, etc. During this period, the real estate agent who has worked with you all along should still be involved in offering information and assisting where necessary.

The stresses of these four periods of relocation can be substantially reduced by a combination of information, preparation, and coordination. A couple of checklists provided in the appendix can help.

Documents Needed in Relocation

The following documents, referring to yourself and all appropriate family members, should be assembled before the move and be kept with you for immediate assessiblility:

❑ Driver's license(s)

❑ Social Security card(s)

❑ Birth certificate(s)

❑ Passport(s)

❑ Vehicle(s) title and registration

❑ Vehicle(s) insurance policy

❑ Health insurance information

❑ Tax returns (last two years)

❑ W-2 forms (last two years)

❑ School transcripts

❑ Medical records

❑ Immunization records (especially children)

❑ Address/telephone book (personal)

❑ Local phone book from old location

❑ Special or general power of attorney from spouse re home purchase

❑ Personal financial statement

Moving Tips

One month before moving . . .

❑ Arrange for a moving firm agent to visit your home to inspect your possessions and give an estimate of moving cost. Check insurance coverage, packing and unpacking labor costs, travel time for the load, and the method and time for payment. Many moving companies require cash or money orders at the destination before unloading, so be prepared.

❑ List items to be moved and those to be discarded.

❑ Notify the post office of moving date and new address.

❑ Send change of address cards to all correspondents.

❑ Terminate memberships—Church, clubs, and civic organizations. Get letters of introduction.

❑ Notify newspapers, creditors, insurance companies, attorney, etc. of your intended move.

❑ Close credit accounts.

❑ Notify schools and collect transcripts or arrange for records to be sent to the new sehool district.

❑ Obtain birth records, baptismal certificates, etc.

Two weeks before moving . . .

❑ Check with moving company and confirm moving date.

❑ Update insurance coverages to include possessions at the new home and enroute.

❑ Transfer bank accounts and ask for credit references to be sent to your new bank.

❑ Begin packing things you intend to move yourself.

❑ Take things to the cleaners as necessary, and have them wrapped for moving.

❑ Make or confirm travel arrangements—include arrangements for pets.

One week before moving . . .

❑ Collect items from cleaners, in storage, at repair shop, or loaned out.

❑ Return borrowed items.

❑ Clean appliances for shipping—remove TV antenna if necessary.

❑ Notify phone company, arrange for all utility meters to be read prior to your move, and arrange for any refunds due you.

❑ Gather appliance warranties and instructions and put them in a kitchen cupboard for new tenants.

Two days before moving . . .

❑ Drain power tools of fuel if necessary.

❑ Label paint cans you're leaving for new tenants— they may want to have touch-up paint.

❑ Remove curtains, drapes, and other fixtures you're taking with you.

❑ Buy traveler's checks for funds while enroute.

❑ Pack lightweight clothing in dresser drawers for ease in moving and unpacking upon arrival.

One day before moving . . .

❑ Arrange to spend tomorrow night in a motel— your beds will be on the moving truck.

❑ Give friends or relatives your schedule, travel route, and expected arrival time at your destination.

❑ Defrost refrigerator/freezer—place charcoal or baking soda inside to dispel odors.

❑ Check all cabinets, closets, attic, basement, crawl space, etc., for overlooked items.

❑ Select items needed for immediate housekeeping at your new home—pack all in one box and label accordingly.

On moving day . . .

❑ Accompany moving man through the house as he tags furniture—you should mark it for room location in the new house.

❑ Specify what is to be moved and what is to stay.

❑ Sign and get copy of the bill of lading (freight bill) from the operator and put it in a safe place for future reference.

❑ Check exact destination directions with the operator and verify estimated date and time of arrival.

❑ Double-check closets, drawers, shelves, etc. to be sure they are empty.

❑ Leave keys needed by new tenant with Realtor or agent.

Upon arriving at your new home . . .

❑ Plan for inspection of your new home prior to closing of title.

❑ Notify police if your new home will be vacant for any length of time before you move in.

❑ Check furniture for damage immediately upon arrival, preferably while the mover is still there.

❑ Make sure utilities are connected and service is started.

❑ Register children in school.

❑ Have locks changed in new home; make sure you have adequate insurance.

❑ Obtain necessary licenses (driver, pet); register car with the state if necessary.

❑ Revise wills.

❑ Open checking and savings accounts.

❑ Register to vote.

Appendix B—Toll-Free Hotlines

Aging and Adult Services 1-800-422-3263

AIDS/HIV Information Hotline 1-800-272-2437

Alcohol & Drug Help 1-800-562-1240

American Cancer Society 1-800-729-1151

Arthritis Foundation 1-800-542-0295

Attorney General (Consumer Protection) 1-800-551-4636

Beach Closure—Shellfish Toxins 1-800-562-5632

Better Business Bureau 1-800-955-5100

Cancer Information 1-800-442-6237

Child Find 1-800-426-5678

Child Protective Services 1-800-562-6926

Domestic Violence Hotline 1-800-562-6025

Ferry Information 1-800-843-3779

Human Rights Commission 1-800-233-3247

Internal Revenue Service/Federal Tax Information 1-800-829-1040

Insurance Claims (Consumer Protection) 1-800-562-6900

Labor & Industries Client Relations Hotline 1-800-547-8367

Legislative Hotline 1-800-562-6000

Long-Term Care Ombudsman 1-800-562-6028

Lottery Winning Numbers 1-800-545-7510

Medicaid Information 1-800-562-3022

Missing Children 1-800-543-5677

Puget Sound Air Pollution Control 1-800-552-3565

Puget Sound Water Quality 1-800-547-6863

Realtors Association 1-800-562-6024

Recycling Hotline 1-800-732-9253

Snowmobile Association 1-800-784-9772

Tourist Information Hotline 1-800-544-1800

Utilities Consumer Services 1-800-562-6150

Veterans Affairs 1-800-562-2308

Washington State Parks 1-800-233-0321

Washington State Patrol/Report Drunk Drivers 1-800-223-7865